ENGAGING IMAGES FOR RESEARCH, PEDAGOGY, AND PRACTICE

ENGAGING IMAGES FOR RESEARCH, PEDAGOGY, AND PRACTICE

Utilizing Visual Methods to Understand and Promote College Student Development

Edited by Bridget Turner Kelly
and Carrie A. Kortegast

Foreword by Peter Magolda

STERLING, VIRGINIA

Published by Stylus Publishing, LLC.
22883 Quicksilver Drive
Sterling, Virginia 20166-2102

Library of Congress Cataloging-in-Publication Data

Names: Kelly, Bridget Turner, 1973- editor. |
Kortegast, Carrie A., 1975-editor.
Title: Engaging images for research, pedagogy, and practice :
utilizing visual methods to understand and promote college student
development / edited by Bridget Turner Kelly and Carrie A.
Kortegast.
Description: First edition. |
Sterling, Virginia : Stylus Publishing, LLC, [2017] |
Includes bibliographical references and index.
Identifiers: LCCN 2017025543|
ISBN 9781620365892 (pbk. : alk. paper) |
ISBN 9781620365885 (cloth : alk. paper) |
ISBN 9781620365908 (library networkable e-edition) |
ISBN 9781620365915 (consumer e-edition)
Subjects: LCSH: Visual literacy--Study and teaching (Higher) |
College student development programs. |
College teaching--Methodology. |
Student affairs services--Methodology.
Classification: LCC LB1068 .E64 2017 |
DDC 378.1/98--dc23
LC record available at https://lccn.loc.gov/2017025543

13-digit ISBN: 978-1-62036-588-5 (cloth)
13-digit ISBN: 978-1-62036-589-2 (paperback)
13-digit ISBN: 978-1-62036-590-8 (library networkable e-edition)
13-digit ISBN: 978-1-62036-591-5 (consumer e-edition)

Printed in the United States of America

All first editions printed on acid-free paper
that meets the American National Standards Institute
Z39-48 Standard.

First Edition, 2018

10 9 8 7 6 5 4 3 2

To Alex and Addison

CONTENTS

FOREWORD

In 2015 I retired from higher education after spending 37 years as a student, administrator, or professor. Since then I have embraced leisure activities that I shunned while working. Despite being a self-taught amateur photographer for three decades, during the summer of 2017 I finally attended a photography conference in Chicago, Illinois, that included instructional seminars and photo walks/critiques. More recently, I returned from a vacation where I applied the skills that I honed in Chicago to photographing Canadian Rockies landscapes. During these trips, I read *Engaging Images for Research, Pedagogy, and Practice* as a precursor to writing this foreword. This book, which contains exemplars of visual methods that promote college student development, transcended and enriched my understanding of both my scholarly and leisurely worlds. It is germane to university educators, researchers, and practitioners (its intended audiences) as well as amateur photo enthusiasts like me, which is a testament to the book's importance and utility.

During my Chicago photography seminars, instructors projected visual images onto screens and invited participants to consume, relate to, and critique the subject matter. This pedagogy, rooted in collaborative learning, was superior to simply listening to lectures or acquiring helpful hints from experts. I marveled at the diverse reactions and interpretation of these images—resulting in potent learning opportunities.

During photo walks, photographers' life experiences and values influenced the subject matter they deemed photo-worthy (e.g., people, architecture, nature). Later in small groups, we honed our visual literacy skills by uncovering the photographic and political agendas embedded in the images. Shooting a long exposure black-and-white photograph of a city skyline at night that included a building with a light display that read "Pride" was a purposeful act that aligns with my (and the creators' of the light display) values celebrating gay pride (Figure F.1).

Engaging Images for Research, Pedagogy, and Practice helped me to appreciate and optimize my photography workshop as well as my scholarly pursuits. Contributors discuss the (a) purpose, perils, and power of arts-based research methods and pedagogies (e.g., improving analytical skills, encouraging self-reflexivity); (b) benefits of generating, disseminating, consuming, and critically examining visual acts (i.e., visual literacy); and (c) need to promote

Figure F.1. Chicago skyline, June 2017.

visual arts research and pedagogies with the hope of embracing untapped and compelling teaching and learning possibilities. These are timely and important contributions.

In the Canadian Rockies the book's content was again relevant and disorienting by challenging conventional wisdom about photography. On the tour bus and at various stops, cell phone cameras leveled the proverbial playing field, allowing those with cellphones to produce photos of scenes as stunning as those with professional gear (like me). This widely available technology provided individuals innovative and easy ways to narrate their travels using visuals to recount spectacular scenes difficult to describe in writing. The power to record history no longer rested with those with professional equipment. Every participant could take, interpret, and post their photos online, making them accessible worldwide. My photograph of two fathers using cellphones to photograph their children standing on the ledge of a mountaintop documents the fathers' goal of telling a story about the children's excitement as well as my agenda of juxtaposing tourists with the stunning surroundings to convey majestic grandness of the mountains. Collectively we produced two different images and interpretations of the same scene (Figure F.2).

Online photo galleries preserved tour participants' visual artifacts and provided space for a virtual community of photographers to collaborate and teach and learn from each other long after the tour concluded. Emancipatory technologies such as cellphones and social media decenter power and redress inequities in photography.

Figure F.2. Jasper, Alberta, 2017.

Note. Blurring applied to protect identities.

Editors Bridget Turner Kelly and Carrie A. Kortegast and the contributors document the multiple ways visual methods (e.g., photovoice, photo-elicitation, or critical media studies) enhance higher education research, pedagogy, and practice. The book contains specific examples of ways that educators can leverage the use of images to optimize student learning and encourage students' critical engagement in and understanding of campus cultures.

An explicit goal of this book is to nudge higher education to broaden conventional notions of educational research (e.g., scientific inquiry) by embracing arts-based methods. Contributors offer compelling cases that arts-based methods can make visible marginalized communities' experiences that conventional research may overlook and cultivate students' critical consciousness by revealing debilitating assumptions and practices in cultural and educational systems that are often hidden in plain view. The historical and theoretical overviews coupled with research and classroom exemplars reveal ways for students to decipher the increasingly visual world in which they live.

As researchers, educators, and even photographers, we have been socialized to exercise our craft the "right" way. We resist urges to innovate or "think different" because the result may be rebuffed by those in power such as supervisors, journal editors, or photography critics. During my photography conference, one presenter argued that when composing a subject, photographers have the option of looking at it with the analytical (i.e., left) or the creative (i.e., right) side of the brain. She lamented, "Students don't look at things as they could be, only as they are." Kelly, Kortegast, and associates recognize we live in a visual world and our research and pedagogies need to keep pace with this reality. They are uneasy with things as they are and provide possibilities of how things can be by encouraging readers to think visually, take risks, self-reflect, and empower students. Their detailed examples, analyses, and cautions ease transition fears. I am grateful these colleagues have championed this agenda, and I am grateful that I am retired so that I have time to reflect on ways to apply their insights to my scholarly and leisurely worlds.

Peter Magolda
Professor Emeritus
Miami University

ACKNOWLEDGMENTS

This book would not have been possible without the support, encouragement, and cheerleading of many people. We would like to thank Katherine Branch and Amanda O. Latz, whom we met serendipitously during an ACPA–College Student Educators International National Convention program session. After the session, the four of us discussed our work using visual methods and exchanged e-mail addresses. This first communication paved the way for multiple presentations and writing opportunities. We would also like to thank Kristin McCann and Chris Linder who joined our collaboration. We are grateful for the support they have provided us as well as the opportunity to learn from them new ways to incorporate visual methods in our own research and pedagogy. We hope our collaboration and friendship continues into the future.

We would also like to thank Ester U. Sihite who helped with the editing of early versions of the chapters and assisted with administrative tasks. Additionally, we would like to acknowledge Adam Gregory who provided technical assistance.

Bridget Turner Kelly

First and foremost, I am grateful to serve an awesome God who sustains and inspires me to be my best self in all endeavors. This book required a lot of prayer and I am so thankful to Carrie for embarking on this journey with me.

I began visual research with the coaching and assistance of Penny Bishop. To her I will ever be grateful for encouraging me to collect data using drawing as an interview method. Getting to know Ann E. Austin and having her model of using drawing to interview graduate students was also a big impetus for my visual research work. I am thankful to both Penny and Ann for leading the way.

I would also like to thank Therese Huston who assisted me in developing my teaching pedagogy and facilitated my incorporating visuals into my practice. Owning my visual learning style has fostered a joy of using visuals such as movies, pictures, and videos in my teaching. My friends Art Munin and John Dugan furthered my knowledge of visual pedagogy by introducing me to photo elicitation in a required course I now teach. I am forever grateful for their friendship and peer mentoring in visual pedagogy and manuscript writing.

Most importantly, I am grateful to my family. To my educator parents, John and Clevonne Turner, who always encouraged my book writing from elementary school through the present, I thank you for the unconditional love, laughter, and wisdom you shower upon me. To Robert Kelly, my life partner, biggest fan, and gentlest critic, your love gives me strength and courage to go boldly into each day. To our amazingly kind, fun, smart, and God-fearing kids, Alex and Addison, your faith in me and joy in Mom writing a book (they do not quite get journal articles), carried me through the years this has taken to complete from conception to publication.

Carrie A. Kortegast

I am thankful for the mentorship, friendship, and opportunity to collaborate with Bridget on this book. I am also grateful for the encouragement of Ryan Everly Gildersleeve to explore the use of visual methods in my dissertation study. As my major professor, he challenged me to explore how visual methods might enhance my work, as well as the possibilities of the use of visuals in qualitative research.

I would also like to thank Sarah Westfall for her ongoing support, mentorship, and friendship. She taught me a lot about what it means to be a student affairs professional and the role and responsibility we have toward students. I am also grateful to Sarah for connecting me with Flo Hamrick who served as my first doctoral faculty adviser at Iowa State University. Flo provided me with my first opportunity to do qualitative research, mentoring me through data collection, analysis, and the publication process. This experience launched my love of qualitative research.

To Claire Robbins and Chris Linder, thank you for making my experience as an assistant professor a little less lonely. While officially we have organized as a writing group, that does not fully capture the depth of our relationship or friendship. Thank you for the support, encouragement, and laughter. #mountainonthecabin4ever

Lastly, I would like to thank my spouse, Katy Jaekel. She has been a constant source of support, guidance, cheerleading, and love. I cannot thank her enough for her encouragement with this book and for being my in-house editor. I am grateful to have her as my partner, friend, and colleague. She brings a tremendous amount of joy into my life.

INTRODUCTION

Bridget Turner Kelly and Carrie A. Kortegast

Reflections

We begin this book with reflections on the motivation we had for conducting visual research, pedagogy, and practice. Each contributor to this volume somewhat surreptitiously found his or her way to utilizing visual images, and we hope this book increases the chance that educators, researchers, practitioners, and students will see the power of engaging visual images. The purpose, overview, and need for the book follow these reflections.

Bridget

Two women influenced my first foray into conducting visual methods in qualitative research. The first was Ann E. Austin. I watched her deliver her presidential speech to the Association of the Study of Higher Education's (ASHE) annual international conference in November 2001. She included participant-generated drawings created by graduate students and early career faculty in a study called "The Development of Graduate Students as Prospective Teaching Scholars" (Austin, 2002). The speech was given to the entire assocation and later published in *The Review of Higher Education*, a top-tier higher education journal. The drawings elicited a visceral reaction of instant recognition and understanding of the meaning the participants sought to convey. As Austin explained how the drawings were collected during interviews, I was inspired by this new-to-me way to elicit data that were meaningful to the participant and could convey an emotion in an instant. When I came back from the conference I began thinking more about studying faculty life and understanding my own new role as assistant professor.

The second woman who influenced me to take the plunge into conducting visual methods research was Penny Bishop, an assistant professor in K–12 education. In her K–12 research, participant-generated drawings were a common way to understand middle school students' experiences. Bishop and I began our careers together in a cohort of new assistant professors in the

1

College of Education. We talked often about our experiences as new female professors and I shared the study that Austin discussed at the conference. Bishop wanted to understand more about the women faculty experience but because it was not a research interest related to K–12 or middle school students she was unsure how she could pull it off on a new tenure-track line. I convinced Bishop that her role in the research we sought to conduct on women faculty could be a methodological one, using participant-generated drawings to get at the experiences in new ways. After all, females were leaving the tenure track at research universities in disproportionate numbers to male faculty, and their number of 35% of all full-time faculty members had not increased in the past 75 years, despite their increasing numbers in bachelor's, master's, and doctoral programs. Something was causing female faculty to depart the tenure track before tenure and I thought perhaps drawing could get at the reasons in ways that numbers and the written word had not unearthed. If K–12 researchers could ask students to draw about their experiences, and a full professor and president of ASHE could ask graduate students and early career faculty to draw their experiences, I thought Bishop and I could include drawings as a component in our qualitative interview protocol for women faculty members.

Now that the 10-year longitudinal study of women faculty experiences is complete and I have published numerous research articles on the findings from the interviews, incorporating the drawings into a research article has still eluded me. One of the reasons for this book is to explore how I and others who conduct visual methods research or use visual methods in pedagogy and teaching struggle to make it relevant and an everyday occurrence in student development.

Carrie

The summer of 2009, I set off to Spain to collect data for my dissertation on a short-term study abroad program. The previous year, I had started to develop an interest in the use of photographs in research inspired by the work of Sarah Pink, Douglas Harper, Caroline Wang, and Mary Ann Burris. Their research spoke to me, as did the photographs they shared. Their use of photographs resonated and connected with me as the images provided entry points into the lives and experiences of others. With this in mind, I set off to Spain with a new digital SLR camera and institutional review board (IRB) approval to collect participant photographs and to document events through my own photographs.

During the six-week program, the student participants could choose to participate in a photovoice style interview where they recorded daily experiences or in a more traditional semistructured interview that did not include photographs. Although only seven students chose to participate in the photo-voice style interviews, the quality of these interviews were better. Their photographs provided important insights and windows into their experiences living and learning in another country that often felt missing from the more traditional style interviews. Having photographs to discuss served as an important memory prompt. The students provided detailed stories about how they were navigating living in a new culture and some of the everyday challenges associated with learning a new language and culture.

Moreover, the photographs provided access to spaces and places I was not allowed. For a variety of reasons, I was not able to observe students in their host family's apartments. This was due partly to students' housing contracts regarding no guests but mostly due to cultural practices about not having guests in the home. Accordingly, student photographs became a window into their experiences living with host families. For instance, Figure I.1 is a photograph shared by Daisy (a pseudonym) of when her host mother taught her how to cook cucumber and cheese soup. The photograph became a prompt to discuss Daisy's interactions with her host mother, how the study abroad experience contributed to her career aspirations as a nutritionist, and her observations of cultural differences. Overall, the photographs students shared with me and the subsequent conversation regarding their experiences were invaluable to me as a researcher.

Because of my interest in the use of visual methods in research, I started to find ways to incorporate visuals methods into my teaching pedagogy. At first, I was nervous that students, and more so my colleagues, would not

Figure I.1. Daisy learning to cook cucumber and cheese soup from her host mother.

Note. Photograph by Daisy.

see value in using arts-based methods in the classroom. Like many other faculty members, I was socialized to privilege exams, paper writing, and data analysis as the standards for the evaluation of student work and knowledge. I was concerned that my credibility would be undermined and the use of arts-based pedagogy would be seen as "arts and crafts" or juvenile. Instead, I found that the use of visual methods such as digital storytelling, campus art audits, infographs, and reflective collages provided students with opportunities to develop visual literacy and analytical and multimodal communication skills and connect theory with practice. For example, in my student development theories course, I had students create digital stories as a way to use their own experiences as sites to analyze using the theories we studied (Figure I.2).

The process of creating and sharing a digital story provided students with an opportunity to engage in self-reflexivity as well as demonstrate the ability to use theory as an analytical tool (for more details, see Kortegast & Davis, 2017). Given that higher education and student affairs administration is an applied field, students needed opportunities to grapple with how to use theory in their practice. The use of visual methods in pedagogy provided new opportunities for applied and experiential learning.

Figure I.2. Screenshot of digital story created by Jonathan Davis (Kortegast & Davis, 2017).

Note. Scan QR code to view video (www.youtube.com/watch?v=vJpWq3E-yyg&feature=youtu.be).

My use of visual methods in research and pedagogy has evolved over time and often through trial and error. Over the years, I have grappled with issues of confidentiality, interpretation, and representation of participants in my studies that have used visual methods. In regard to teaching, I have wrestled with how to evaluate work that is often personal in nature when using digital storytelling or reflective collages. Although their work often related to the course topic, sometimes students would miss the mark regarding engagement in the theories we were learning. Validating their student experiences but holding them accountable for meeting the learning outcomes can be tricky. These challenges in the use of visual methods in research and pedagogy bear consideration and attention. However, the use of visual methods has enhanced my pedagogy and research. My hope is that this book will serve as a resource for others to learn about how visuals can enhance their own research, pedagogy, and practice.

Purpose and Overview

As our preceding reflections show, living in an increasingly visual world opens up new opportunities to leverage visual methods in enhancing student learning, success, and belonging. The purpose of this book is to provide informative, rich examples of the use of visuals to understand and promote college student development research, pedagogy, and practice. With the increased accessibility of cameras, the ability to engage in image production has become more available to individuals. Individuals, including college students, faculty, and administrators, narrate the social world in new ways using visuals. This is evidenced through the widespread use of social networking outlets such as Facebook, Twitter, Flickr, Tumblr, DrawSomething, Pinterest, and Instagram (Duggan & Smith, 2013). Individuals and institutions of higher education are using images to narrate everyday events through the aforementioned means, among others (e.g., posters, videos, videoblogs). Increasingly, we are seeing students mobilize around social issues on campuses using images (e.g., *Hidden Dores* at Vanderbilt [anchorlink.vanderbilt .edu/organization/hiddendores]) and posting videos regarding issues of campus climate (e.g., *The Black Bruins* by Sy Strokes [www.youtube.com/ watch?v=BEO3H5BOlFk]). Moreover, institutionally produced visual arti- facts send messages about institutional culture and values (Magolda, 2001; Strange & Banning, 2001). There are new opportunities for student development administrators and faculty to utilize the visual sensory modality and image-based artifacts to promote student success and belonging, which are critical outcomes of higher education.

This book is divided into three parts (research, pedagogy, and practice). Each part has a theoretical and methodological introductory chapter followed by three or four chapters focusing on application.

Part One: Visual Methods and Research

The field of college student development research often privileges the written word and numerical data in the analysis and representation of knowledge. Because of the limitations of word-based and quantitative research, several scholars have called for the development of alternative approaches, objectives, and methodologies to social science research (MacDougall, 1997; Metcalf, 2012). Visual methods can provide new insights into researching and promoting student learning and development and understanding the campus environment. Chapter 1 by J. Michael Denton, Carrie A. Kortegast, and Carrie Miller describes how visual methods have been used in higher education and makes a case for including visual methods in a researcher's toolbox. Katherine Branch and Amanda O. Latz's chapter 2 outlines a different theoretical approach to visual methods and methodologies in higher education research. David J. Nguyen's chapter 3 examines using visual methods to develop new understandings of student success. Chris Linder's chapter 4 focuses on the use of social media in higher education research. Taken together, the chapters illustrate how visual methods can be incorporated in studies to enhance our knowledge of student development and learning.

Part Two: Visual Methods and Pedagogy

Visual methods have also been used inside the classroom to develop pedagogical practices that can enhance student learning and development. The focus on visual methods allows for different and creative ways for educators to think about how subjects, such as social justice, might be taught and how educators can draw on new, changing modalities in their existing pedagogies and frameworks. For instance, an instructor's pedagogy in a diversity-related course can affect how and what students learn about race (Gurin, Dey, Hurtado, & Gurin, 2002). Pedagogies dedicated only to imparting knowledge about issues of diversity might not be as effective at promoting cognitive growth as pedagogy that is also aimed to increase empathy and reduce anxiety (Bowman, 2010; Pettigrew & Tropp, 2008). Therefore, one could reasonably argue that the ways in which students learn about social justice depends upon such contextual factors as *how* a teacher teaches. Visual methods in pedagogy provide students opportunities to unpack the images they encounter on a daily basis and develop important critical literacy regarding visuals. As part of twenty-first-century skills and a knowledge-based economy, increasingly, students are being asked to analyze, produce, and repurpose visuals. In chapter 5, Bridget Turner Kelly and Ester U. Sihite review how visual methods have been used in the classroom to enhance student learning and include examples from their own classroom in student development. Amanda O. Latz and Keri L. Rodgers's chapter 6 outlines photovoice and visual life writing as a pedagogical tool to incorporate participatory research into graduate pedagogy. Kathryn S. Jaekel's chapter 7 addresses the importance of students developing visual literacies to meet the needs of an ever-changing world. Paul Eaton's chapter 8 illustrates how an instructor can go from using isolated visual techniques in the classroom to fully integrating his or her course with visual methods. Natasha H. Chapman and James McShay's chapter 9 examines the use of digital stories to deconstruct and reconstruct leadership. This part of the book provides readers with windows into using visual-based pedagogies that have the potential to meet students where they are and move them to new understanding about the content of their course of study.

Part Three: Visual Methods and Practice

Student development professionals can also utilize visual methods to provide students with out-of-classroom learning opportunities. The meanings ascribed to images are socially constructed; therefore, we need to be "concerned with the perception and the meanings attributed to them" (Prosser, 2011, p. 479). Student development professionals can assist students in comparing, defining, and understanding how and what meanings are ascribed to images, such as photographs (Harper, 2002). Through the process of engaging with images and visuals outside of the classroom, students have the opportunity to reflect on their own and others' meaning-making of the image. Engaging students in the process of producing and reflecting upon images can promote important learning outcomes that can enhance what they learn in the classroom. In chapter 10, Carrie A. Kortegast highlights how incorporating visual methods into student development practice may enhance student learning. Elizabeth A.M. McKee's chapter 11 discusses how she uses visuals in service-learning and civic engagement to assist students in reflecting on issues such as homelessness, hunger, race, and racism. Jillian A. Martin's chapter 12 describes the use of visual methods as a way for student development professionals to reflect on their professional practice and use of theory in their work. Heather C. Lou's chapter 13 details how creative and artistic pedagogy can be helpful tools for students' identity development outside the classroom. In Chapter 14, Bridget Turner Kelly and Carrie A. Kortegast conclude the book with where we may go from here, discussing implications and future directions for visual methods in research, pedagogy, and practice.

Several chapters in this book, including the introduction, include QR codes to web-based content. We encourage readers with smartphones to download a QR scanner onto their devices. There are several different QR scanner applications available, and many are free to use. In chapters with linked material, readers can scan the QR code to be routed to the video, image, or website. The goal is to create a more interactive experience.

The three parts of this book underscore that we are living in a visual world and are constantly surrounded by images and visuals that often go underexplored, underutilized, and unrecognized. Attention on visuals and the messages visuals send are at times minimized as "just a picture," passively consumed, and/or considered less conceptual than other forms of information. Schwartz (2007) argued that our skills at interpreting and understanding images are underdeveloped, stating, "[v]iewing images is a learned, skill-based activity" (p. 319). Images send important nonverbal messages regarding cultural values, norms, and expectations. Additionally, visuals have the "capacity to evoke as well as create collective and personal memory" (Prosser, 2011, p. 484). Images such as photographs, participant-generated drawings, or art can provide opportunities to "reflect upon larger cultural realities" (Harper, 2000, p. 727) and prepare college students for the visual world they inhabit. The authors of these chapters provide a roadmap for helping students gain skills at exploring, utilizing, and recognizing the relevance of visual images.

Audience and Need

The primary audience for this book includes higher education educators, researchers, and practitioners who teach, research, and promote college student development and learning. This book could be a resource for student affairs and higher education courses required for undergraduate- or graduate-level students, one-time professional development workshops for undergraduate or graduate students, and/or administrators at all ranks, as well as students in educational research courses and college teaching and learning courses. We believe those most interested in this book will be new and seasoned educators who are looking for effective, innovative, and creative ways to utilize visual methods in research, teaching, assessment, and practice. Additionally, utilizing visual methods are not limited to the face-to-face classroom, as they are also appropriate for the burgeoning online course offerings in higher education as well as for use outside of class in student, faculty, and staff groups.

James Elkins (2007), stated that "images are central to our lives . . . [and] it is time they are central to our universities" (p. 8). Student development researchers, practitioners, and faculty have paid inadequate attention to the use of visuals in research, pedagogy, and practice. Visuals can provide new insights into college student learning and development, campus climate and environments, and student success that words and numerical data cannot capture alone. Moreover, developing visual literacies and the ability to analyze, produce, and reproduce images is an important skill for the twenty-first century. We hope this sourcebook will inspire researchers, practitioners, and faculty to reconsider how they engage with visuals as well as how to leverage visuals in order to increase student success and learning.

References

Austin, A. E. (2002). Preparing the next generation of faculty: Graduate school as socialization to the academic career. *The Journal of Higher Education, 73*(1), 94–122.

Bowman, N. A. (2010). College diversity experiences and cognitive development: A meta-analysis. *Review of Educational Research, 80*(1), 4–33.

Duggan, M., & Smith, A. (2013, December 30). *Social media update 2013. Pew Research Center.* Retrieved from http://www.pewinternet.org/files/2013/12/PIP_ Social-Networking-2013.pdf

Elkins, J. (2007). *Visual literacy.* New York, NY: Routledge.

Gurin, P., Dey, E. L., Hurtado, S., & Gurin, G. (2002). Diversity and higher education: Theory and impact on educational outcomes. *Harvard Educational Review, 72*(3), 330–366.

Harper, D. (2000). Reimagining visual methods: Galileo to *Neuromancer.* In N. K. Denzin & Y. S. Lincoln (Eds.), *Handbook of qualitative research* (2nd ed., pp. 717–732). Thousand Oaks, CA: Sage.

Harper, D. (2002). Talking about pictures: A case for photo elicitation. *Visual Studies, 17*(1), 13–26.

Kortegast, C. A., & Davis, J. (2017). Theorizing the self: Digital storytelling, applying theory, and multimodal learning. *College Teaching, 65*(3), 106–114. doi:10.1080/87567555.2016.1255584. Retrieved from https://www.youtube.com/ watch?v=vJpWq3E-yyg&feature=youtu.be

MacDougall, D. (1997). The visual in anthropology. In M. Banks & H. Morphy (Eds.), *Rethinking visual anthropology* (pp. 276–295). New Haven, CT: Yale University.

Magolda, P. M. (2001). What our rituals tell us about community on campus: A look at the campus tour. *About Campus, 5*(6), 2–8.

Metcalfe, A. S. (2012). Imag(in)ing the university: Visual sociology and higher education. *The Review of Higher Education, 35*(4), 517–534.

Pettigrew, T. F., & Tropp, L. R. (2008). How does intergroup contact reduce prejudice? Meta-analytic tests of three mediators. *European Journal of Social Psychology, 38*(6), 922–934.

Prosser, J. (2011). Visual methodologies: Toward a more seeing research. In N. K. Denzin & Y. S. Lincoln (Eds.), *The Sage handbook of qualitative research* (4th ed., pp. 479–496). Thousand Oaks, CA: Sage.

Schwartz, D. (2007). If a picture is worth a thousand words, why are you reading this essay? *Social Psychology Quarterly, 70*(4), 319–321.

Strange, C. C., & Banning, J. H. (2001). *Educating by design: Creating campus learning environments that work.* San Francisco, CA: Jossey-Bass.

PART ONE

VISUAL METHODS AND RESEARCH

I

OVERVIEW OF THE USE OF VISUAL METHODS IN RESEARCH

J. Michael Denton, Carrie A. Kortegast, and Carrie Miller

Visuals are embedded in our everyday lives. Increased access to cameras has changed how we use images to communicate and record observations of the world around us. With increased access to visuals both as consumers and producers, new possibilities open for how visuals can be used in higher education research. Although using visual methods and methodologies in research has become more mainstream in a general sense, published higher education scholarship seldom includes visual methods such as photovoice, photo elicitation, visual ethnography, visual discourse analysis, or critical media studies (Metcalfe, 2012). Yet, images have the power to evoke new understandings and information about institutions and individuals within higher education.

As an interdisciplinary field, higher education researchers have a long history of incorporating methods and methodologies from other disciplines to understand topics and issues related to students, faculty, governance, policy, and learning. Similarly, higher education researchers who have incorporated visual methods into their research practices have drawn inspiration primarily from the disciplines of sociology, anthropology, psychology, cultural and media studies, and health sciences. Broadly, visual methods in higher education have been incorporated in the following primary ways: researcher analysis of existing images or artifacts (e.g., visual content analysis), participant analysis of existing visuals (e.g., photo elicitation, using a visual prompt during interviews), researcher-generated visuals (e.g., documentary photography), and participant-generated visuals (e.g., auto-driven photo elicitation, photovoice, diagramming, drawings; Kortegast et al., in press). Although there are individual examples of the use of a variety of different visual methods, photographic methods such as photo elicitation, photovoice, and visual content analysis are the dominant methods in higher education research.

This chapter reveals ways that visual images provide researchers a unique opportunity to find the interesting in the ordinary, foreground taken-for-granted assumptions, engage participants as cocreators of research, and gain deep insights into how the production of images impacts campus cultures. In this chapter, we discuss the following: (a) visuals as communicators of cultural messages, (b) subjective messages of visuals, and (c) uses of visual methods in higher education research.

Visuals as Communicators of Cultural Messages

The use of visuals in research is not new; however, qualitative researchers rarely foreground visual images, such as photographs, in data collection, analysis, and representation of information. Yet, often a goal of qualitative research is to uncover, unpack, and come to understand social and cultural complexity. Erwitt (*The Daily Telegraph*, 2010) stated:

> To me, photography is an art of observation. It's about finding something interesting in an ordinary place. . . . I've found it has little to do with the things you see and everything to do with the way you see them.

Often, it is not what researchers see, but how they make sense of it that matters—the *why* matters more than the *what*. Moreover, although the range of possibilities of human expression is vast, "the idea that research can be conducted using nondiscursive means such as pictures, or music, or dance, or all of those in combination, is not an idea that is widely practiced in American research" (Barone & Eisner, 2012, p. 1). Visuals and other arts-based methods can elicit information not always captured by numerical or word-based data.

Sociologists and anthropologists have used photographs as a tool to study, represent, and understand culture (Harper, 1988). The first comprehensive use of photography in representation of ethnographic knowledge was Bateson and Mead's (1942) book *Balinese Character: A Photographic Analysis*. In this text, Bateson and Mead argued they were trying "a new method of stating the intangible relationships among different types of culturally standardized behavior by placing side by side mutually relevant photographs"

(p. xii). The book attempted to catalog cultural practices, rituals, and artifacts through the use of photographs supplemented by written description. The use of photographs helped describe cultural traditions that are often difficult to convey in written text.

Photographs incorporated into the interview process have been used to elicit information about participant experiences. The method of photo elicitation developed out of Collier's (1957) work studying the mental health needs of a changing ethnically diverse community in the Maritime Provinces in Canada. Collier found that introducing photographs into the research process produced richer and more detailed responses from interview participants than traditional interviews. Additionally, the incorporation of photographs provided an opportunity for the research team to explicitly discuss their taken-for-granted assumptions about housing and residents' perceptions of their community. The use of photo elicitation has been expanded to other fields and disciplines (for a review, see Harper, 2002) as a method to understand individual experiences in various social and cultural contexts including higher education.

Although sociological and anthropological approaches of visual methods have used visuals, particularly photographs, as a way to document and explore cultural practices, media studies have a long history of providing analysis of print images, films, and advertisements. Derived from cultural and media studies, visual content analysis and critical visual analysis focus on examining the messages texts and images send about a particular topic. In higher education, institutions' social media accounts, websites, and college viewbooks all use visual imagery to convey an often carefully curated message about the campus values, culture, and environment. Hartley and Morphew (2008) argued the following:

> College and university viewbooks are selling to prospective students in the same way that print ads, billboards, and television screens do: This product will make you happy, meet your every need, help you succeed—even make your [sic] rich. (p. 688)

Viewbooks are not merely a collection of photographs of a campus but instead carefully constructed on the part of the creator to convey a particular message about campus culture. Consumers of viewbooks may or may not interpret the viewbook in the way that the creators intended—they impart their own meaning on the viewbook. Thus, visual content analysis and critical visual analysis provide methodological approaches to exploring and uncovering cultural practices, values, and messages embedded within these images.

Subjective Messages of Visuals

When utilizing visual methods, it is important to remember that images can be viewed and understood in many and, at times, contradictory ways. The meanings ascribed to photographs are subjective and arbitrary and depend on the viewer of the image (Pink, 2007). Individuals ascribe different meanings to images based on their own cultural understandings and subjective lens. Barthes argued that all nonphotographic images (e.g., drawings, paintings, film) contain both denoted and connoted messages. *Denoted* messages are the things reproduced or shown in the image, or the literal meaning of the image (i.e., the objects, persons, or landscapes captured in the image). *Connoted* messages are stylistic choices regarding how meaning is conferred to the objects in the image through social and cultural significance and interpretation (Barthes, 1977). However, according to Barthes (1977), photography makes distinguishing between denoted and connoted messages impossible, as people tend to focus on the image as the actual, real thing reproduced, rather than what the image represents (Barthes, 1977, 1980/1981).

The denoted message, or subject of the photograph, is often perceived as the actual thing depicted, creating a kind of "illusionary presence" (Shurkus, 2014, p. 71). Berger (2005) discussed this as the "ambiguity of the photograph" (p. 85). To illustrate this point, Berger shared a photograph of a man and a horse. He stated that "the photograph offers irrefutable evidence that this man, this horse and this bridle existed. Yet it tells us nothing of the significance of their existence" (p. 86). Drawing on this example, in Figure 1.1, what is known is that these individuals were on a sailboat. To use Berger's term, then, the individuals *existed*.

Figure 1.1. Study abroad students on a sunset cruise around Port of Valencia.

This picture confers that these individuals were on a sailboat at sunset. However, this tells us very little about who these individuals are, where they are, why they were on the sailboat, or what cultural or social meaning is attached to this photograph. As Berger (2005) stated, "the photograph begs for an interpretation" (p. 92).

The connoted message happens during the creation of the image as well as individual viewers' reception of the image. *Connotation*, imbuing an image with social or cultural significance, is a dual process occurring both during the creation of the image and during the consumption of images. Viewers bring their particular cultural lenses, experiences, histories, relationships, and knowledge to their interaction with an image (Pink, 2007). As such, no viewer is sure to have the same response to or interpretation of the image. One viewer of an image may impart more meaning or importance or have different understandings of the image than other viewers or even the creator of the image.

As an example, the photograph in Figure 1.1 was taken by a student during a study abroad program in Spain (Kortegast, 2011). The educational practice of studying abroad in Europe is laced with social and cultural significance. Depending on the viewer's orientation, the interpretation of this photograph might vary. It could be seen as a unique educational opportunity to experience another culture or it could be seen as a form of cultural tourism. Here, the creator of the image might attach different social and cultural meaning to this image. The creator, Daisy (a pseudonym), shared that the photograph represented both an experience she had never had before, sailing, as well as "living the European dream" (Kortegast & Kupo, 2017). Because forms of representation influence perception, the employment of multiple forms of representation, such as the visual, has an epistemological justification; it has the potential to enhance what can be known from multiple perspectives.

However, higher education professionals should be critical consumers of the images they consume and create. The meanings of photographs are situated meanings constructed by different viewers and not "given" or "natural" (Pink, 2007, p. 129). Embedded within photographs are symbols of class, gender, time and travel, and labor that can be used to evoke stories and experiences (Bell, 2002). The image that Daisy shared is linked to the larger social, cultural, and educational practice of study abroad. Who studies abroad, where they go, and what they do while they are overseas are tightly coupled with issues of privilege. These latent meanings are embedded in Daisy's photograph of a sunset cruise on the Mediterranean Sea but are often not critically examined. Thus, the connoted and denoted messages are difficult to extricate from one another in photography. Photographs are "a powerful ideological weapon because photography works to naturalize a view of the world that is in fact always political and interested" (Batchen, 2009, p. 7). Thus, when constructing materials or interpreting images careful attention should be taken to consider what taken-for-granted (i.e., hegemonic) assumptions and ideologies are being conveyed in images selected. Asking questions about *what* and *whose* purposes and interests such representations serve are important ethical and educational considerations.

Uses of Visual Methods in Higher Education Research

As mentioned, the use of visuals in higher education research does not reside within one particular theoretical or methodological tradition, but rather cuts across a variety of different traditions. There is a small but growing body of research that has utilized visual methods to explore higher education research topics. The predominant methods are photo elicitation, photovoice, visual content analysis, and arts-based inquiry. The following section provides an overview of these methods and examples from studies related to higher education.

Photo Elicitation

Photo elicitation is the dominant visual method used in higher education. This method has been used to study a wide range of different types of students, student subcultures, and topics with higher education. Photo elicitation is a method of interviewing that involves the use of images, researcher- or participant-generated photos, archival photos, or advertisements during the interview process to elicit information from respondents. These images serve as visual prompts to guide the research interview to gain information from participants about a particular topic. For instance, Harper (2001) shared aerial photos, archival images, and researcher-produced photographs during his interviews with farmers in order to explore how farming has changed over time. The photographs served as prompts to discuss how industrialization and modernization has changed the structure of farming and the family farm. In general, photo elicitation is a method that utilizes photographs to explore meanings individuals attach to particular topics. Higher education research has typically focused on the use of either researcher supplied photographs (see Harper, 2002) or participant-generated photographs (e.g., auto-driven; see Clark-Ibanez, 2004).

There are several examples in higher education research of the use of photo elicitation through including visuals prompts during interviews to solicit thoughts and opinions from participants on a particular topic. Harrison and Lawrence's (2003) study used photographs as prompts to explore African

American student athletes' perceptions of an athletic career transition. Participants were asked to review a student athlete profile that included two photographs and provide written responses. Information gained from the written responses provided insight into students' understanding of a transition into an athletic career.

Similarly, Comeaux's (2013) photo elicitation study used a vignette accompanied by a photograph of either a Black man or White man in a cap and gown to explore faculty perceptions of high-achieving college men. Comeaux stated, "the use of photo elicitation methodology was able to evoke thoughts, feelings, and conflicts concerning faculty perceptions of Black and White male collegians' academic accomplishments" (p. 460). Additional studies include Johnson, Hallinan, and Westerfield (1999) and Harrison (2002) that used photo elicitation to explore racial stereotyping of college male athletes. Cumulatively, the use of a visual image provided participants with prompts to contextualize their comments as well as explore their thoughts and understandings about potentially sensitive topics.

Participant-Generated Photo Elicitation

There are several examples of participant-generated photo elicitation in higher education research across different contexts, student populations, and subjects. Some examples include Birnbaum's (2013) study exploring students' representation of self and student subcultures via Facebook profiles, Blinn and Harrist's (1991) study of nontraditional age college women's reentry experience, and Mayhew's (2004) study exploring students' understandings of spirituality. Additionally, Branch (1997) used photo elicitation to explore how African American students attending a large public research university experienced the campus environment during their first few weeks of their first year. Branch found that the student-produced photos provided insight into students' lives and perspectives that an interview protocol alone would not typically generate.

In Hobbs and Klare's (2010) study of the use of the library by students, they stated that photographs provided students with the opportunity to "show, rather than just tell us" (p. 350). Additionally, the use of participant-generated photographs provided them with "concrete and specific examples to answer our questions about what makes a space comfortable, confusing, or conducive to studying" (p. 350). For instance, an example they shared was of a photograph of a pair of the participant's shoes. While discussing the photograph and the reason the student included his shoes, the student shared that he was from a poor family and could not afford much new clothing. He discussed extensively how using the library collection, reserve materials, and interlibrary loan saved him money on books and readings assigned for class.

Hobbs and Klare concluded that "this conversation gave us a new perspective on his answers, which we would not have had without the discussion about his shoes" (p. 350).

Photovoice

Developed out of the field of public health, Caroline Wang and Mary Ann Burris (1997) introduced the concept of *photovoice*. Photovoice is a form of emancipatory and action-oriented research that encourages participants to serve as experts and documenters of their community through the use of photography and dialogue. The photographs generated by participants served as a catalyst for dialogue with fellow community members, researchers, and agencies (public and nonprofit) that interact with the community. Photovoice, as envisioned by Wang and Burris (1994), explores communities and their needs through engaging in meaningful dialogue with community members in their capacities as experts. Photovoice is an expansion of photo elicitation (Kong, Kellner, Austin, Els, & Orr, 2015). Although both use participant-generated images, photovoice studies typically adopt emancipatory outcomes and goals for participants and may engage participants in analysis and critical reflection (Kong et al., 2015; Wang & Burris, 1997).

Often a goal of photovoice within research designs is to assist participants in developing "critical consciousness" (Freire, 2001, p. 73) through the examination of their communities. Participants are asked to share photographs to "record and reflect their community's strengths and concerns" (Wang & Burris, 1997, p. 370) with the overtly political purpose of generating change and influencing policy (Prosser, 2011, p. 484). However, not all photovoice projects result in an increase of critical consciousness or the examination of communities among participants. For instance, Latz (2012) argued that participation in her study exploring the educational lives of community college students promoted high levels of reflective consciousness. Through the process of taking, selecting, and explaining participant-generated photographs, individuals are able to reflect and make meaning of their own thoughts, memories, and experiences.

Several higher education scholars have used photovoice to explore the experiences of marginalized populations. For instance, researchers studying gay and lesbian students of color have found the photovoice method useful for ethical research with students who "often find themselves at an intersection of cultures, identities, and value systems called 'borderlands' that collide and conflict" (Anzaldúa, 1999, 2010, cited in Means & Jaeger, 2015, p. 11). Means and Jaeger's (2015) study of Black gay men found this method useful in understanding the intersections of participants' racial, sexual, and spiritual identities as they related to different contexts including higher education.

Blending constructivist and quare (i.e., Black queer) theoretical frameworks, their participants took photographs of meaningful spaces in their life.

Similarly, Peña-Talamantes (2013) studied the complex lives of Latina/o gay and lesbian college students. Provided with disposable cameras, participants were asked to take pictures salient to their racial and sexual identities. These photographs served to illuminate themes that were important to the participants but not otherwise identified in interviews and reflections (Peña-Talamantes, 2013).

Visual Content Analysis

As discussed previously, visual content analysis and critical visual analysis focus on examining the messages texts and images communicate about a particular topic. For example, Hartley and Morphew (2008) analyzed the text and images of 48 different college and university viewbooks to explore the representation and marketing of higher education. They concluded that viewbooks "commodif[y] college choice" (p. 688) by communicating the following message:

> This product will make you happy, meet your every need, help you suc-
> ceed—even make your [sic] rich. It is the rare viewbook that goes beyond
> the sales pitch to try to connect with something more cerebral, spiritual, or
> educational. (p. 688)

Ultimately, the images that colleges and universities choose to use communicate important messages about the institution. Examples of other studies that use visual content analysis include Saichaie and Morphew's (2014) analysis of college and university websites; Hum and colleagues' (2011) analysis of Facebook profile pictures; and Osei-Kofi and Torres (2015) and Osei-Kori, Torres, and Lui's (2013) critical visual analyses of the representation of race and gender in college viewbooks.

Arts-Based Inquiry

Although arts-based inquiry often incorporates art forms that are language-based (e.g., narratives, poetry), there are several forms of arts-based methods that employ "nonverbal media," such as drawings, paintings, or photography (Barone & Eisner, 2006, p. 96). Arts-based research "adapt[s] the tenets of the creative arts in order to address social research questions in *holistic* and *engaged* ways in which *theory and practice are intertwined*" (Leavy, 2009, p. ix; emphasis in original). The methods arose to advance an ethic of care and mutuality between researchers and participants and can provide participants opportunities to be "collaborators or even co-researchers" (Finley, 2005,

p. 682). These researchers often use these methods as a way to address power inequities and ethical quandaries not only about the populations they seek to understand but also about research itself.

An expressed purpose of arts-based inquiry is to challenge traditional conventions and methods of scientific research. Thus, it primarily concerns itself with representing findings in an aesthetic manner (that is, either beautifully or through certain artistic conventions) with an aim toward the *"enhancement of perspectives"* (Barone & Eisner, 2006, p. 96; emphasis in original). Unlike other forms of research, arts-based researchers are not necessarily concerned with providing singular, definitive meaning about their topic but with opening up various possible interpretations and understandings. Arts-based research seeks to forge new avenues for creating knowledge; as Finley (2005) asserted, "there are varied ways in which the world can be known" (p. 685). Ultimately, the construction of art is a way to generate knowledge as well as a way for researchers to present knowledge (Vaughn, 2005).

Drawings, Painting, and Graphic Elicitation
Although more prominent in other disciplines, the use of nonphotographic drawings and graphics in higher education research is relatively rare; however, some examples of such scholarship do exist. Like photographic methods, some of these methods are used toward more social justice–oriented aims than others. Although this small body of scholarship differs in its degree of criticalness (i.e., the degree to which these studies interrogate power structures), these scholars share a common belief that new kinds of knowledge and insight can be accessed through drawings, paintings, and graphics.

Interested in community college students' meaning-making after transferring to a four-year institution, Rodriguez and Kerrigan (2016) utilized a graphic elicitation method in which participants developed relational maps. Participants were provided with maps resembling a bullseye with the word "me" at the center. Participants were asked to write words that described their identity as a college student, with the least descriptive or salient words on the outer rings. This activity augmented data from semi-structured interviews regarding the students' identity, development, and engagement (Rodriguez & Kerrigan, 2016). To the researchers' surprise, during the interviews, one participant illustrated how the phrases and words he chose would move or change on his map compared to his time in community college. This student's creativity compelled the researchers to modify their protocol, actively soliciting other participants to engage the map in a similar manner. The change in protocol provided a more complex and nuanced understanding of students' identities. As Rodriguez and Kerrigan (2016) stated, the map "helped participants in conceptualizing distance and expressing aspects of themselves in ways that they perhaps could not verbalize" (p. 1063).

Welkener and Baxter Magolda (2014) used nonverbal methods to explore college students' developmental journey toward self-authorship. They asked junior and senior undergraduate students to use various two- and three-dimensional materials (e.g., magazines for collage, sculpting material) to create self-portraits; they supplemented this method with interviews and a free-writing exercise. Using one participant's artwork as an exemplar, they concluded that "the rich metaphors she [the student] shared through imagery, combined with her verbal and written descriptions, provide a unique window into her view of self, relationships, and knowledge that is, as her opening quote conveys, 'so much more intense'" (Welkener & Baxter Magolda, 2014, p. 584) than without the self-portrait.

A coauthor of this chapter (Denton, 2014) conducted research with gay college men living with HIV using a poststructural (specifically, queer theory) lens. In addition to participating in in-depth interviews using a life-story protocol, participants created various forms of artwork to express their relationship to HIV/AIDS (Denton, 2014). The choice to do an arts-based study with these men rose from many considerations. First, AIDS activists have a long tradition of using artwork to counteract and reframe oppressive cultural and political representations (Crimp, 1988). Second, art provided a method for involving participants more in the research process and foregrounding their voices, an important element derived from The Denver Principles (1983), ethical guidelines developed by people living with HIV. And finally, the theoretical framework called for finding a way to allow participants to express multiple voices or selves. Given the choice to create any kind of artwork reproducible on a page, two participants created linguistic pieces (e.g., poetry), three created paintings or drawings, and one shaped a bonsai tree. The art produced by the participants portrayed the complexity of living with HIV as a gay man in the United States, amplified their narratives, and illuminated tensions and contradictions not always evident in their verbal narratives.

Although higher education researchers have not drawn as much from other graphic methods, other disciplines offer insights into what such research could encompass. For instance, Ketchen Jr., Short, and Terrell (2011) used a graphic novel format to represent research about academic journal review processes. Hidalgo (2015) combined photographic images with comic book style fonts, formats, and captions to create a visual experience that uses photographs and video stills to create a graphic experience called an *augmented fotonovela*. Fotonovelas are a critical intervention designed to subvert colonizing anthropological research by drawing on a traditional Latino/a format that combines photographic or video images with other graphics (Hidalgo,

2015). Rippin (2012) used portraits as a way of understanding the cultural impact of an influential national business leader. Her portraits encompassed the use of a variety of methods, including not only drawing and painting but also textiles and collage.

Conclusion

The use of visual images in higher education research and practice can allow participants to illuminate their life experiences as well as otherwise taken-for-granted or invisible aspects of their institutions. Arts-based methods, and especially photovoice, have been used to highlight and explore marginalized communities' experiences of their everyday worlds and manifest aspects of participants' lives that researchers may not otherwise notice.

The public health and urban planning scholars who implemented the first documented photo-based studies did so because they were interested in understanding the communities they were studying through the eyes of their participants. These studies often focused on understanding the physical objects in participants' neighborhoods, schools, and homes that had cultural or personal significance. The research questions ultimately centered on understanding how individuals construct and understand their immediate social environments. As illustrated by Means and Jaeger's (2015) study of gay Black college men, the same basic questions that motivated early photo-based studies are equally relevant to higher education communities today.

Such questions include the following: How do students make sense of and understand their campus communities (e.g., residential communities) and the broader contexts in which they live, work, and study? What are the safe or comfortable spaces for students? What spaces are alienating or marginalizing? How do the surrounding communities to universities welcome or reject certain students? Using student-led photography, projects could help clarify and correct assumptions held by student affairs educators and higher education administrators.

Drawings, collages, and other visual methods are useful for exploring identity, development, emotions, and other complex phenomena. Visual methods can enhance other research methods and prove to be more inclusive, not to mention enjoyable, experiences for participants. Experiencing joy, as hooks (1994) reminded us, should be part of the educational endeavor. Further, visual methods can serve social justice–oriented purposes, as well as evaluative, supervisory, and self-reflective purposes. Although often seen as marginal compared to more conventional research methods, studies demonstrate that visual methods enhance and complement other means of producing knowledge, often producing the kind of information not otherwise available or discernable. Those interested in infusing visual methods into research or practice should anticipate resistance and develop solid rationales for their use.

As we discussed, images abound in higher education, many of which are controlled and produced by those in various institutions. Images, and photographs in particular, convey explicit (or denoted) information—such as presenting actual students attending the institution—but also implicit (or connoted) messages, such as what kind of students are welcome and important at that institution. Given the power of images and photographs to evoke strong feelings and to import a sense of naturalness (Barthes, 1977, 1980/1981), those producing images should carefully consider and reflect on the assumptions, biases, and unexamined ideologies of such images at every stage, from production to display.

References

Anzaldúa, G. (1999). *Borderlands: La frontera* (2nd ed.). San Francisco, CA: Aunt Lute Books

Anzaldúa, G. (2010). La conciencia de la mestiza: Towards a new consciousness. In M. Adams, W. J. Blumenfeld, C. Castaneda, H. W. Hackman, M. L. Peters, & X. Zuniga (Eds.), *Readings for diversity and social justice* (pp. 94–98). New York, NY: Routledge.

Barone, T., & Eisner, E. (2006). Arts-based educational research. In J. L. Green, G. Camilli, & P. B. Elmore (Eds.), *Handbook of complementary methods in education research* (pp. 95–109). Washington, DC: American Educational Research Association.

Barone, T., & Eisner, E. W. (2012). *Art-based research*. London, England: Sage.

Barthes, R. (1977). *Image music text* (S. Heath, Trans.). New York, NY: Hill and Wang.

Barthes, R. (1981). *Camera lucida* (R. Howard, Trans.). New York, NY: Hill and Wang. (Original work published 1980)

Batchen, G. (2009). Palinode: An introduction to photography degree zero. In G. Batchen (Ed.), *Photography degree zero: Reflections on Roland Barthes's camera lucida* (pp. 1–30). Cambridge, MA: MIT Press.

Bateson, G., & Mead, M. (1942). *Balinese character: A photographic analysis*. New York, NY: New York Academy of Sciences.

Bell, S. E. (2002). Photo images: Jo Spence's narratives of living with illness. *Health*, 6(1), 5–30.

Berger, H. (2005). *Situated utterances: Texts, bodies, and cultural representations*. New York, NY: Fordham University Press.

Birnbaum, M. G. (2013). The fronts students use: Facebook and the standardization of self-presentations. *Journal of College Student Development*, 54(2), 155–171.

Blinn, L., & Harrist, A. W. (1991). Combining native instant photography and photo-elicitation. *Visual Anthropology*, *4*(2), 175–192.

Branch, K. (1997). *Pictures and perceptions: First-year, African American students' impressions of a predominantly white university* (Doctoral dissertation). Indiana University, Bloomington, IN.

Clark-Ibanez, M. (2004). Framing the social world with photo-elicitation interviews. *American Behavioral Scientist*, *47*(12), 1507–1527. doi:10.1177/00027 64204266236

Collier, J. (1957). Photography in anthropology: A report on two experiments. *American Anthropologist*, *59*, 843–859. doi:10.1525/aa.1957.59.5.02a00100

Comeaux, E. (2013). Faculty perceptions of high-achieving male collegians: A critical race theory analysis. *Journal of College Student Development*, *54*(5), 453–465.

Crimp, D. (1988). AIDS: Cultural analysis / cultural activism. In D. Crimp (Ed.), *AIDS: Cultural analysis, cultural activism* (pp. 3–16). Cambridge, MA: MIT Press.

Denton, J. M. (2014). *Living beyond identity: Gay college men living with HIV* (Unpublished doctoral dissertation). Miami University, Oxford, OH.

Finley, S. (2005). Arts-based inquiry: Performing revolutionary pedagogy. In N. K. Denzin & Y. S. Lincoln (Eds.), *Handbook of qualitative research* (3rd ed., pp. 681–694). Thousand Oaks, CA: Sage.

Freire, P. (2001). *Education for critical consciousness*. London, England: A&C Black.

Harper, D. (1988). Visual sociology: Expanding sociological vision. *The American Sociologist*, *19*, 54–70.

Harper, D. (2001). *Changing works: Visions of a lost agriculture*. Chicago, IL: University of Chicago Press.

Harper, D. (2002). Talking about pictures: A case for photo elicitation. *Visual Studies*, *17*(1), 13–26. doi:10.1080/14725860220137345

Harrison, B. (2002). Seeing health and illness worlds—Using visual methodologies in a sociology of health and illness: A methodological review. *Sociology of Health & Illness*, *24*(6), 856–872.

Harrison, C. K., & Lawrence, S. M. (2003). African American student athletes' perceptions of career transition in sport: A qualitative and visual elicitation. *Race Ethnicity and Education*, *6*(4), 373–394.

Hartley, M., & Morphew, C. C. (2008). What's being sold and to what end?: A content analysis of college viewbooks. *The Journal of Higher Education*, *79*(6), 671–691. doi:10.1353/jhe.0.0025

Hidalgo, L. (2015). Augmented fotonovelas: Creating new media as pedagogical and social justice tools. *Qualitative Inquiry*, *21*(3), 300–314.

Hobbs, K., & Klare, D. (2010). User driven design: Using ethnographic techniques to plan student study space. *Technical Services Quarterly*, *27*(4), 347–363.

hooks, b. (1994). *Teaching to transgress: Education as the practice of freedom*. New York, NY: Routledge.

Hum, N. J., Chamberlin, P. E., Hambright, B. L., Portwood, A. C., Schat, A. C., & Bevan, J. L. (2011). A picture is worth a thousand words: A content analysis of Facebook profile photographs. *Computers in Human Behavior*, *27*(5), 1828–1833.

Johnson, D. L., Hallinan, C. J., & Westerfield, R. C. (1999). Picturing success: Photographs and stereotyping in men's collegiate basketball. *Journal of Sports Behavior, 22*(1), 45–53.

Ketchen Jr., D. J., Short, J., & Terrell, W. (2011). Graphic truth: Some hidden realities of the review process. *Journal of Management Inquiry, 20*(1), 88–94.

Kong, T. M., Kellner, K., Austin, D. E., Els, Y., & Orr, B. J. (2015). Enhancing participatory evaluation of land management through photo elicitation and photovoice. *Society and Natural Resources, 28*, 212–229.

Kortegast, C. A. (2011). *Picturing learning: A visual ethnography of social learning during a short-term study abroad program* (Unpublished doctoral dissertation). Iowa State University, Ames, IA.

Kortegast, C., & Kupo, V. L. (2017). Deconstructing underlying practices of short-term student abroad: Exploring issues of consumerism, postcolonialism, cultural tourism, and commodification of experience. *International Journal of Critical Pedagogy, 8*(1), 149–172.

Kortegast, C. A., McCann, K., Branch, K., Latz, A. O., Kelly, B. T., & Linder, C. (in press). Enhancing ways of knowing: Participant-generated visual methods in higher education research. *Review of Higher Education.*

Latz, A. O. (2012). Understanding the educational lives of community college students: A photovoice project, a Bourdieusian interpretation, and habitus dissonance spark theory. *Current Issues in Education, 15*(2), 1–25.

Leavy, P. (2009). *Method meets art: Arts-based research practices.* New York, NY: Guilford Press.

Mayhew, M. J. (2004). Exploring the essence of spirituality: A phenomenological study of eight students with eight different worldviews. *NASPA Journal, 41*(4), 647–674.

Means, D. R., & Jaeger, A. J. (2015). Spiritual borderlands: A Black gay male college student's spiritual journey. *Journal of Student Affairs Research and Practice, 52*(1), 11–23.

Metcalfe, A. S. (2012). Imag(in)ing the university: Visual sociology and higher education. *The Review of Higher Education, 35*(4), 517–534.

Osei-Kofi, N., & Torres, L. E. (2015). College admissions viewbooks and the grammar of gender, race, and STEM. *Cultural Studies of Science Education, 10*(2), 527–544.

Osei-Kofi, N., Torres, L. E., & Lui, J. (2013). Practices of whiteness: Racialization in college admissions viewbooks. *Race Ethnicity and Education, 16*(3), 386–405.

Peña-Talamantes, A. E. (2013). Empowering the self, creating worlds: Lesbian and gay Latina/o college students' identity negotiation in figured worlds. *Journal of College Student Development, 54*(3), 267–282.

Pink, S. (2007). *Doing visual ethnography* (2nd ed.). Thousand Oaks, CA: Sage.

Prosser, J. (2011). Visual methodology: Toward a more seeing research. In N. K. Denzin & Y. S. Lincoln (Eds.), *The Sage handbook of qualitative research* (pp. 479–496). Los Angeles, CA: Sage.

Rippin, A. (2012). Eliza, Anita, and me: An art investigation using portraiture as a research method in organization studies. *Culture and Organization, 18*(4), 305–322.

Rodriguez, S. K., & Kerrigan, M. R. (2016). Using graphic elicitation to explore community college transfer student identity, development, and engagement. *The Qualitative Report, 21*(6), 1052–1070.

Saichaie, K., & Morphew, C. C. (2014). What college and university websites reveal about the purposes of higher education. *The Journal of Higher Education, 85*(4), 499–530.

Shurkus, M. (2014). Camera lucida and affect: Beyond representation. *Photographies, 7*(1), 67–83. Retrieved from http://dx.doi.org/10.1080/17540763.2014.896276

The Daily Telegraph. (2010). Magnum photographer Elliott Erwitt's favourite photographs, in pictures. Retrieved from http://www.telegraph.co.uk/news/picturegalleries/uknews/11393014/Magnum-photographer-Elliott-Erwitts-favourite-photographs-in-pictures.html?frame=3189131

The Denver Principles. (1983). Retrieved from http://www.actupny.org/documents/Denver.html

Vaughan, K. (2005). Pieced together: Collage as an artist's method for interdisciplinary research. *International Journal of Qualitative Methods, 4*(1), 1–21.

Wang, C., & Burris, M. A. (1994). Empowerment through photo novella: Portraits of participation. *Health Education & Behavior, 21*(2), 171–186. doi: 10.1177/109019819402100204

Wang, C., & Burris, M. A. (1997). Photovoice: Concept, methodology, and use for participatory needs assessment. *Health Education & Behavior, 24*(3), 369–387. doi:10.1177/109019819702400309

Welkener, M. M., & Baxter Magolda, M. B. (2014). Better understanding students' self-authorship via self-portraits. *Journal of College Student Development, 55*(6), 580–585.

2

UTILIZING PHOTO ELICITATION TO EXPLORE BELONGING AND SPACE IN CAMPUS ENVIRONMENTS

Katherine Branch and Amanda O. Latz

Imagine the following scenario: You are interested in physical spaces on campus where students who identify as people of color engage in identity work. To do this, you engage students of color in a focus group and ask the following questions: Where do you feel most like yourself on campus? Why does that particular space make you feel most like yourself? What does that space look like? What do you do in that space? What do you not do in that space? Who is with you in that space? Who is absent in that space? You also ask the following questions: Where do you feel most unlike yourself on campus? Why does that particular space make you feel most unlike yourself? What does that space look like? What do you do in that space? What do you not do in that space? Who is with you in that space? Who is absent in that space? These questions would likely generate a rich and robust conversation related to campus physical spaces and the identity work that happens in those spaces.

However, it is one thing to talk or describe a specific space, and it is quite another to *show* and tell about a specific space (Branch, 2003). If, ahead of that focus group, the researcher had given those participants cameras and asked them to respond to those questions with photographs, the nature of that focus group may have changed remarkably, as the presence of images could have augmented and influenced the conversation. According to Harper (2002), "exchanges based on words alone utilize less of the brain's capacity than do exchanges in which the brain is processing images as well as words" (p. 13).

Now, consider ways in which electronic social media has changed the landscape of human sociality and practices of life narration. Most social media platforms are highly visual, and with the advent and affordances of digital photography and smartphone technology, it has never been easier to communicate visually. College students are engaging in identity development vis-à-vis social media (Junco, 2014). That said, why not engage them in inquiry in ways with which they are familiar? Refer back to the previous example. Imagine the richness of data that students could generate if asked to respond visually—with no other parameters—to exploring identity development, investigating belongingness, and assessing influences of their collegiate environment. What might we see and discover if students make use of myriad and ever-expanding technologies to engage in these tasks?

We contend, based on our own research experiences, that visual inquiry is ripe with opportunities for both learning about and fostering college student development. Thus, in this chapter we describe visual methodologies and methods used in research we have carried out, provide details of how one method (i.e., photo elicitation) was implemented, and explicate connections between using participant-generated visual materials in research with college students and student development.

Visual Methodologies and Methods

The collective knowledge base related to college student development is recent compared with academic disciplines that initially contributed to research on students in postsecondary settings (e.g., anthropology, history, psychology, sociology). In the United States, the emergence of the profession of college student affairs in the twentieth century (see American Council on Education, 1937) resulted in the establishment of a body of scholarship that is specific to understanding human development and learning in relationship to participation in higher education. As Gillon, Beatty, and Davis (2012) noted,

> Whereas *The Student Personnel Point of View* authors could not identify existing agencies to pursue scholarly efforts, the field now boasts a range of professional organizations and associations with members who have committed their careers to exploring college student experiences. (p. 71)

Today's scholarship is interdisciplinary, in that it draws upon knowledge from numerous academic disciplines, yet uniquely examines the interactions among diverse students and the collegiate environments they frequent.

Historically, although psychological approaches to understanding college student development may be prominent, we argue that interdisciplinary approaches will yield more comprehensive and authentic understandings related to how students develop during and through their collegiate experiences. A wide range of parent disciplines inform the study of higher education, and student affairs specifically, and visual inquiry within many of these parent disciplines has been used for decades (e.g., Bateson & Mead, 1942) and even for more than a century in some cases (e.g., Riis, 1890). However, the use of visual methodologies and methods within the field of student affairs remains relatively nascent. According to Pink (2012), the start of the twenty-first century marked an emergence of visual methods and methodologies "as a field of interdisciplinary scholarship and practice" (p. 6). Although many studies within the field of student affairs draw on interdisciplinary knowledge, the research methodologies and methods have yet to fully embrace use of the visual. Furthermore, much of the work done to advance what is known about college student development was generated from a logocentric (Drucker, 2014) perspective, which privileges words as representations of an external reality. Visual methods broaden this perspective and call for the inclusion of additional forms of representation.

Within this chapter, we define *methodologies* as overarching approaches to research projects. We define *methods* as the means through which those methodologies are carried out. For example, as part of a study grounded in a phenomenological methodology (e.g., Vagle, 2014), a researcher could use the method of a participant-generated graphic elicitation exercise during face-to-face interviews (e.g., Crilly, Blackwell, & Clarkson, 2006). Here, we are most concerned with participant-generated visuals—those that are attentive to and grounded in the participants' perspectives of their lives, regardless of medium (e.g., photography, self-portraiture, drawing, collage making).

Although we are beginning to see the infusion of visual methodologies (e.g., Latz, 2012) and methods (e.g., Welkener & Baxter Magolda, 2014) within studies of student development, this area requires additional scholarly attention. There are many reasons for this. Foremost, there are limits to what can be conveyed through language. Interviews, focus groups, and even surveys or questionnaires are often necessarily bound to the conventions of verbal and written language in regard to what and how ideas are expressed. Additionally, contemporary life is highly visual. This includes the ubiquity of social media and its visual affordances such as making, sharing, narrating, and editing photographs, animated gifs, videos, memes, and so on. Again, why not blend research approaches and practices with manners of expression congruent with college students' everyday life experiences?

Utilizing Photo Elicitation to Explore Campus Environments

Some of my (Katie's) first memories focus on the visual. Perhaps this is because of the eye surgery I had when I was young and the accompanying "games" that I played to improve my vision—including one using photographic slides. Later, in adolescence, I had an interest in photojournalism; I pursued this interest in my undergraduate education. While an undergraduate I also became connected with student affairs work and eventually became a residential staff member. My residence hall director, an African American man, influenced my decision to begin graduate studies in higher education and student affairs. He also became a mentor to me; he helped increase my knowledge and skills with people whose racial identity was different from my own, which is White. Because of my work with students of color as a student affairs professional, I tended to focus on race and ethnicity as a facet of identity, and how collegiate environments interacted with racial and ethnic aspects of self.

Combining my interests, knowledge, and skills in visual imagery, diverse student populations, and person–environment interaction was important to me as I prepared during doctoral studies to potentially transition from a student affairs practitioner to a full-time faculty member. In addition, I had a strong desire to conduct inquiry that could improve both bachelor degree attainment and the experiences of diverse college students. Thus, I designed a qualitative research study investigating first-year, African American undergraduates' transitions into a predominantly White research university. At the time of this study (and currently), the majority of African American undergraduates were enrolled at predominantly White universities (National Center for Education Statistics, 1995, 2016). More details about my positionality and how I addressed my racial privilege throughout this study are in my dissertation (Douglas, 1997).

The overarching approach I took in this scholarly inquiry was symbolic interactionism, which is akin to phenomenological-oriented methodology that seeks understandings from the viewpoints of participants. A sociological perspective, symbolic interactionism "seeks to explain action and interactions as the outcomes of the meaning actors attach to things and social actions" (Jary & Jary, 1991, p. 508; see also Blumer, 1969; Mead, 1934). Because of my student affairs work experiences, awareness of the importance of visual images to students, and desire to open up dialogue with students who differed from my racial identity, I looked for ways to incorporate alternative forms of data representation and semiotic perspectives. In communication systems, linguistic expression as written and spoken word tends to dominate as ways of conveying and acquiring information. Thus, emphasis on using a broader range of human sensory modalities lacks prevalence (Eisner, 1982).

In my study, photographs were used to readily generate data antecedents and re-present data via the visual sensory modality.

Furthermore, I wanted both the production and interpretation of these photographs to be consistent with a semiotic perspective, in which the visual images could provide symbolic meaning as part of a broadly defined language system (Bruner, 1990). I knew that asking participants to interpret their photographs to me was integral to the research process. Photo elicitation interviews use reflexive photographs produced previously by research study participants or generated by participants for specific research purposes (Harper, 1987, 1988). Ziller (1990) noted that having meaningful interview conversations about participant-generated photographs can assist with cross-cultural communication; therefore, this method potentially could assist with communication between African American student participants and me as a White researcher. Additionally, I could find only one published study that used reflexive photographs taken by college students and employed photo elicitation interviews (Perka, Matherly, Fishman, & Ridge, 1992); thus, I wanted to understand more about the use of these visually based research methods.

The primary purpose of my study was to investigate first-year, African American undergraduates' impressions of the campus environment at a predominantly White research university. I wanted to both understand the students' meanings of those impressions and discover attributions for their impressions (Branch Douglas, 1998a; Douglas, 1997). Because the methodology and methods utilized in this study were new at that time to higher education researchers, a secondary purpose was to explore the usefulness of participant-generated photographs that later served as stimuli in interviews in qualitative inquiry. I used purposive, maximum variation sampling to select participants (Lincoln & Guba, 1985; Stake, 1994), who were five first-year African American women and five first-year African American men. Selection criteria were being from a variety of in-state and out-of-state hometowns, living in differing on-campus residential settings, and being (or not being) affiliated with the institution's three programs linked with minority undergraduate recruitment and retention. Students could create pseudonyms for identification purposes.

Impressions were defined as the "thoughts, feelings, ideas, or images remaining with a person as a result of perceptions stemming from some type of experience(s)" (Douglas, 1997, p. 9). To allow for impression formation of the campus environment without knowing they might partake in a research study, participants were contacted after the end of the 6th week of the fall semester and generated photographs during the 11th and 12th weeks. Each participant was given a disposable, 27-exposure, 35-mm camera with a built-in flash and preloaded color film. In the mid-1990s, this technology for generating photographs was widely available in the consumer marketplace, and even today this technology can be used in similar studies. The undergraduates were given the following task: "Take pictures that illustrate your impressions of [the university] or that will help you to describe your impressions of [the university]" (Douglas, 1997, p. 38). Participants also were asked to record in a provided notebook the day of the week and time the photo was taken, what they were photographing in each frame of film, what that photo meant to them, the thoughts and feelings they had about that impression, and what might have influenced those thoughts and feelings.

After participants completed their generation of photographs, they were given a set of prints of their photographs and a photo album and asked to arrange the photos in the order they preferred to talk about them during an approximately two-hour individual interview. I began the individual photo elicitation interviews by asking participants to describe each photo and what that image meant to them; when needed, I encouraged students to use the comments from their notebooks as prompts in talking about their images. Additional preplanned questions were as follows:

- What are some of your strongest impressions?
- Do you consider that impression positive, negative, or neutral?
- How, if at all, do you think your impressions influenced your behavior?
- How, if at all, did the visual component of the study affect you?

After preliminary data analysis, I developed constructs about the students' impressions of this predominantly White research university and conducted three small-group interviews with the study participants. In addition to discussing the constructs in these small groups, I asked if the students would recommend this university to other African American prospects and what advice they would give if an African American student planned to start his or her collegiate career at that institution.

With the more detailed and member-checked information after the small-group interviews, I continued with data analysis until six themes emerged. These themes related to the following aspects of this campus environment: (a) natural, physical environment; (b) institutional size; (c) racial consciousness; (d) Greek-letter organizations; (e) racial and cultural interactions; and (f) preparation for the future. Racial consciousness, Greek-letter organizations, and racial and cultural interactions were the themes that the use of participant-generated visuals and photo elicitation interviews seemed to both draw out and elaborate on in terms of the complexity of impressions that students had. For example, Simone made an entry in her notebook to accompany the image she took of a house where Greek-letter organization members resided (Figure 2.1). She wrote, "This house is absolutely beautiful! My parents' house doesn't even *compare* to this one. White kids can come to school and virtually pick which mansion they want to live in. Wow!" When talking about this image, she said, "They live here and for generations. . . . It's just amazing. I don't understand that. . . . But, I guess they can afford to do it." Monique took a similar photo of a sorority house and commented,

> African Americans are very underrepresented on [this] campus. We don't even have a sorority house. Why? Also, why is it I only hear about White Greek organizations doing things in the community? Do the Black Greeks do things, but they aren't reported or shown publicly? . . . The only reason I would want to pledge is to live in one of these big fancy houses, but that won't happen because Blacks don't even have a house.

A number of participants took photographs related to White Greek chapters to show their impression that the White Greek chapters dominated campus social life, contributing to their own racial consciousness as well as indicating a lack of interactions among racial and other cultural subgroups on campus.

Photo elicitation interviews demonstrate the importance of researchers not assuming the meanings of the visuals generated by study participants. As Pauwels (2011) stated, "It is important to note that the respondent-generated material, while offering a unique (insider) perspective, is never an end product, but just an intermediate step in the research" (p. 8). Although

Figure 2.1. Greek fraternity house, 1995.

Note. Taken by Simone.

Simone's and Monique's similar images of a White Greek fraternity and sorority house show the convergence of impressions that students wanted to convey, another example shows how similar images had entirely different meanings when explained by each photographer. Both Tiffany and James took photographs that focused on a sculpture by a museum that is on campus (Figure 2.2.). James took the photo to show how physically beautiful he thought the campus was and how that reflected positively on the students who went there. He also took a photo of a baseball diamond visible from his residence hall window to show this beauty. However, to Tiffany, who took a similar photograph, the image was representative of how money was spent at this campus. She commented, "The red thing [sculpture] is something I know my money went to, but I have no idea what it is. . . . It seems like this school tries to take you for everything."

Six years after the completion of the initial research, I reconnected with 7 of the 10 study participants to discover the potential impact of campus impressions on these individuals' subsequent development and bachelor's degree attainment (Branch, 2004). Five of the students had graduated, and 2 others had left the university after 2 or 3 years and were working on their degrees elsewhere. All agreed that their initial impressions of the campus environment were lasting, although the influence of the impressions was wide-ranging. Perhaps the greatest change was in relationship to Greek-letter organizations, as participants reported they had lower regard for White Greek-letter organizations and higher regard for historically Black Greek-letter organizations. Overall, 6 of the 7 participants said they would

Figure 2.2. On-campus red sculpture, 1995.

Note. Taken by James.

recommend the university to other African Americans. The participant who would not recommend the institution indicated wanting more diverse opportunities and a better social experience. Lastly, in regard to the photo elicitation aspect of the original study, all participants reported they enjoyed being part of a study that involved a visual research method.

Despite the value that photo elicitation can add to the research process, there are few published studies on its use in higher education settings, especially those that involve students. Lapenta (2011) wrote,

> Although it remains fairly marginal to mainstream research, photo-elicitation has recently gained broader recognition for its heuristic and collaborative potential. Indeed, it is becoming an established element in the methodological toolbox of the visual anthropologist or sociologist and is increasingly popular in a range of interdisciplinary research studies. (p. 202)

Given the interdisciplinary nature of researching human development in the context of higher education settings and the potential to learn differently when incorporating photo elicitation into the research process, the next section identifies some of what Amanda and I learned when conducting participatory visual research with college students.

Connections With Student Development

Incorporating participant-generated images into the research process was an intentional choice for us as qualitative researchers and as practitioners who are knowledgeable about student development theories and models. Both the inquiry methodologies and research methods we selected for our scholarship on exploring belonging and space in campus environments was guided by this knowledge and prior applications with diverse students. Through our work using participant-generated visuals, we also discovered links to student development perspectives and gained insights from students about how such methods influenced not only their development but also their enthusiasm about taking part in research.

Power Dynamics

When using participant-generated visuals in the research process, we were keenly aware of sharing power with the participants in our studies. As the primary researchers, we recognized that we held both responsibility and authority for making decisions about study design, data analysis, and tangible products (e.g., dissertations, scholarly articles, exhibits). In terms of understanding the phenomena of interest and conveying insights to others, we recognized that student participants were coresearchers. As such, we selected methodologies, methods, and theories grounded in perspectives that guided us in the use of shared power. Because of the nondominant nature of the research methodologies and methods that we utilized in our studies, we explicated reasons for their selection. One of the reasons that I (Katie) selected the photo elicitation method was to lessen my power as not only a primary researcher but also a White woman collaborating with African American students. As Ziller (1990) suggested, it is noteworthy that this method did draw out elaborate information that related to race (i.e., racial consciousness, Greek-letter organizations, and racial and cultural interactions).

More tacit in our research was our knowledge of how approaches to sharing power during the research process interfaced with, and potentially enhanced, college student development. For example, in the study on African American students' impressions of a predominantly White research university, theories of identity development were used to address how differences in racial identity might impact recruitment of participants and information shared with the researcher (e.g., Bennett, 1990; Cross, 1991). To foster trust and model open communication, it was important that prospective participants had the opportunity to talk with me (Katie) about why I was interested in the topic and in what ways I intended to share data. When conducting photo elicitation interviews, I used intellectual development theories to guide how to phrase additional, clarifying questions (e.g., Baxter Magolda, 1992; Perry, 1968/1970). During the small-group interviews, I noticed how some students' ways of thinking were challenged positively by other students in the groups. During one group conversation, students vigorously debated the terms *segregation* and *separation* when discussing how African American and White students rarely mingled socially. It was evident through comments made that students not only learned from each other but also reconsidered or expanded their definitions of these terms. Although this debate might occur in a traditional focus group, the photographic images brought out the nuances in students' rationales for utilizing intentionally different words for what they observed and experienced.

Student Engagement

Time on task, both physically and psychologically, is a factor that can promote college student development (Astin, 1984; Kuh, 2009). Therefore, because of the use of shared power in research processes that include participant-generated visual materials, the amount of time on task required from study participants can be both substantial and purposeful. For example, the time study participants spent on arranging their photo albums in preparation for photo elicitation interviews required more time and mental energy than merely showing up at an interview. It also signaled that the photo elicitation interview would require more than showing up; there would be active participation in knowledge cocreation versus selecting predetermined response options, like on many questionnaires or surveys.

Engagement is the first of two themes that I (Katie) identified when gathering data specific to the use of reflexive photographs and photo elicitation interviews in the impressions study; the second theme was reflection (Branch, 2003; Branch Douglas, 1998b). These two themes were not mutually exclusive and appeared to align closely and augment each other. For example, Simone commented, "I thought it [participating in a study that involved taking photos] was fun. It gave me a chance to think about different things about myself as well, so it was a learning experience for me." The intrigue of being able to take photographs led to investment, which I thought of as an aspect of engagement. Simone commented this method made participating in the project more creative and increased her enthusiasm for participating. Marie said, "Before I took a picture, I had to think about, why am I taking this? I'm not just going around taking pictures just for the heck of it." Reflection was evident when one participant, Xavier, expressed surprise at realizing that he was taking pictures "of the same thing" (i.e., an impression) but at different times of the day and in different physical surroundings. He said, "I think that was eye-opening about the whole thing," and further noted "I think it [taking photos] was good. . . . I tend to get pessimistic in my writing." My (Amanda's) work on a photovoice (Latz, 2012) study related to how community college students construct their educational lives included a similar finding related to reflection, with connections to student identity development similar to what we discussed earlier. For example, one of my participants described how participation in my study caused her to really think about why she was in college, "to really think about it and to break it down" (Latz, 2012, p. 55). This intense level of reflection and concomitant extended meaning-making gave way to moments ripe for various kinds of student identity development.

Conclusion

We contend that the use of visual methodologies and methods in the pursuit of understanding college student development is illuminating, yet underutilized and undertheorized. We urge other student affairs scholars to engage in research and assessment that identifies methodological assumptions of visually based inquiry. We specifically advocate for the use of participant-generated visuals as an inquiry method because of its attentiveness to power dynamics as well as influence on student engagement and reflection; college student development is both knowable and encouraged by the use of this method. By being intentional in our use of such methods, as a group of institutional agents who influence students every day and as a field of student affairs researchers, we are better able to serve college students today and in the future.

References

American Council on Education. (1937). *The student personnel point of view* (American Council on Education Studies, Series 1, Vol. 1, No. 3). Washington, DC: Author.

Astin, A. (1984). Student involvement: A developmental theory for higher education. *Journal of College Student Personnel, 25,* 297–308.

Bateson, G., & Mead, M. (1942). *Balinese character: A photographic analysis.* New York, NY: New York Academy of Sciences.

Baxter Magolda, M. B. (1992). *Knowing and reasoning in college: Gender-related patterns in students' intellectual development.* San Francisco, CA: Jossey-Bass.

Bennett, C. I. (1990). *Comprehensive multicultural education* (2nd ed.). Needham Heights, MA: Allyn & Bacon.

Blumer, H. (1969). *Symbolic interactionism: Perspectives and methods.* Englewood Cliffs, NJ: Prentice-Hall.

Branch, K. (2003). Visual methods. In F. K. Stage & K. Manning (Eds.), *Research in the college context* (pp. 115–128). New York, NY: Brunner-Routledge.

Branch, K. (2004). *Lasting impressions? How initial environmental perceptions impacted African American students.* Emerging Scholar presentation at the annual convention of the American College Personnel Association, Philadelphia, PA.

Branch Douglas, K. (1998a). Impressions: African American first-year students' perceptions of a predominantly White university. *The Journal of Negro Education, 6,* 416–431.

Branch Douglas, K. (1998b, November 7). *Seeing as well as hearing: Responses to the use of an alternative form of data representation in a study of students' environmental perceptions.* Paper presented at the annual meeting of the Association for the Study of Higher Education, Miami, FL.

Bruner, J. (1990). *Acts of meaning.* Cambridge, MA: Harvard University Press.

Crilly, N., Blackwell, A. F., & Clarkson, P. J. (2006). Graphic elicitation: Using research diagrams as interview stimuli. *Qualitative Research, 6,* 341–366. doi: 10.1177/1468794106065007

Cross Jr., W. E. (1991). *Shades of Black: Diversity in African-American identity.* Philadelphia, PA: Temple University Press.

Douglas, K. B. (1997). *Picture and perceptions: First-year, African American students' impressions of a predominantly White university* (Unpublished doctoral dissertation). Indiana University, Bloomington, IN.

Drucker, J. (2014). *Graphesis: Visual forms of knowledge production.* Cambridge, MA: Harvard University Press.

Eisner, E. (1982). *Cognition and curriculum: A basis for deciding what to teach.* New York, NY: Longman.

Gillon, K. E., Beatty, C. C., & Davis, L. P. (2012). A critical examination of student affairs research: 75 years of "progress"? In K. M. Boyle, J. W. Lowery, & J. A. Mueller (Eds.), *Reflections on the 75th anniversary of the student personnel point of view* (pp. 67–71). Washington, DC: American College Personnel Association-College Student Educators International.

Harper, D. (1987). The visual ethnographic narrative. *Visual Anthropology, 1,* 1–19.

Harper, D. (1988, Spring). Visual sociology: Expanding sociological vision. *The American Sociologist, 19,* 54–70. doi:10.1007/BF02692374

Harper, D. (2002). Talking about pictures: A case for photo elicitation. *Visual Studies, 17*(1), 13–26.

Jary, D., & Jary, J. (1991). *The Harper Collins dictionary of sociology.* New York, NY: HarperCollins.

Junco, R. (2014). *Engaging students with social media.* San Francisco, CA: Jossey-Bass.

Kuh, G. D. (2009). What student affairs professionals need to know about student engagement. *Journal of College Student Development, 50,* 636–706. doi:10.1353/csd.0.0099

Lapenta, F. (2011). Some theoretical and methodological views on photo-elicitation. In E. Margolis & L. Pauwels (Eds.), *The Sage handbook of visual research methods* (pp. 201–213). Thousand Oaks, CA: Sage.

Latz, A. O. (2012). Toward a new conceptualization of photovoice: Blending the photographic as method and self-reflection. *Journal of Visual Literacy, 31*(2), 49–70.

Lincoln, Y., & Guba, E. (1985). *Naturalistic inquiry.* Beverly Hills, CA: Sage.

Mead, G. H. (1934). *Mind, self, and society: From the standpoint of a social behaviorist.* Chicago, IL: The University of Chicago Press.

National Center for Education Statistics. (1995). *Digest of Education Statistics 1995* (U.S. Department of Education Publication No. NCES 95-029). Washington, DC: U.S. Department of Education Office of Educational Research and Improvement.

National Center for Education Statistics. (2016). *Digest of Education Statistics 2015* (U.S. Department of Education Publication No. NCES 2016-014). Washington, DC: U.S. Department of Education & the Institute of Education Science.

Pauwels, L. (2011). An integrated conceptual framework for visual social research. In E. Margolis & L. Pauwels (Eds.), *The Sage handbook of visual research methods* (pp. 3–23). Thousand Oaks, CA: Sage.

Perka, P., Matherly, C., Fishman, D., & Ridge, R. (1992). Using photographs to examine environmental perceptions of African-American and White Greek members: A qualitative study. *College Student Affairs Journal, 12*(1), 7–16.

Perry Jr., W. G. (1970). *Forms of intellectual and ethical development in the college years: A scheme.* New York, NY: Holt, Rinehart & Winston. (Original work published 1968)

Pink, S. (2012). Advances in visual methodology: An introduction. In S. Pink (Ed.), *Advances in visual methodology* (2nd ed., pp. 3–16). Los Angeles, CA: Sage.

Riis, J. A. (1890). *How the other half lives: Studies among the tenements of New York.* New York, NY: Charles Scribner's Sons.

Stake, R. E. (1994). Case studies. In N. Denzin & Y. Lincoln (Eds.), *Handbook of qualitative research* (pp. 236–247). Thousand Oaks, CA: Sage.

Vagle, M. D. (2014). *Crafting phenomenological research.* Walnut Creek, CA: Left Coast Press.

Welkener, M. W., & Baxter Magolda, M. B. (2014). Better understanding students' self-authorship through self-portraits. *Journal of College Student Development, 55,* 580–585. doi:10.1315/csd.2014.0057

Ziller, R. C. (1990). *Photographing the self: Methods of observing personal orientations.* Newbury Park, CA: Sage.

3

USING VISUAL RESEARCH METHODS TO UNLOCK NEW UNDERSTANDINGS OF STUDENT SUCCESS

David J. Nguyen

In this chapter, I draw on a combination of visual and interview data from the National Study of Lesbian, Gay, Bisexual, Transgender, and Queer (LGBTQ+) College Student Success (NSLGBTQCSS) to excavate new understandings of student success. This chapter melds student-generated data sources to reconceptualize *success* as defined and depicted by students. The visuals provided by students diverge significantly from normative definitions of *success* and offer new meanings of student life as well as pathways for visual research.

Within the field of higher education, there is no shortage of research on the topic of college student success. Enter "college student success" into any image search on any search engine, and results overwhelmingly comprise pictures of caps thrown into the air, students lined up for graduation, or students engaged in classroom discussions. These images demonstrate how representational practices of student success emphasize *academic* success; however, distilling a narrow imagery of student success omits other campus-based experiences that also prepare students for their futures. Scholars and educators have reinforced these notions of success. Although researchers have not reached consensus on what outcomes constitute student success, conversations surrounding the subject typically center on how students benefit from postsecondary experiences revolving around select academic barometers (Kuh, Kinzie, Schuh, & Whitt, 2010). These academic barometers often measure success through retention and persistence outcomes, deeming graduating and credentialing students a reasonable metric for defining *success* (Lumina Foundation, 2012). However, these conceptions of success often focus on institutional measurements overlooking how individual students define *success*.

Visual research methods have been employed within many academic disciplines; however, most higher education scholars have resisted adopting these types of qualitative research methods. Visual tools within higher education settings present scholars and practitioners with the opportunity to illuminate new understandings of often-studied social phenomena, such as college students and postsecondary institutions. Weber and Mitchell (1995) argued that using visual research methods can "offer a different glimpse into human sense-making than written or spoken texts do because they can express that which is not easily put into words: the ineffable, the elusive, the not-yet-thought-through, the subconscious" (p. 34). Visual research methods can challenge spoken or written texts by offering uniquely rich vantage points. For example, Branfman (1972) incorporated voices from people living within the Plain of Jars in southeastern Asia. For years, Western countries denied having any military involvement with this local territory. Yet, when Branfman asked the people living in this area about the Laotian Civil War, numerous drawings depicted U.S. involvement in the substantial bombing and destruction of the territory. Through the visual representations presented by people living within the Plain of Jars, previously concealed meanings were excavated and provided new beliefs about the area.

How a person, event, or attribute is presented frames a person's thinking (Kahneman & Tversky, 1979). In essence, the way something is represented also serves as a political act. Culture studies scholar Stuart Hall examined the politics associated with acts of representation. Hall (1997) posited that representation "is an essential part of the process by which meaning is produced and exchanged among members of a culture. It does involve the use of language, of signs and images which stand for or represent things" (p. 15). The meanings attached to specific words, phrases, and images can become fixed and normative. For example, Shahjahan, Morgan, and Nguyen (2015) utilized Hall's concept of representation to interrogate how narrow distillations of students in the production of large-scale international assessments only emphasized objective knowledge required for students. When the term *student success* circulates, the meaning becomes fixed. In this chapter, I discuss how the use of visual research methods within the NSLGBTQCSS program attempts to destabilize simplistic understandings of student success.

National Study of LGBTQ+ College Student Success

Recognizing the growing value visual research methods present for enhancing understanding of experiences, this chapter foregrounds the importance of visual elements incorporated into the research design of NSLGBTQCSS. This research study utilizes two discrete databases and mixed- and multi-methods aimed at understanding student success for students minoritized on the basis of sexual orientations and/or gender identities. Here, I begin by discussing the tenets of the student success literature. Then, I discuss extant empirical studies depicting the experiences of LGBTQ+ collegians. Finally, I summarize why visual elements provide a missing puzzle piece to the study of LGBTQ+ student success.

Student Success

Although the concept of student success has received significant attention from scholars and policymakers, what student success really looks like remains relatively opaque. Even before Barack Obama declared that by the year 2020 the United States will produce 5 million additional college graduates and once again possess the highest proportion of college graduates in the world, policymakers and administrators were focused on a singular conceptualization of student success (United States Department of Education, n.d.). That is, student success was equated to their retention and, ultimately, graduation (Rutherford & Rabovsky, 2014). Given the significant monetary investment federal and state policymakers have infused into postsecondary education, these constituencies sought to evaluate the efficiency of higher education institutions.

In crafting evaluation criteria for higher education accountability, policymakers have created financial incentives to encourage institutions to think more clearly about how students can succeed within collegiate spaces (Dougherty, Natow, & Vega, 2012; McKeown-Moak, 2013). These financial incentives are often referred to as *performance funding*, a mechanism which "uses a clearly specified formula to tie funding to institutional performance on indicators such as student retention, attainment of certain credit levels, and other student outcomes" (Dougherty & Reddy, 2013, p. 1). States have established metrics in different ways but point to graduating students and graduating them within a timely manner as the way to measure student success. These policy perspectives and metrics play an important role in appropriating limited federal and state funding, but this picture of student success neglects the population most affected by the way *success* is defined: students. Thus far, very few student success studies have incorporated student perspectives, and, more central to this chapter, no studies have integrated visual portrayals of how students envision success.

LGBTQ+ College Students

Studies involving LGBTQ+ student populations demonstrate that these student populations face particular challenges that might impact normative measurements of *student success* as defined by scholars and policymakers. Until recently, most national data sets (e.g., the Higher Education Research Institute at the University of California, Los Angeles or the National Survey of Student Engagement at Indiana University) and institutions did not collect information about students' sexual orientations or gender identities. Without knowing specific identity markers, good measurements of persistence and retention of LGBTQ+ students cannot be tracked. What is known is that LGBTQ+ students experience campus environments differently than many student populations. In particular, campus climate studies paint the collegiate environment as negative, hostile, and discriminatory for LGBTQ+ students (Garvey, Taylor, & Rankin, 2015; Rankin, 2005; Rankin, Blumenfeld, Weber, & Frazer, 2010). For example, Rankin and colleagues (2010) used quantitative research methods to identify that approximately one-third of LGBTQ+-identified students considered leaving their institutions because of the hostile and chilly campus environment for LGBT people. These negative environments can have a profound impact on a student's overall academic experience, including retention and graduation success.

Other researchers using a range of quantitative and qualitative methods found that as LGBTQ+ students felt increasingly marginalized on campus, they struggled more academically, participated in fewer high-impact practices, and suffered more from mental health issues (Kilgo et al., 2015; Meyer, 2003; Pryor, 2015; Woodford & Kulick, 2015; Woodford, Kulick, & Atteberry, 2014; Woodford, Howell, Silverschanz & Lu, 2012). In the past few years, Michael Woodford's quantitative scholarship has been particularly insightful for exploring relationships between the campus environment and a range of academic and social outcomes in LGBTQ+ student populations. For example, Woodford and Kulick (2015) studied multiple dimensions of psychological and experiential campus climate with academic and social integration for sexual minority students at a single institution. The results of this quantitative study highlighted the effects of negative campus experiences, particularly heterosexist behaviors, on academic and social integration. Sexually minoritized students were more likely to become academically disengaged, and they performed worse academically the more they felt harassed on the basis of heterosexist norms (Woodford & Kulick, 2015).

A number of studies have also used qualitative research methods, particularly interview and ethnographic methods, to highlight the experiences of LGBTQ+ people (Abes, 2011; Longerbeam, Inkelas, Johnson, & Lee, 2007; Means & Jaegar, 2013, 2015, 2016; Nicolazzo, 2016; Nicolazzo & Marine, 2015; Pitcher, Camacho, Renn, & Woodford, in press; Pryor, 2015). These qualitative studies documented student interactions, obstacles, and student engagement. Only recently have studies with LGBTQ+ students paired traditional qualitative approaches, such as ethnography and case study, with visual tools. Findings from these studies nuance previous understandings of LGBTQ+ students. For example, Kortegast (2017) paired storytelling with photovoice data to explore the concepts of safety, support, and inclusion with LGBTQ students. Means and Jaegar (2013, 2015, 2016) conducted several studies that integrated semistructured interviews and photovoice prompts. The combination of visuals and interview data yielded powerful insights. For example, a participant in Means and Jaegar's (2013) study discussed feeling loneliness on campus. In addition to simply telling the interviewer about these feelings, the participant took a picture of a dark hallway to capture this feeling. Although the participant's description was important to the study, the participant-generated data added new depth to understanding loneliness. Including visual research methods not only complicated the researchers' understandings of different campus-based phenomena but also furnished scholars and student affairs professionals, who consume this research, with an enhanced understanding of how some students may experience campus life. Visual research methods pair well with existing qualitative research traditions to produce a more holistic picture and undo previous axioms regarding LGBTQ+ students.

Bridging Student Success and LGBTQ+ Student Experiences

As discussed in the preceding sections, nearly all student success studies have shied away from asking students how they conceptualize success, and few LGBTQ+ studies have incorporated visual research methods. The NSLGBTQCSS research group sought to bridge understandings of student success and LGBTQ+ collegians. In recent years, this research group observed campuses working to eradicate negative campus environments by engaging LGBTQ+ collegians. They also wanted to shift the conversation within the scholarly literature to focus on how students are overcoming challenges and operationalizing success, not necessarily on the negative environmental attributes. Employing an antideficit approach encouraged researchers to contemplate how asset-based approaches might illuminate differences in the ways in which LGBTQ+ students tend to be depicted. This research group sought to disrupt what have become normative understandings of the LGBTQ+ collegiate experiences. As political climates for people marginalized on the basis of sexual orientations and/or gender identities continue to shift, research should move from a deficit perspective to an appreciative approach.

To advance the overall study's aims, NSLGBTQCSS project investigators wanted to make at least two scholarly contributions: longitudinal research design and multiple visual research methods. Renn (2010) encouraged researchers to consider longitudinal designs with LGBT student populations to capture the fluctuations in salience of their identities and to delve more deeply into their college-going experience. Given the increase of technology in many facets of life and the ease of access, visual research methods provided a new avenue for nuancing current understandings of how students conceptualize and operationalize individual definitions of *success*. A longitudinal research design incorporating visual research methods presented this research group with the opportunity to repeal extant deficit perspectives about LGBTQ+ students and replace those previously held notions with more appreciative approaches focusing on how LGBTQ+ students successfully navigate the collegiate environment. In short, incorporating visual research methods would enhance prior understandings and advance new conceptualizations of LGBTQ+ students and student success.

Study Data

This section discusses the visual research methods utilized and the data collected through NSLGBTQCSS to illustrate how these methodological tools can excavate new understandings of student success. NSLGBTQCSS is a mixed- and multi-methods research project exploring how environmental, institutional, and personal factors promote success for sexually minoritized students. Much of the scholarship about LGBTQ+ college students operates from a deficit perspective, assuming that this student population is lacking in some way. Countering this consistent narrative, NSLGBTQCSS employed an appreciative, antideficit approach to disentangle factors supporting LGBTQ+ collegians as they navigate postsecondary education. Empirical studies emanating from NSLGBTQCSS data identified varying sources of support, such as institutional policy, faculty, kinship, and environmental factors, that might foster a student's ability to success attributes within collegiate contexts (Linley, Nguyen, Brazelton, Becker, Renn, & Woodford, 2016; Nicolazzo, Pitcher, Renn, & Woodford, 2017; Pitcher, Camacho, Renn, & Woodford, in press).

The overall research design of NSLGBTQCSS centers Bronfenbrenner's (1993) person-process-context-time (PPCT) ecological perspective as its theoretical foundation. Visual research methods are well-suited for studying ecological systems because ecological perspectives furnish researchers with opportunities to evaluate "changing properties of the immediate setting in which the developing person lives, as this process is effected by the relations between these settings, and by larger contexts in which the settings are embedded" (Bronfenbrenner, 1989, p. 188). In short, individuals are nested within larger systems responsible for shaping an individual's development. Using visual research methods presents researchers with the opportunity to capture attributes proximal or distal to the individual. For example, an important attribute for a student may be to make friends with people who have similarly minoritized identities because the student came from a homogenous hometown lacking other openly LGBTQ+ people. In contrast, the U.S. Supreme Court marriage equality ruling, a distal occurrence, shapes the individual's macrosystem. The interconnectedness and interaction among the different contextual layers lend themselves well for researchers to utilize visual tools to explore phenomenon at a single layer or across multiple layers.

The NSLGBTQCSS data consist of the following two components: a concurrent mixed-methods quantitative and qualitative data set and a longitudinal, qualitative data set. During the first data collection, a multi-institutional group of researchers collected nearly 1,000 usable survey responses from LGBTQ+ collegians attending a regional conference for sexually minoritized and allied students. In addition to the collected quantitative data, these researchers conducted 60 semistructured interviews. Data collected during this phase of the project involved understanding participant experiences with high school and collegiate environments, academic contexts, student engagement (e.g., study abroad, faculty research, living-learning communities), on-campus resource usage, and health outcomes (e.g., suicide, alcohol usage). Although LGBTQ+ studies have become more robust in both quantitative and qualitative methodologies, few studies have integrated a visual research approach as a tool for eliciting deeper reflection and responses. Using visual research methods offered a unique lens into studying both student success and LGBTQ+ students, as I discuss in the following section.

The second data collection phase utilized a longitudinal, qualitative design to interrogate findings from the first phase of the study and to explore success experiences of queer-identified students at Michigan State University (MSU). The second phase began with a cohort of LGBTQ+ collegians beginning in their first year. This phase, now entering its fourth year of data collection, has involved more than 10 interviews with each study participant. This study evidences how students conceptualize and make strides toward their own unique definitions of *personal, social,* and *academic success.* Interview transcripts document the trial-and-error nature of the collegiate environment while providing a space for students to discuss different understandings of their evolving social identities. To unearth new understandings of LGBTQ+ collegians' experiences, we incorporated an array of visual research methods, such as photo elicitation, campus map drawing, identity illustrations, and other identity-centric visual activities. The research team discussed the importance of encouraging study participants to reflect on their experiences of success. In thinking about the concept of success, discussions centered on how success changes over time, as does one's identity. In the next section, I focus attention on the photo elicitation research methods.

Photographing Success

NSLGBTQCSS explores how students conceptualize and operationalize success. Although NSLGBTQCSS researchers have incorporated a number of visual research methods into the overall study, I focus on one visual research method, photo elicitation, which I have found to be helpful in understanding nuanced definitions of *student success*. In this section, I discuss how we collected the data and the new insights we derived.

Photo Elicitation Data Collection Procedures

In this study, we were interested in capturing how students define *success* through their collegiate careers. The study's focus centered on the concept of *success*, with a specific emphasis on how students operationalize this term in their academic, personal, and social lives. Throughout NSLGBTQCSS, the team of researchers believed the ways in which students contemplate and operationalize success changes over time. We centered this belief by embedding questions about success within every interview protocol over the course of the study. Specifically, we asked students to talk about what success meant to them during interviews occurring within the first few weeks and last few weeks of the fall and spring semesters. A challenge in asking people about success is that the narratives tend to revolve around ideas with the most salience at the time of interviews and minimize or overlook potentially significant, less immediate moments (Levin, 2006).

As a research group, we discussed some of the challenges we faced in better understanding student success from the student's own perspective. At this particular juncture, the project investigator (Kristen Renn) encouraged us to think about a visual research method as a heuristic for reflection. To encourage a reflective state, one week prior to the final academic-year interview (typically, two weeks before the end of semester), we asked all participants to bring an object or photo representing their success from the current academic year. More specifically, we queried all interview participants as follows: "Before today's interview, I asked you to bring an object or photo that represents your success this year. Tell me about your example of success from this year." Study participants used this interview question to recount stories of different highs and lows experienced during a specific academic year. The interviewer focused the interview on why the image represented success to the student.

An important consideration within the research group was how to collect and interpret the interview and visual images. Having a consistent interview protocol across multiple researchers provided an opportunity for each interviewer to inquire about the individually generated image of success while asking the same questions. Being consistent across researchers presented an opportunity to not only identify variations in the ways *success* can be defined but also to see patterns across the collage of images. Furthermore, consistent questioning allowed the researchers to ensure the validity of participant responses. When considering how to analyze the visual data, it was important to review the interview transcripts at the same time as locating the visual image. Pairing the verbalized narrative and image allowed for rich and thoughtful conversations about emergent observations within the data while also allowing the researchers to triangulate findings across disparate experiences. In the next section, I discuss new insight derived from the study data collection.

New Insights Derived

The multifaceted intent of using visual research methods was to complicate linear notions of student success. In this section, I present *student success* as a multifaceted concept consisting of personal and social success in addition to academic success. To capture the richness of each student's evolving definition, we paired our visual research data with traditional qualitative interview data. In this section, I discuss how student-generated images uncovered new understandings of student success and campus life.

More Than Academic Success

Every study participant interviewed shared images of their success, which extended beyond traditional ways scholars and administrators think of student success, namely academics. For example, Brett discussed the image he brought to his interview (Figure 3.1). He was singing on stage with his a capella group. He shared that "success isn't always about academics to me. Just getting into a group and fitting in and finding friends who like you— [for] who you are." Pairing his image with the interview data, Brett described having the opportunity to challenge himself through joining a student organization. The thought of joining such a group at the beginning of his first year would have been unthinkable. Now at the end of his first year, he joined a

Figure 3.1. Brett's image of student success, joining an a capella group.

student group and achieved his version of success through feeling accepted and finding a place of belongingness on campus. He noted, "Each person in the group is very different from each other and we're just all one family. [Through social interaction] you discover each other person and how they're unique."

Here, Brett discussed the importance of feeling a connection and a place of belonging in college. Having grown up in a small community lacking social acceptance for LGBTQ+ people, Brett wanted to succeed socially and find support lacking from his personal life.

Student Success Combines Personal and Social Aspects
Many study participants expressed success as a function of personal and social success. During the concluding interview at the end of the second year, Joe shared an image of a new romantic interest that developed during the latter part of his sophomore year. Joe shared,

> That's been my success. [This picture] of my boyfriend from a date we had a while ago. That was a pirate exhibit at the museum. That was a very great image. I like it a lot. He's been a very positive force in my life and made me very happy. It's a pretty significant, I guess, milestone, sort of. It's the first time I've done anything [dating] like this.

During Joe's earlier interviews, he expressed frustration in lacking the ability to make connections with other people in the LGBTQ+ community.

During subsequent interviews, he suggested feeling symptoms of depression and anxiety due to his difficulty in meeting new people. As the year progressed, Joe's definition of *success* evolved to engaging in a romantic relationship, his first one.

Another example complicating traditional notions of college student success emanated from a series of interviews with Lovely. She started the final interview of her first year talking about how she had come a long way personally since enrolling at MSU. In particular, in her interview she shared a video of her learning how to swim as how she defined *success*, described as the following:

> In the beginnin' I would not even go out of the shallow end. I was like, "Nope, nah, I'll just stay over here." Now I'll go in 10 feet, 8 feet, and stuff, so that's in the video. It's us swimming, doin' a whole lap.

Lovely seized the opportunity to learn how to swim because she recalled an earlier memory about being terrified of water. She shared,

> When we had a family reunion in 2006, it was all this water, and I jumped in the water, and it was 11 feet. I just thought it was the end of my life right then and there. I just never learned how to swim when I was younger, and so I really was not tryin' to go any deeper than 5 feet.

If the study only verbally interviewed students about their student success, answers may have been more consistent than the menagerie of images utilized to demonstrate success. The difference in simply defining *success* may have yielded answers based on the participants' interpretation of success, or even pointed to the normative definitions surrounding degree completion. Furthermore, if the participant was asked only to produce an image without pairing it with interview questions, then the nuance of Lovely's triumph could have been rendered invisible, or even worse, lost.

Student Success Requires External Support
The nuanced depictions of success demonstrate that student success requires a combination of support and resources during the collegiate journey. Shelly selected a light bulb to represent her second year of college because she "operated this year in a turn-on turn-off kinda fashion. I wake up, do the same thing, and I go to bed. That's how I've operated, and it worked" (Figure 3.2).

When probed further about the selection of a light bulb and repetition of college life, she mentioned that she picked a high-efficiency light bulb,

Figure 3.2. Shelly's student success image, a high-efficiency lightbulb.

because I was pretty efficient. Then, light bulbs, they work in a sorta fashion that there's energy at one side of the terminal. That's what I feel myself with every day, so just basic things. Then, electrons go and bang against the filament, so it's a pretty rough ride, and then it ends up glowing, so I end up doing whatever I'm supposed to be doing. The glass part just shields the filament. That would be metaphorically my friends and my family that keep me from overheating, which is what the glass does on a light bulb. That's why I picked it. I was just, like . . . I needed my friends and family. I do my own work. I put in the work myself, which is the energy in the beginning. Then, at the end, I get a product, which is light.

Numerous participants like Shelly discussed the importance of having support beyond campus boundaries to fulfill their narratives of success. Understanding the ecological system for students is instrumental to fostering student success. Because higher education institutions are continuously investing in and developing student success programs, the field can benefit from the understanding that students regularly consult people external to student services. Integrating external communities with internal campus communities can strengthen these types of programs, as well as shed the linear assumption that students can succeed on their own accord.

The introduction of a visual tool distilled nuanced and complicated understandings of success. Throughout the longitudinal study, the

NSLGBTQCSS research team frequently discussed student definitions of *success*. We noticed many students discussed success concepts relative to what was happening at a particular point in time. Participants did not feel that they had achieved or even understood success, but when we asked them to produce an image capturing student success, they produced eclectic images and rich descriptions to which we would not have otherwise been privy. The student-generated information departed significantly from how policymakers and administrators have discussed and distributed knowledge around the concept of student success. Simply introducing a photo elicitation data point illustrated the messiness of student success and why different stakeholder groups need to incorporate student voices and imagery in their decision-making processes.

Conclusion

In this chapter, I demonstrated that previous representations of "student success" affix the meaning to simply graduation, while forgetting to ask how *students* conceptualize *success*. The present study gathered visual evidence countering the notion that academic and social integration are required determinants of success (Tinto, 1993). Much of what the study data illustrate are counternarratives to traditional linear notions of college student success. The visual research method illustrated in this chapter crystallizes a departure from success simply as degree completion. Visual methods elicited new understandings of student success through offering a complicated and melded meaning of success. In essence, student success constitutes more than simply graduating or achieving a specific grade in a class. Instead, a more holistic picture comes into view of how students visualize, make progress toward, and achieve success.

References

Abes, E. S. (2011). Exploring the relationship between sexual orientation and religious identities for Jewish lesbian college students. *Journal of Lesbian Studies*, *15*(2), 205–225.

Branfman, F. (1972). *Voices from the Plain of Jars: Life under an air war*. Madison, WI: University of Wisconsin Press.

Bronfenbrenner, U. (1989). Ecological systems theory. In R. Vasta (Ed.), *Six theories of child development* (pp. 187–249). Greenwich, CT: JAI Press.

Bronfenbrenner, U. (1993). The ecology of cognitive development: Research models and fugitive findings. In R. H. Wozniak & K. W. Fischer (Eds.), *Development in context: Acting and thinking in specific environments* (pp. 3–44). Hillsdale, NJ: Lawrence Erlbaum Associates.

Dougherty, K. J., Natow, R. S., & Vega, B. E. (2012). Popular but unstable: Explaining why state performance funding systems in the United States often do not persist. *Teachers College Record, 114*(3), 1–42.

Dougherty, K. J., & Reddy, V. (2013). Performance funding for higher education: What are the mechanisms? What are the impacts? *ASHE Higher Education Report, 39*(2), 1–134.

Garvey, J. C., Taylor, J. L., & Rankin, S. (2015). An examination of campus climate for LGBTQ community college students. *Community College Journal of Research and Practice, 39*(6), 527–541.

Hall, S. (1997). *Stuart Hall: Representation and the media* [VHS]. Northampton, MA: Media Education Foundation.

Kahneman, D., & Tversky, A. (1979). Prospect theory: An analysis of decision under risk. *Econometrica: Journal of the Econometric Society, 47*(2), 263–291.

Kilgo, C. A., Nguyen, D. J., Brazelton, G. B., Mollett, A. L., Linley, J. L., Renn, K. A., & Woodford, M. (2015). *LGBTQ+ students: The relationship between outness and social acceptance by peers on participation in high-impact practices.* Paper presented at the Annual Meeting of the Association for the Study of Higher Education (ASHE), Denver, CO.

Kortegast, C. A. (2017). "But it's not the space I would need": Narrative of LGBTQ students' experiences in campus housing. *Journal of College and University Student Housing, 43*(2), 58–71.

Kuh, G. D., Kinzie, J., Schuh, J. H., & Whitt, E. J. (2010). *Student success in college: Creating conditions that matter.* San Francisco, CA: Jossey-Bass.

Levin, K. A. (2006). Study design III: Cross-sectional studies. *Evidence-Based Dentistry, 7*(1), 24–25.

Linley, J. L., Nguyen, D., Brazelton, G. B., Becker, B., Renn, K., & Woodford, M. (2016). Faculty as sources of support for LGBTQ college students. *College Teaching, 64*(2), 55–63.

Longerbeam, S. D., Inkelas, K. K., Johnson, D. R., & Lee, Z. S. (2007). Lesbian, gay, and bisexual college student experiences: An exploratory study. *Journal of College Student Development, 48*(2), 215–230.

Lumina Foundation. (2012). *Special report: A stronger nation though higher education.* Indianapolis, IN: Author. Retrieved from http://www.luminafoundation.org/publications/A_Stronger_Nation-2012.pdf

McKeown-Moak, M. P. (2013). The "new" performance funding in higher education. *Educational Considerations, 40*(2), 3–12.

Means, D. R., & Jaeger, A. J. (2013). Black in the rainbow: "Quaring" the Black gay male student experience at historically Black universities. *Journal of African American Males in Education, 4*(2), 124–140.

Means, D. R., & Jaeger, A. J. (2015). Spiritual borderlands: A Black gay male college student's spiritual journey. *Journal of Student Affairs Research and Practice, 52*(1), 11–23.

Means, D. R., & Jaeger, A. J. (2016). "Keep pressing on": Spiritual epistemology and its role in the collegiate lives of black gay and bisexual men. *Journal of College and Character, 17*(1), 23–39.

Meyer, I. H. (2003). Prejudice, social stress and mental health in lesbian, gay and bisexual populations: Conceptual issues and research evidence. *Psychological Bulletin, 129*, 674–697.

Nicolazzo, Z. (2016). "Just go in looking good": The resilience, resistance, and kinship-building of trans* college students. *Journal of College Student Development, 57*(5), 538–556.

Nicolazzo, Z., & Marine, S. B. (2015). "It will change if people keep talking": Trans* students in college and university housing. *Journal of College and University Student Housing, 42*(1), 160–177.

Nicolazzo, Z., Pitcher, E. N., Renn, K. A., & Woodford, M. (2017). An exploration of trans* kinship as a strategy for student success. *International Journal of Qualitative Studies in Education, 30*(3), 305–319.

Pitcher, E. N., Camacho, T. P., Renn, K. A., & Woodford, M. R. (in press). Affirming policies, programs, and supportive services: Using an organizational perspective to understand LGBTQ+ college student success. *Journal of Diversity in Higher Education.* doi:10.1037/dhe0000048

Pryor, J. T. (2015). Out in the classroom: Transgender student experiences at a large public university. *Journal of College Student Development, 56*(5), 440–455.

Rankin, S. R. (2005). Campus climates for sexual minorities. *New Directions for Student Services, 2005*(111), 17–23.

Rankin, S., Blumenfeld, W. J., Weber, G. N., & Frazer, S. (2010). *State of higher education for LGBT people.* Charlotte, NC: Campus Pride.

Renn, K. A. (2010). LGBT and Queer research in higher education: The state and status of the field. *Educational Researcher, 39*(2), 132–141.

Renn, K. A., & Arnold, K. D. (2003). Reconceptualizing research on college student peer culture. *Journal of Higher Education, 74,* 261–291.

Rutherford, A., & Rabovsky, T. (2014). Evaluating impacts of performance funding policies on student outcomes in higher education. *The ANNALS of the American Academy of Political and Social Science, 655*(1), 185–208.

Shahjahan, R. A., Morgan, C., & Nguyen, D. J. (2015). "Will I learn what I want to learn?" Usable representations, "students" and OECD assessment production. *Discourse: Studies in the Cultural Politics of Education, 36*(5), 700–711.

Tinto, V. (1993). *Leaving college: Rethinking the causes and cures of student attrition.* Chicago, IL: University of Chicago Press

United States Department of Education. (n.d.). *Meeting President Obama's 2020 college completion goal.* Retrieved from https://www.ed.gov/news/speeches/meeting-president-obamas-2020-college-completion-goal

Weber, S., & Mitchell, C. (1995). *"That's funny, you don't look like a teacher!": Interrogating images and identity in popular culture.* New York, NY: Routledge.

Woodford, M. R., Howell, M. L., Silverschanz, P., & Yu, L. (2012). "That's so gay!": Examining the covariates of hearing this expression among gay, lesbian, and bisexual college students. *Journal of American College Health, 60*(6), 429–434.

Woodford, M. R., & Kulick, A. (2015). Academic and social integration on campus among sexual minority students: The impacts of psychological and experiential campus climate. *American Journal of Community Psychology, 55*(1), 13–24.

Woodford, M. R., Kulick, A., & Atteberry, B. (2014). Positive factors, campus climate, and health outcomes among sexual minority college students. *Journal of Diversity in Higher Education, 8*(2), 73–87.

4

SOCIAL MEDIA AS A TOOL TO EXPLORE STUDENT CULTURES

Chris Linder

In fall 2014, Emma Sulkowicz, a student at Columbia University, used her senior art thesis as a form of activism and resistance. Titled *Carry That Weight*, Sulkowicz's thesis consisted of carrying a mattress with her everywhere she went on campus to represent the weight she carried as a survivor of sexual violence. Sulkowicz was sexually assaulted by another student at Columbia and reported it to her school's authorities, who did not find the accused student responsible (Smith, 2014). Pictures of Sulkowicz carrying her mattress around campus circulated on social media, providing powerful visual representations of her protest (Figure 4.1). Students and sexual violence survivors across the country connected via the #CarryThatWeight hashtag on Twitter, sharing stories of survival, activism, and resistance. #CarryThatWeight became a movement on college campuses across the country and two years later, student activists continue to post pictures of mattress displays on their campuses (Figure 4.1), demonstrating the power of visuals as a form of student activism and connection.

As a scholar interested in campus sexual violence and student activism, movements like the one spurred by Sulkowicz captured my attention. Further, as a user of social media for activism, resistance, and raising awareness, I wanted to better understand how student activists employed social media for their work in addressing sexual violence on campuses. With a team of three additional researchers, I initiated a research project designed to better understand the strategies of anti–sexual violence activists and the role of social media in this movement. Although we did not set out to specifically examine the use of visuals in activism, we quickly learned that visuals played a large

Figure 4.1. Tweet from Stand with Survivors of Emma Sulkowicz carrying her mattress with the hashtag #CarryThatWeight.

Note. Scan QR code to view tweet (https://twitter.com/SWSmovement/status/6011023973652 19329).

role in the effectiveness of social media in raising awareness about sexual violence. Student activists we interviewed discussed being intentional about using pictures to draw attention to their posts. We observed this use of visuals during our data collection on Facebook and Twitter.

In this chapter, I describe how I (along with two different teams of researchers) engaged social media to examine cultures of two distinct student groups: campus anti–sexual violence activists and students who dress up for football games in the southern United States. Although neither study was limited to visual representations, visuals did play a role in both studies. In the following sections, I briefly provide an overview of the research and the context in which the studies took place and describe the specific ways we used social media as a strategy to better understand a student culture. I conclude the chapter with lessons about conducting research using visual methods.

Using Social Media and Visuals to Examine Anti-Sexual Violence Activism

Throughout history, activists have used so-called new media to raise awareness about injustices to a larger scale, often resulting in shifts in public perception, policy, and some attitudes and behaviors. For example, in the post-Civil War south, Ida B. Wells worked with progressive newspapers in the north to call attention to the problems of lynching and the rape of Black women (Giddings, 2008). The newspapers frequently published pictures to accompany text describing the atrocities of lynching. Similarly, during the civil rights movements of the 1960s, television was considered new media. Television, and its use of images, may have contributed to the urgency and increased awareness of racism in the United States during the 1960s (Bonilla & Rosa, 2015). Activists used television to raise awareness about riots in Selma, Alabama, drawing attention to ongoing struggles for equity (Bonilla & Rosa, 2015).

More recently, activists in a variety of movements have employed social media—today's new media—to raise awareness about injustice, connect with other activists with similar goals, and to hold institutions (higher education, media, government, political officials) accountable to address issues of injustice (Linder, Myers, Riggle, & Lacy, 2016). Images and speed are central components of social media, both of which contribute to increased awareness and understanding of the urgency of addressing sexual violence on college campuses.

In our study, we sought to better understand the strategies of campus anti–sexual violence activists and the role of social media, including visuals, in their activism. To do this, we employed an Internet-related ethnography (Postill & Pink, 2012), gathering data from a variety of social media platforms and interviews with campus sexual violence activists. Specifically, a research team of four people formally collected data for six months and paid attention to online media sources long before and after we formally collected data, influencing our data analysis and familiarity with the data. We began the study largely as a result of our own experiences on social media and how we observed what we believed to be a shift in momentum behind addressing sexual violence on college campuses. Each member of the research team was either currently or had been a staff member in a campus-based women's center. We could sense that something was different about the national attention this round of activism was receiving and wanted to better understand what fueled this shift in momentum.

Collecting Data on Social Media

To begin the study, we collected newspaper articles from national media outlets about campus anti–sexual violence activism. We largely relied on our own networks to collect this information. We pulled articles that we saw in our own day-to-day media consumption through daily digests from *Inside Higher Ed* and *The Chronicle of Higher Education* and articles that people in our social networks posted to Facebook and Twitter about anti–sexual violence activism, many of which came from the *Huffington Post* and *USA Today*. We reviewed articles about anti–sexual violence activism to see which students' names came up repeatedly and which social media platforms were frequently highlighted. As a result of observing this information for about three months, we began to formally collect data in the spring of 2014 by collecting posts from the group Know Your IX on both Twitter and Facebook. We chose Know Your IX because it was the most visible and active group we had observed in the previous three months. We also conducted interviews with 23 sexual violence activists between January 2014 and July 2014.

We sought institutional review board (IRB) approval for this study and followed typical consent form protocol for interviewing participants. Additionally, we used only publicly available social media. *Publicly available* means that anyone with a user account could access the tweet or Facebook post. Search tools cannot access accounts set to private, so we did not collect tweets or posts from private user accounts. For example, I might use a common hashtag such as #KnowYourIX to post on my Instagram account, but because my Instagram account is set to private, only people whom I have granted permission to follow me could find that post, even if searching with the known hashtag. Later in the chapter, I describe in greater detail some challenges related to ethics and privacy when conducting social media research, especially focusing on visuals posted by users.

The very nature of using social media as a tool for activism is to respond to current topics and trends in the environment; therefore, data collection for this project was ongoing and fluid. We started by following the hashtag #KnowYourIX and observing the Facebook feed of the Know Your IX group. As we interviewed activists and observed trends through these initial social media observations, we added a few more sources of social media to our data collection. Table 4.1 highlights some data we collected via social media between January 31, 2014, and July 31, 2014, including the electronic resource we used to collect data, which I describe in the following section.

Each member of the research team shared a notebook on Evernote. In this notebook, we posted newspaper articles relevant to the study, researcher reflections immediately after conducting interviews with activists, and additional notes and reflections we had throughout the data collection and analysis part of the study. This is also where we kept the newspaper articles we used to identify potential participants and minutes from our research

TABLE 4.1
Examples of Social Media Data Collected for
Anti–Sexual Violence Activism Study

Hashtag or User	Platform	Date Data Collection Began	Resource for Collecting	Number of Posts Collected
#KnowYourIX	Twitter	1/23/14	Twitter Archiving Google Sheet	591
Know Your IX	Facebook	1/31/14	If This Then That	131
SAFER	Facebook	2/1/14	If This Then That	156
#SAAM*	Instagram	4/11/14	If This Then That	1,915

*SAAM = Sexual Assault Awareness Month (1,571 posts during the month of April).

team meetings. This notebook had 303 notes, including newspaper articles, visual images, scholarly articles, researcher reflections, and additional notes throughout the study.

Electronic Resources Supporting Data Collection

Twitter Archiving Google Sheet (TAGS) is a system developed by a technologically savvy blogger who freely shared the spreadsheet, including codes for collecting tweets in a Google sheet. This was available informally during the time of our study and has since become a Google-supported application with support available. TAGS allows a person to gather tweets based on a hashtag or user. The sheet includes an archive of the tweets, including a link that will take the researcher directly to the tweet and a summary and dashboard of trends associated with the hashtag or user.

If This Then That (IFTTT) is a web-based application that connects a variety of applications and devices to allow people to systemically collect information. IFTTT uses "recipes" that allow a user to set up simple spreadsheets to collect a variety of information from the web. We used IFTTT to gather Facebook and Instagram feeds related to our study. Since our study, however, Instagram has made its Application Program Interface (API) private, which does not allow users to gather information from Instagram in the same way we did.

Importance of Images in Sexual Violence Activism

Through this study, we sought to better understand student activists' use of social media to address issues of sexual violence on college campuses. Although the intention of the study did not center visuals in the research questions or data analysis, images were central to student activists' strategies for raising awareness related to issues of campus sexual violence. Student activists described intentionally using images to draw attention to their posts. They highlighted their belief that people were more likely to read an article or click on a link about an awareness-raising event if the post had an eye-catching visual with it. Further, as we observed engagement on social media, we noted the ways in which images contributed to a sense of community among activists. As noted previously, activists shared almost 2,000 photos on Instagram during the month of April using the hashtag #SAAM for Sexual Assault Awareness Month. These images likely served to develop a sense of solidarity and gave each other ideas for awareness-raising events (see Figure 4.2).

Further, as highlighted at the beginning of this chapter, the #CarryThatWeight campaign relies heavily on a visual image to send a

Figure 4.2. #CarryThatWeight campaign at DePaul University.

Note. Photograph by Dylan Fahoome.

message about the weight sexual assault survivors carry with them. In addition, the visuals included during the past two years indicate activists on many campuses have adapted the #CarryThatWeight campaign to fit their own campuses. A future study could examine the #CarryThatWeight campaign and the use of visuals in its evolution.

Gameday Dress

In the second study highlighted in this chapter, we used Instagram to document and examine the phenomenon of dressing up for football games in the southeastern region of the United States. In the Southeastern Conference (SEC), football is frequently referred to as "religion" and shapes much of the culture of campuses during the fall semester (Mason, 2016, para. 7). One of the many traditions associated with football gameday in the SEC is that many White women dress up for football games. Although a few men and women of color also participate in this ritual, it is a raced, classed, and gendered phenomenon with White, middle-class women participating in the ritual more than other people. One can see evidence of this ritual across many sources. For example, during the late summer and fall, most clothing stores in the college towns in the SEC display gameday dress sections, featuring dresses and accessories in school colors tailored toward women. Further, campus newspapers and yearbooks run stories about this tradition, and television news sources (e.g., CBS [CBS, 2007], CNN [Mason, 2016], ESPN [SEC Fan, 2014]) have special news stories about the phenomenon.

As researchers, we were curious about the ways social media influenced the practice of dressing up for football games, so we collected photos from Instagram and interviewed students about gameday dress at one institution in the SEC. We chose Instagram to examine the phenomenon of gameday dress because Instagram is a platform that centers photos and would allow us to search using a popular hashtag related to the football culture at the institution at which the study took place. Text is limited on Instagram and the focus is on the photo being shared, which allowed us to see the phenomenon under study.

Similar to the sexual violence study, this study was not funded and members of the research team did not have access to expensive or high-tech mechanisms for gathering digital data. We began by gathering all of the photos publicly posted to Instagram using a commonly used hashtag for showing gameday spirit at this institution. We collected these photos by taking screen shots on our phones of every photo posted during a 24-hour period starting at 9:00 a.m. before the second home game of the season in fall 2013. The screen shots resulted in 5,017 photos, 1,592 of which we described as *portraits*, meaning that they were photos that included people who were clearly posing for the camera.

To analyze the photos, we started by coding the photos based on several categories in an attempt to sort and understand the photos. We coded the photos in this study based on the idea that we were examining "hot spots" of data where the information "glows" and "creates a sense of wonder" (Ringrose & Renold, 2014, p. 773). We developed codes as we moved through the data, rather than starting with an a priori set of codes developed before starting the process of coding. For example, prior to starting the coding process, we did not consider *car* as a significant location in which people took selfies on game day. However, as we moved through the data, we began to notice that many selfies appeared to be taken in a car, so we added a code of car to location of the photos.

We coded the photos using the following categories: perceived gender, perceived race, portrait type, clothing, and location. As we coded these photos, we wrestled with the categorization of people based on race and gender because we could not ask people how they identified themselves. The identity constructs of race and gender are much more nuanced than what is visible and more complex than the set, static categories we used to categorize people. Further, identifying a person's race or gender depends on the characteristics the person doing the identifying associates with a particular race or gender, not necessarily congruent with the experience of the person being identified. For example, people often consider wearing makeup to be a feminine characteristic associated with being "woman"; however, some people who choose to wear makeup may not identify their gender as "woman."

However, we wanted to illustrate the ways in which the phenomenon of gameday dress is gendered, raced, and presumably classed, so we did code photos based on our perceptions of gender and race, acknowledging the complicated nature of this. All members of the research team identified as cisgender White women. All engage in feminist research, and one also engages in critical race scholarship. Two of the researchers also identify as working-class, and none of the researchers has participated in the ritual of dressing up for football games, despite the fact that all three attended and participated in undergraduate institutions with significant football cultures.

After we coded the photos, we came together to discuss what we saw. The photos collected from Instagram were very similar, highlighting a distinct formula for posting gameday photos to Instagram. Selfies overwhelmingly featured a similar head tilt; long, straight hair; and chunky jewelry matching the school colors. Similarly, group photos included women with long, straight hair; chunky jewelry; dresses in school colors with cowboy boots; and a hand on the hip. This pose is commonly referred to as the "skinny arm," in which the woman puts her hand on the smallest part of her waist in order to emphasize that part of her body. Although we had permission to collect and analyze these photos because they were publicly available on Instagram, printing the photos required a different level of permission, which we found difficult to obtain. To view photos similar to what we observed, readers can enter #GoDawgs into an Instagram search and see similar results.

After coding the photos collected through Instagram, we conducted focus groups with undergraduate women at the institution where the study took place to better understand what we observed through the photos. We asked participants to discuss whether they dressed up for football games and what kinds of things influenced their decisions. We also asked them about how they used social media to document their experiences at football games if they attended them. Overwhelmingly, the discussions in the focus groups indicated that the students who chose to dress up for football games (most of the students who participated in the focus groups) did so because it was "tradition" and that it represented their desire to be seen as a "classy lady." The focus group discussions confirmed what we thought we observed on social media; namely, that the phenomenon was largely part of White middle-class culture, rooted in heteronormativity. Even if students did not identify as middle- or upper-class, they chose to participate in the ritual as a way to perform White middle-class womanhood. Additionally, participants discussed the importance of dressing up at football games as a way to attract men. They described the importance of finding a husband while at college and that tailgating at football games was a prime place to attract men based on their attractiveness and interest in football.

Using Instagram (visual social media) to examine the phenomenon of gameday dress at one institution in the SEC yielded important insight that may not have come through had we only talked with students about their experiences. By viewing photos of the phenomenon, we identified patterns we would not have thought to ask students about. For example, noting how women frequently posed in a particular manner for selfies was something that we saw, but not something that students probably would have shared with us had we only interviewed them. Additionally, the visual representations showed how strikingly similar group photos were and the significance of straight hair and chunky jewelry in women's outfits. Both of these visual observations led us to understand the significance of the ways in which women followed very specific formulas of womanhood when participating in this ritual. In talking with students, they shared with us the importance of community in the ritual of dressing up for football games, but they did not describe the ways they followed specific patterns in their dress and picture behavior—that is something we observed through visuals. Observing these common behaviors led us to a feminist analysis regarding ways college women may feel pressure to conform to even more rigid standards of beauty than we otherwise thought.

Implications and Lessons Learned

Social media can assist researchers in better understanding student cultures and phenomena. Visual representations of student experiences on social media, paired with their description and discussion of the experience, provide insight and nuance to student experiences. Photos of student rituals and posts to social media illustrate how students experience campus cultures in new ways and allow researchers to quickly see and understand a phenomenon in real-time. Engaging social media as a mechanism for better understanding student culture requires attention to detail and examination of the ethics involved in observing student culture in publicly available spaces. In the following sections, I highlight some lessons learned from engaging social media as a visual research method for better understanding student cultures.

Research Using Digital Tools Is Messy

Technology and the ways students use it are constantly shifting. Collecting data through social media is messy and often not as systematic as more traditional forms of research. For example, although researchers may collect tweets with a particular hashtag or Facebook posts from a particular group, a new hashtag or group may pop up during data collection that draws attention away from the hashtag originally examined. When we started the sexual assault activism study, the Know Your IX group was one of the most visible activist groups in the movement. However, as we engaged in data collection, several other groups began to emerge, and as we interviewed participants, we learned of additional hashtags and organizations activists supported. Although we could not formally collect data from all of the hashtags and groups mentioned, we could observe the groups and hashtags through social media, still informing our understanding of the culture of student activism. A more traditional form of data collection may stipulate that only the data collected through the formal mechanism (e.g., IFTTT or TAGS) should be included in the analysis. Our methodology, Internet-related ethnography (Postill & Pink, 2012), allowed us to consider activism around sexual violence as a whole, not limiting us to only the data we formally collected on spreadsheets as part of our analysis. We continued in our regular practice of online engagement while we formally and systematically collected data, which resulted in a deepened understanding of the ways social media served as a tool for activism and awareness, rather than the activism itself.

Researchers using social media as a way to better understand student cultures may need to let go of postpositivist notions of strict data collection and analysis, recognizing that patterns can be detected in daily observations of social media, rather than strict data collection and analysis using tools designed to count specific words or phrases. Similarly, researchers who typically employ interpretivist or constructivist paradigms for research may benefit from allowing themselves to use some numbers to describe the trends they see in their data. For example, in the gameday dress study, we were committed to a postmodern framework for the study, intentionally choosing to code "hot spots" in the data rather than using only a priori codes to categorize data. However, we also chose to categorize and count particular aspects of the phenomenon to better understand and illustrate the ways in which identity (gender and race) influenced the experience of dressing up for game days. Because social media is a relatively new mechanism for collecting data, researchers may need to take some risks and develop some new strategies for data collection and analysis.

Taking Risks Can Be Rewarding

As highlighted previously, using social media to collect data can be messy and overwhelming. As researchers, we have often been socialized that we must do research the "right" way. As a result, we fail to try new things because that novelty may not be received well by reviewers and journal editors; however, taking risks, trying new things, and creating new avenues for understanding student cultures can be quite rewarding and uncover new ideas and phenomena. Although no one on either research team had a deep understanding of the technology behind the social media platforms we sought to engage in our research, our intuition led us to examine the ways students used social media to participate in a particular student culture. Despite the fact that we did not have formal technological training, we were savvy enough to develop our own strategies for collecting data. As a result, we learned about technology and discovered new ways to engage with research participants. Taking risks to examine social media as a phenomenon in both of these studies resulted in richer, more complete data and a deeper understanding of the nuances of student cultures. For example, using Instagram in the gameday dress study allowed us to visualize the consistent ways that women posed for pictures at football tailgates, prompting us to ask students about these practices. If we had not observed the hand-on-the-hip phenomenon, we may not have known to ask student participants about the pose, which led us to understand the idea of the "skinny arm" in ways we may not have had we not previously observed it. As mentioned previously, observing photos led to a contribution to feminist scholarship, highlighting rigid beauty and gender expectations many college women strive to uphold.

Social Media Can Serve as a Primary or Secondary Form of Data

In the studies described here, data collected on social media served as both the primary and the secondary form of data. In the gameday dress study, the photos collected from Instagram served as the primary data collected from the project. Most of the data analysis for the project happened through reviewing the photos collected. We conducted focus groups with students as a form of secondary data analysis, a way to dig deeper into what we saw in the photos. The campus sexual violence activism study centered the voices of the activists, and the data collected from social media complemented the perspectives of the activists. Although we collected the data simultaneously, the ways the activists described their use of social media was clearer than what we could see just from reviewing the posts on social media. The data collected on social media illustrated the activists' perspectives. The visual media triangulated or crystallized the data (Ellingson, 2008), resulting in increased confidence and additional evidence to support our findings about social media as a tool for activism.

As with most qualitative research, researchers should engage in *triangulation* or *crystallization,* defined as collecting data from more than one source as a way to illustrate and deepen the data. Social media research can serve as an avenue for doing this. Using data from social media can be an important way to understand student cultures in addition to talking with students. As with any data collection, the researcher's perspective often informs the interpretation of the data; therefore, talking with students about their perceptions of what is happening on social media is an important way to strengthen the research by raising a variety of perspectives and interpretations of a particular set of data. Although researchers should talk with members of the population or the student culture they seek to understand, they do not necessarily need to talk with the same members of the population they study on social media. For example, in the campus sexual violence activism study, we talked with student activists and we collected data from social media, but we did not connect the two groups. The activists we talked to were not necessarily the same social media users we followed. Instead, the activists we talked to shared their perspectives about using social media, and our social media data complemented or illustrated the strategies that the activists shared in their interviews. Similarly, in the gameday dress study, we talked with students about using Instagram to celebrate and participate in gameday culture, yet we did not use their specific photos to match what they said. Instead, we studied an overall culture, and the photos and focus groups served to help us understand the culture as a whole, rather than specific students' experiences with that culture.

Ethics

Through both of these studies, we gathered publicly available social media data, meaning that anyone with a Facebook, Twitter, or Instagram account (and in some cases without) could access the information we accessed. We pursued IRB approval for both studies. Those sections of the studies were considered exempt because the information on social media was publicly available. The interviews and focus groups followed typical recruitment and informed consent procedures. However, just because the IRB did not require additional information about collecting data from social media does not mean we did not wrestle with ethical issues. Even though people (presumably many students) posted their photos to Instagram without privacy settings, they likely did not think about research as a reason people would review their photos. Further, as we presented sessions on the campus at which the study took place, we worried about potentially embarrassing students who may have seen themselves in the study if we used the photos we collected from Instagram. In that study, we were critiquing a system of patriarchy, a system in which many people, women included, participate, and we did not want to shame or embarrass anyone for their choices. In addition, photos from Instagram and Twitter are copyrighted and we could not reproduce those photos in written and published materials about our study. As a result, we were not able to include many visuals in chapters such as this one. To address this issue, we hired a model to reenact some of the most common poses we saw on Instagram to illustrate our points about what we saw in the data.

Similarly, in the activism study, many of the posts we gathered from social media included usernames and photos. Although we were not explicitly studying the users in the social media posts in this study, the same ethical concerns applied. Did they know their information might be used in a research study? Is it different for a social media post to be shared in a journal article than in an online space with thousands of other users? What if someone whose social media post we used was in the audience of a presentation we gave? How would that person feel about being on the screen without knowing it prior to arriving? At the same time, the posts provide meaningful insight into a phenomenon and may assist educators in better understanding and working with students.

As we continue to analyze data from both studies, I still wrestle with these ethical challenges. I wonder how to balance the potential concerns about privacy with the educational benefit people will receive. Further, I think about the ways privacy is changing. As I started to contact social media users to request permission to use their photos in a publication, the effort felt futile. In the age of tweeting, retweeting, posting, and reposting, most people who share photos on social media have an expectation that those images will be shared and used in a variety of ways. In fact, some people share on social media with the very intention of something going *viral*, meaning that it is shared over and over again. Asking for permission to use the image in these cases seems to serve more to raise red flags for the user than address issues of consent and privacy. Many social media users employ social media specifically to draw attention to their issue or cause. They are intentionally seeking followers and attention and to create awareness about an issue. It could be that those of us in the academy are holding on to traditional views of privacy and using our lenses and experiences to inform our interpretation of the practice of students, without considering their perspectives. Students frequently choose to openly engage in a public arena and often desire to draw attention to themselves and the issues for which they are advocating. For these reasons, we chose to use only social media posts publicly available and considered the purpose of the posts as we thought about the privacy of the users. For example, in social media activist studies, the very purpose of sharing on social media is to draw attention to the cause, resulting in our choice not to blur usernames or photos and directly cite the location of the tweet or post. However, given that the Instagram photos for the gameday study likely were not posted with the intention of researchers engaging in a critical analysis of the practice, we chose to blur the faces and usernames of the posts because the intention of the posts was not to raise awareness.

Conclusion

Social media provides a unique way for researchers to gather data about student cultures and phenomena. Social media combines text and visuals, resulting in opportunities for researchers to examine and deepen their understanding of issues with which college students are wrestling. Social media allows researchers to gather significant amounts of data quickly, which is both a challenge and a benefit. The quick capture of data allows researchers to have access to current data, yet the bulk of the data may be overwhelming to manage. Similarly, the access to publicly available spaces presents some unique challenges related to privacy and confidentiality. As researchers continue to refine their approaches to using visuals as data, findings from visual methods will enhance our understanding of students' experiences, allowing us to improve campus environments for students from a variety of perspectives and experiences.

References

Bonilla, Y., & Rosa, J. (2015). #Ferguson: Digital protest, hashtag ethnography, and the racial politics of social media in the United States. *American Ethnologist, 42*(1), 4–17. doi:10.1111/amet.12112

CBS. (2007). *Georgia's hottest coeds* [Video]. Retrieved from https://www.youtube .com/watch?v=qRevRq-enXc

Ellingson, L. L. (2008). *Engaging crystallization in qualitative research: An introduction.* Thousand Oaks, CA: Sage.

Giddings, P. (2008). *Ida: A sword among lions: Ida B. Wells and the campaign against lynching.* New York, NY: HarperCollins.

Linder, C., Myers, J. S., Riggle, C., & Lacy, M. (2016). From margins to mainstream: Social media as a tool for campus sexual violence activism. *Journal of Diversity in Higher Education, 9*(3), 231–244. doi:10.1037/dhe0000038

Mason, S. (2016). *Gameday in the South? No t-shirts, please* [Video]. Retrieved from http://www.cnn.com/2014/12/05/living/irpt-sec-football-fashion/index.html

Postill, J., & Pink, S. (2012). Social media ethnography: The digital researcher in a messy web. *Media International Australia, 145*, 123–134.

Ringrose, J., & Renold, E. (2014). "F**k rape!": Exploring affective intensities in a feminist research assemblage. *Qualitative Inquiry, 20*(6), 772–780. doi: 10.1177/1077800414530261

SEC Fan. (2014). *Wives of the SEC* [Gameday segment; video]. Retrieved from http://www.saturdaydownsouth.com/sec-football/video-wives-sec-gameday-segment/

Smith, R. (2014, September 21). In a mattress, a lever for art and political protest. *The New York Times*. Retrieved from https://www.nytimes.com/2014/09/22/arts/design/in-a-mattress-a-fulcrum-of-art-and-political-protest.html

PART TWO

VISUAL METHODS AND PEDAGOGY

5

OVERVIEW OF THE USE OF VISUAL METHODS IN PEDAGOGY

Bridget Turner Kelly and Ester U. Sihite

If visual research—as discussed in the first part of this book—can deepen examinations of individuals, dynamics, and institutions within higher education, then visual pedagogy—a specific method and practice of teaching—can help facilitate the ways in which educators and students engage in these topics in the classroom context. As the previous chapters articulate, images have the power to evoke (generally) new understandings about the world around us and (specifically) the multifaceted topics of higher education and student affairs. Part two explores the following question: How can educators best leverage the use of images to optimize student learning and critical engagement in the topics of higher education and student affairs? In exploring pedagogy in this chapter, we give weight to the premise that how students learn depends largely on such contextual factors as how a teacher teaches. We offer an interdisciplinary and theoretical basis for the potential of visual methods to promote student learning. We then share some examples from the literature of visual pedagogical methods used in higher education. Next, we discuss our experience of implementing a photo elicitation project in a graduate-level course. The photo project prompts students to share reflections and photographs focused on multiculturalism for social justice in higher education. Finally, we end with potential implications for the use of visual pedagogical methods in the higher education field.

Learning Styles

For decades, research on learning styles has sought to identify how people learn best and how these findings can inform pedagogy (Brown, 1998; Cassidy, 2004). Keefe (1987) described learning style as the set of "cognitive, affective, and physiological factors that serve as relatively stable indicators of how learners perceive, interact with, and respond to the learning environment" (p. 2). These theories include models on brain hemisphericity (Asselin & Mooney, 1996), personality factors (e.g., Myers-Briggs; Myers, 1976), and information processing (e.g., experiential learning; Kolb, 1984). Acknowledging the plethora of ways in which learning styles can be understood, some scholars have also taken the approach of offering more comprehensive models that identify the different dimensions of learning, such as perceptual, cognitive, and affective (James & Gardner, 1995); information processing, instructional preference, and learning strategy (Cassidy, 2004); or the analogous onion layers Curry (1983) used to refer to various levels of a person's characteristics or learning style.

For the purpose of this discussion, we center one area of the learning styles research: sensory modalities. A number of scholars have conceptualized and categorized sensory modalities over the years, most commonly utilizing models such as the VARK (visual, aural, reading-writing, and kinesthetic; Fleming, 1995, 2001) and the Barsch learning style inventory, which specifies the visual, auditory, and kinesthetic modalities (Barsch, 1991). These models posit that individuals differ in the "sense modality of stimuli from which they best absorb, retain, and process new information" (Krätzig & Arbuthnott, 2006, p. 238). Although few studies have conclusively explained the science of sensory modalities—specifically how sensory modality preferences are distributed among people and which modalities are most effective at facilitating learning—there are pockets of information from which educators can potentially glean effectiveness.

Some evidence suggests that the majority of individuals learns best through visual stimuli. Fleming (1995) explained that visual learners prefer for "information to arrive in the form of graphs, charts, and flow diagrams," "sometimes draw maps of their learning sequences or create patterns of information," and are "sensitive to different or changing spatial arrangements, and can work easily with symbols" (p. 309). Brown (1998) and Bradford (2004) argued that roughly 65% of the general population fits this category (followed by 30% who are auditory and 5% who are kinesthetic learners), which means that the majority of people need to *see* what they are learning.

There may be a reason for this distribution, centering on the notion that vision is the single most powerful sensory tool human beings have for processing and retaining information, taking up about half of the brain's resources (Medina, 2009). In his book *Brain Rules,* Medina (2009) highlighted experiments indicating that people more efficiently learn and better retain certain types of information when pictures, as opposed to solely text or oral presentations, are used. This is likely due to the fact that "our evolutionary history was never dominated by text" (p. 234) and that pictorial information better "sticks" to our neurons. Two additional findings also have the potential to contribute to our understanding of how students learn. Medina (2009) indicated that multisensory exposure, or the engagement of multiple senses, leads to better learning than does unisensory exposure. For example, it is better to have verbal narrative and animation combinations, or sight and touch combinations, rather than just one or the other. Additionally, an emotionally charged event or experience is the best processed and recalled type of external stimulus. These types persist much longer in our memories than "neutral memories" (Medina, 2009, p. 80).

Although the findings on sensory modalities are informative and compelling, taken altogether the research suggests that—far from a one-size-fits-all or one-model-fits-all tactic—educators can enhance their pedagogical approaches by understanding that learning comprises multiple, contextual elements that interact with one another. For example, in a study by Krätzig and Arbuthnott (2006), undergraduate students indicated a contextual factor contributing to their learning was whether they thought the material was interesting. This example speaks to the importance of *what* is being delivered, not just *how* it is delivered. In summarizing these dynamics, Brown (1998) stated that "the brain performs many functions simultaneously—thoughts, emotions, imagination, and predispositions—which are continually interacting within social and cultural contexts" (para. 14).

What are some take-aways from all of this research on learning? One of the biggest themes that stands out to us is that students learn in dynamic, multifaceted, and diverse ways. Simply put, there are multiple ways of knowing and learning. Some students may gravitate to visual learning and others to auditory or kinesthetic learning. At the same time, in much of the U.S. postsecondary education system, methods of teaching and learning have not been equally valued, let alone utilized in classrooms (Moore, 1999; Rendón, 2009). In terms of learning style, Fleming (1995) noted that "society rewards read-writers in our schools and tertiary systems. The instruction, the textbooks and the assessment programs are usually in print. We suspect that many tertiary teachers are clones of the read-write teachers who taught them" (p. 312). As educators, we have witnessed the reliance on text-heavy reading and writing in higher education settings—including in student affairs programs—and we note the contrast between the lived practice and what learning theory proposes. We propose delivering content that is interesting; emotionally charged; and uses a variety of tactics, especially visual pedagogy.

Beyond sensory modalities, some of the literature on learning styles also suggests that a wider variety of intelligences and kinds of "truths" should be allowed, recognized, and fostered in higher education. For example, Moore (1999) noted that dominant paradigms within higher education regard visual thinking as "idiosyncratic, subjective, non-linear . . . [and] typically unrelated to intelligence" (para. 3), while also being distinct from "objective facts (logic and science)" (para. 4). However, Moore argued this tradition of thinking is unhelpful because people essentially go through similar ways of interpreting, judging, decision-making, and trying to make sense of what they see and feel—the only difference may be what type of discourse they engage in and what is privileged depending on the discipline. In a similar vein, Kussrow (1997) suggested that teachers' repertoires of techniques need to accommodate and reflect students' diverse learning styles and multiple intelligences; for example, logical-mathematical and linguistic intelligences must no longer be "given preferential treatment over musical, spatial, bodily-kinesthetic, interpersonal, intrapersonal, and natural intelligences" (p. 10). What all of this says to us is that the power of visual pedagogy has not been tapped for the potential it could have for students' learning and development. If roughly two-thirds of students retain information from or are more stimulated through visual stimuli, why not include more visual pedagogy in higher education?

Visual Pedagogical Methods in Higher Education

Although there has been a substantial amount of research on learning styles, there are sizeable gaps in the literature, specifically on visual learning and/or visual pedagogy, and an even larger dearth of literature on the use of visual pedagogical methods in higher education and student affairs programs. We seek to help address these gaps, undergirded by the central premises that visual methods can play unique and important roles in how we teach and can promote different and active kinds of learning among students. In this section, we highlight several examples of how postsecondary educators have employed visual pedagogical methods within their classes.

Digital Storytelling

Digital storytelling has been used in a variety of settings not limited to higher education classrooms. The products of digital storytelling can include video games, advertisements, PowerPoint presentations, and electronic photo albums (Vinogradova, Linville, & Bickel, 2011). Within pedagogy, *digital storytelling* generally refers to the process of using media technology to construct a multimodal, personal narrative. Digital storytelling has been used in the fields of cultural production, education, counseling, and language learning. As one of the studies we reviewed highlighted, the Center for Digital

Storytelling in Berkeley, California, offers a model for digital storytelling that emphasizes the potential democratizing nature of this method, as student authors are able to control the story and the entire production process. Students learn the technologies and techniques, often utilizing symbols, and ultimately even creating "the basis for students to become more critical consumers of media who can therefore cast a more analytical gaze on media texts" (Vinogradova et al., 2011, p. 176). Students choose from a variety of sources to create a multimodal product, including photographs, animations, short digital videos, drawings, music, and sound. Often, students are tasked to express a story reflecting an important or life-changing experience, exploring "connections between people, events, and places," as well as "develop[ing] connections between the author, the story, and the audience" (Vinogradova et al., 2011, p. 176). This example highlights how digital storytelling pedagogy can be interesting to the students, evoke emotionally charged reactions by focusing on life-changing experiences, and utilize multiple visual methods.

We found two cases of digital storytelling in the education literature. The first case highlighted pedagogical approaches involving arts-integrated, multimodal writing tasks used within an English (as a foreign language) classroom at a junior college in Taiwan. Lee (2014), the instructor of the course and author of the study, documented the trajectory of two students whom Lee taught. The two students' levels of motivation, confidence, engagement, and mastery of writing tasks noticeably increased once they were encouraged to integrate the arts into their responses (after they had initially been discouraged by conventional language learning instruction). The writing tasks included an online literature circle, a series of first-person narratives with images, and digital storytelling—providing students with a fun, "alternative and richer way to voice [their] thoughts and construct meanings" (Lee, 2014, p. 64). Lee connected these findings to the extant literature, which suggested that multimodal, arts-integrated pedagogical approaches (particularly in language classrooms) can serve to harness different types of intelligences (e.g., visual intelligence), as well as encourage students to take risks, express themselves, and engage meaningfully with ideas, classmates, and teachers.

The second case was by Vinogradova and colleagues (2011). Similar to Lee's (2014) article, the authors also discussed pedagogical practices used in an English language learning classroom among a group of geographically diverse students studying in the United States. The authors examined the use of digital storytelling as a student-centered project that "create[d] inclusive classroom communities of practice and foster[ed] development of multiliteracies" (p. 174). Within the projects described in this article, students developed and produced their personal stories; chose topics, visual images, and music materials; and collaborated with classmates, friends, and family. Students learned production tools and techniques and created and delivered their story using symbolic means. Digital storytelling in this classroom invited students to "take charge of their learning" and "learn how culturally rich information can be designed, composed, transmitted, and interpreted using multimodal means" (Vinogradova et al., 2011, p. 181). The authors posited that digital storytelling fit into their inclusive pedagogy which calls for the holistic participation of each student and critical attention to how learning is designed and facilitated.

Photo Elicitation
Another visual method that has been used in inclusive pedagogy is photo elicitation. Photo elicitation has been increasingly used in qualitative research across disciplines and revolves around the basic idea of inserting a photograph into a research interview. Photo elicitation is based on the notion that "images evoke deeper elements of human consciousness than do words" and that the process of elicitation capitalizes on the "information, feelings, and memories that are due to the photograph's particular form of representation" (Harper, 2002, p. 13). Although the literature more commonly discusses photo elicitation in research methods, there is also great potential for its use in pedagogy, as illustrated in one article and in the example from our classroom teaching, which we share later in this chapter.

Gil-Glazer (2015) reported on a study of college students' experiences and perceptions of having been a part of an academic course that integrated photo elicitation. More specifically, students in the course were exposed to and discussed photographs that conveyed *difficult knowledge,* addressing topics such as violence, human suffering, pain, and extreme sexuality and gender identity. Research about the pedagogical method was based on interviews and questionnaires administered to 14 undergraduate students who took a course in an education program at a college in Israel. The author discussed several themes that emerged. The first theme focused on how photographs often stimulated emotion–thought conflict in students. While sometimes uncomfortable, students expressed the importance of the photographs as part of the educational discourse on society and culture. A second theme centered on students' guided, empathic, and critical discussions about the photographs. Discussions helped students "cope" with the emotions stirred by the photographs and fostered critical visual literacy, such that students could answer the questions: "What are we seeing? What were they trying to show us here? Who was trying to show us?" (Gil-Glazer, 2015, p. 270). Students discussed having previously been bombarded with and desensitized to graphic images in the media, while not having had a basis for processing them. The educational framework of the class, as cofacilitated by the teacher and students, allowed them to make meaning of the photographs, draw implications to social issues, and connect to others through both cognitive and emotional learning.

Arts-Based Inquiry

Similar to photo elicitation, the use of arts-based inquiry in the pedagogy within higher education has been seldom discussed in the literature. Borrowing from the general definition of *arts-based inquiry* (largely used within research), this form of inquiry "adapt[s] the tenets of the creative arts in order to address social research questions in holistic and engaged ways" (Leavy, 2015, p. 4). Arts-based inquiry utilizes the creation and discussion of drawings, concept maps, paintings, photography, or other nonverbal media (Barone, 2006). Jung (2015) facilitated a study at the University of Georgia that highlighted arts-based inquiry as a pedagogical method. The class-based project utilized the frameworks of critical race theory and confrontational pedagogy. Students created postcard art that visually represented their personal stereotypes about people from identity backgrounds other than their own, with the knowledge that the postcards would be publicly and anonymously displayed. The author discussed how the class project prompted students to engage in "complex and uncomfortable revelations of personal beliefs" (Jung, 2015, p. 214) that would have otherwise likely remained unknowable. Following this display of postcards, students discussed the shared images and wrote reflection papers regarding how this project transformed their perceptions of stereotypes. Students created follow-up postcards about ways to "deconstruct institutionalized perceptions of Others" (Jung, 2015, p. 214). This article highlighted the ways in which pedagogy that incorporated arts and images weaved into a broader pedagogical effort to confront knowledge in critical and transformative ways.

Image Theater

Another pedagogical visual method that helps students consider content from an inclusive and critical perspective is Image Theater. The practice of Image Theater was first conceptualized and developed by Augusto Boal (1985) as part of *Theatre of the Oppressed*, a range of theatrical forums and techniques based on Paulo Freire's (1970) *Pedagogy of the Oppressed*. Image Theater centers on "an opportunity for spect-actors to challenge and blur the boundaries that exist between art and life in order to engage in and challenge historical ideologies of democracy, stereotypes, symbols, icons, norms, and values embedded in such images" (Powell & Serriere, 2013, p. 7). To date, there is a dearth of literature on the use of Image Theater in the higher education classroom setting. One article discussed the pedagogical use of Image Theater within a university setting (albeit taking place outside of the classroom walls) among students, in efforts to engage performance of and discourse about democracy. In this study, the investigators facilitated Image Theater in the student union of a university. In this iteration, undergraduate students were organically recruited as spectactors in a theatrical portrayal of the construct of democracy. A participatory strategy such as Image Theater was thought to position students as experts and cocreators of knowledge who are "capable of elaborating and modifying existing knowledge" and "unframing perceptions of reality" (Powell & Serriere, 2013, p. 21). This article highlighted the notion that people learn best—and even contribute to democratic participation of knowledge creation—when *multimodal* as well as *participatory* pedagogical strategies are enacted.

With the scant examples of visual pedagogy we found in the literature, we want to underscore that student development and learning in higher education can be increased by aligning visual pedagogy with the approximately two-thirds of students who identify with a visual learning style. Next we share our own example of incorporating one of the methods, photo elicitation, into a graduate preparation program curriculum.

Photo Elicitation Example

Other than showing videos in class presentations, allowing students to include visuals in reports they made to class, and having students create professional posters for classes, I (Bridget) had not incorporated visuals into a major assignment in my graduate classes. However, because I saw the power of participant-generated drawings in my research, I was open to trying the photo project in my section of the Multiculturalism for Social Justice course. Another faculty member created the photo project assignment and taught the course as an elective when I began teaching it. It is now a required course for every master's student in the higher education program, and the photo project is the major assignment that bookends the course.

The photo project involves photo elicitation, a pedagogical approach to exploring concepts of social justice, privilege, and oppression through pictures. Photo elicitation is a powerful means to address emotional and affective understanding of complex social justice issues that cannot be gleaned through traditional papers and dialogue in class. Although applied in the context of a course, the photo project has broader implications for student development work. Photo elicitation is a relatively new method for getting students beyond awareness to multicultural knowledge and skill development. Additional benefits and tenets of photo elicitation make it ideal for addressing social justice and inclusion in the classroom. Everyone is positioned as a knower, encouraged to personalize broad intellectual concepts and get in touch with feelings pictures evoke. The project stimulates in-depth awareness that can lead to students' knowledge about themselves in larger systems of oppression, privilege, and social justice.

The photo project consists of two parts. In the first part at the start of the semester, before they read anything in class about oppression, privilege, or social justice, students are asked to take photographs representing these major core concepts and document why these pictures are reflective of oppression, privilege, and social justice. In the second part of the project at the end of the semester, the photos from the first part of the project are revisited, and additional photos are added that reflect new interpretations of the core concepts that may have arisen as a result of participation in the course. In addition, a final short paper documents the student's journey as it relates to understanding and representing the core concepts and connecting the student to course literature, exercises we did in class, and dialogues students facilitated with each other.

Figure 5.1 is an example from a student with the accompanying following paragraph written about a train system in Chicago:

> I ride the train multiple times a week, but it was only a few weeks ago that I realized that not all stations are handicap accessible. I included this as a representation of oppression because the station limitations discriminate against individuals who do not fit the normalized costumer [*sic*] profile. This prevents all customers from fully participating in the [Chicago Transit Authority] train system, leaving many needing to make additional transportation plans and allow for more travel time between their destinations.

In my feedback from the first part of this sample project, which the student turned in during the second week of school, I asked "What do you think motivates these decisions? How are you connected to this as a temporarily able-bodied and able-minded individual?" This is typical of the feedback I provide to students in the first part of the project. Students tend to take pictures of things they believe represent privilege (e.g., golf courses, mansions, bandages that only come in beige color), oppression (e.g., Barbie dolls, check

Figure 5.1. Oppression on the train.

cashing stores, staircases), and social justice (e.g., gender-neutral bathrooms, nonprofit organizations, universities) in their daily commute to work, home, and school without any thought of how those images are connected to them personally or in their work with students. The fact that students generate/take the photos themselves without any input from me as an authority or assigned readings gives students freedom to decide how to define terms. Taking photos also gives students an object (e.g. the photograph itself) on which to focus rather than themselves. It feels safer for the students to talk about the photo in the paragraph in small groups in class. That distance slowly falls away as I provide feedback on their photo project assignment and as their classmates ask them prompts I have developed for those small-group class sessions. On the day we discuss oppression and the first part of their photo project is due for week two, students answer the following questions in class in groups of three or four:

- What disturbed or surprised you about oppression photos of your classmates?
- What reading can you connect to photos and why?
- How are photos connected to one of your identities (target or agent) or a cultural group to whom you belong?

In week four, we discuss social justice. Students are asked to bring their social justice photos in from the first part of the photo project and are given the following prompts to discuss in class in groups of three or four:

- Describe one of your social justice photos, the feelings it evoked, and why you believe those feelings emerged.
- Did those feelings connect to any of your target or agent identities?
- How did the pictures connect to your understanding of social justice from our designated reading?

Finally, in week five we discuss privilege, and students are given the following guidelines for their small-group work in class:

Pull out one of your privilege pictures and reexamine it. Do you see it any differently now than when you first took it? Note answer down for yourself.

Break into pairs:

1. Show your picture to the other person and ask them to describe what they see in the picture (i.e., people, buildings, signs, etc.).

2. Ask them whether they think it represents privilege, and why or why not. Note down your feelings/reactions, but do not share them yet.
3. Switch and redo Steps 1 and 2.
4. Discuss how different/similar your perspectives of the pictures were, and what that made you feel/think/believe. Was it affirming, dismissing, triggering?
5. How do your privileged identities connect to ideas in readings?
6. What will you do with the knowledge of your privilege?

With structured, focused time in class that I gave for the students to reflect on the photos they took for each core concept, students were able to use the photos as a point of departure for moving from abstract, theoretical concepts, to deeply personal and work-related meanings. We do not revisit the photos in class until week 13 when I go over the second part of the photo project and assist students in preparing for that final assignment. For the second part of the photo project, students can take new photos, use the same photos, or combine old and new photos to document their new understanding of oppression, privilege, and social justice. The paragraphs they write accompanying each of the three to five photos they take for each core concept must include evidence from readings, and the project concludes in an eight-page paper in which they write their own definition of the concepts, how they came to this definition during the semester, and what action/social change they wish to take or make as a result of their learning. Figure 5.2 and the accompanying paragraph are from the same student who submitted Figure 5.1. Figure 5.2 was submitted for the second part of the photo project.

Figure 5.2. Ableism at the gym.

This is a photo of the gym of which I am a member. The Orange Theory method is one of the newest "trends" in exercise in this country and my newest workout obsession. It is also an example of many privileges I hold. But the one that I have come to a greater understanding of through this course is that as a temporarily able-bodied person, there is great privilege in my ability to participate in a rigorous workout routine. Furthermore, the fact that I work out first thing in the morning, often elicits remarks insinuating that I must be highly motivated, productive, and driven. These comments are directly connected to the social construction of ableism in our culture, as we value a continuously increased pace of life as an indicator of productivity. "When the pace of life in a society increases, there is a tendency for more people to become disabled . . . because fewer people can meet expectations of 'normal performance'" (Wendell, 2013, p. 482). Before our course, I considered such comments a compliment. Now, I see them as a form of ableism because we live within, "a world of strength, the positive (valued) body, performance and production, the non-disabled, and young adults" (p. 483).

This submission for the second part of the photo project was in stark contrast to the photo of the train sign and paragraph about "other" people with disabilities who faced oppression. By the end of the class the student decided to include a new photograph that better captured the understanding of privilege in relation to ableism as oppression. The photo project provided a visual way for the student to demonstrate enhanced understanding of core concepts in the class and how the concepts hit cognitive as well as affect domains.

The photo elicitation assignment is something students hear about from previous cohorts of master's students in our program and look forward to each year. They are mostly excited about using an alternative way to express themselves early on in class—as I am known for strict enforcement of writing style standards and grammar, and the first part of the photo project is not graded based on these elements. Rather, students are assessed minimal points (5 out of a total 25 points for the entire project) for the first part of the photo project, which is based on following format and rules for taking photos solely for this class's purpose, including at least two or three photos for each concept, and keeping their paragraph concise. Most students also look forward to the second part of the photo project at the end of the semester and relish the opportunity to demonstrate what they learned through photographs.

Implications

As much as the students enjoy the photo elicitation project we discussed in the preceding sections, we, as educators, like facilitating their learning using different pedagogical tools. It can be quite dull to read 20 or 40 papers at the end of a 15-week semester-long course, but quite interesting to view photos taken by and analyzed by students. This is one of many implications for utilizing visual pedagogy in higher education classrooms. Engaged learners and teachers foster learning and development. Students are better able to retain knowledge they help cocreate and generate. Another implication is one that ties to the central argument of this book: Helping students connect to and analyze visuals in class enables them to decipher the increasingly visual world in which they live. Instagram, Snapchat, Facebook Live, selfies, and images in the media come at students in a fast-paced 24/7 format. Giving students the skills, as illustrated in the small-group activities shared in our example, to examine the cognitive (What messages are being conveyed, by whom, for what purpose, from which lens are you making those assumptions?) and the affective (What feelings does the image evoke, why, what feelings do others have when viewing the image?) aspects of images increases their visual literacy. Visual pedagogy has the potential to enhance student development and learning with tools for students to be critical of their world and shape ideas for social change.

References

Asselin, S. B., & Mooney, M. (1996). *Diverse learners: Strategies for success.* Glen Allen, VA: Virginia Vocational Curriculum and Resource Center. (ERIC Document Reproduction Service No. 406 529)

Barone, T. (2006). Arts-based educational research then, now, and later. *Studies in Art Education, 48*(1), 4–8.

Barsch, J. (1991). *Barsch learning style inventory.* Novato, CA: Academic Therapy.

Boal, A. (1985). *Theatre of the oppressed.* New York, NY: Theater Communications Group.

Bradford, W. C. (2004). Reaching the visual learner: Teaching property through art. *The Law Teacher, 11,* 12–16.

Brown, B. L. (1998). *Learning styles and vocational education practice.* Clearinghouse on adult, career, and vocational education. (ERIC Document Reproduction Service No. ED422478)

Cassidy, S. (2004). Learning styles: An overview of theories, models, and measures. *Educational Psychology, 24*(4), 419–444.

Curry, L. (1983). *An organization of learning styles theory and constructs.* Paper presented at the Annual Meeting of the American Educational Research Association, Montreal, Canada.

Fleming, N. D. (1995). I'm different, not dumb. Modes of presentation (VARK) in the tertiary classroom. In A. Zelmer (Ed.), *Research and development in higher education: Proceedings of the 1995 Annual Conference of the Higher Education and Research Development Society of Australasia* (pp. 308–313). Canterbury, New Zealand: Higher Education and Research Development Society of Australasia.

Fleming, N. D. (2001). *Teaching and learning styles: VARK strategies.* Christchurch, New Zealand: IGI Global.

Freire, P. (1970). *Pedagogy of the oppressed.* New York, NY: Herder and Herder.

Gil-Glazer, Y. A. (2015). Photography, critical pedagogy and "difficult knowledge." *International Journal of Education Through Art, 11*(2), 261–276.

Harper, D. (2002). Talking about pictures: A case for photo elicitation. *Visual Studies, 17*(1), 13–26.

James, W. B., & Gardner, D. L. (1995). Learning styles: Implications for distance learning. *New Directions for Adult and Continuing Education, 1995*(67), 19–31.

Jung, Y. (2015). Post stereotypes: Deconstructing racial assumptions and biases through visual culture and confrontational pedagogy. *Studies in Art Education, 56*(3), 214–227.

Keefe, J. W. (1987). *Theory and practice.* Reston, VA: National Association of Secondary School Principals.

Kolb, D. (1984). *Experiential learning.* Englewood Cliffs, NJ: Prentice Hall.

Krätzig, G. P., & Arbuthnott, K. D. (2006). Perceptual learning style and learning proficiency: A test of the hypothesis. *Journal of Educational Psychology, 98*(1), 238–246.

Kussrow, P. G. (1997, July). *From pedagogy through andragogy to holosagogy.* (ERIC Document Reproduction Service No. ED412213).

Leavy, P. (2015). *Method meets art: Arts-based research practice.* New York, NY: Guilford Publications.

Lee, H. C. (2014). Using an arts-integrated multimodal approach to promote English learning: A case study of two Taiwanese junior college students. *English Teaching: Practice and Critique, 13*(2), 55–75.

Medina, J. (2009). *Brain rules: 12 principles for surviving and thriving at work, home, and school.* Seattle, WA: Pear Press.

Moore, K. (1999). How real is visual thinking? (Architectural teaching methods). *Architects' Journal, 210*(5), 59–61.

Myers, I. (1976). *Introduction to type.* Gainesville, FL: Center for the Application of Psychological Type.

Powell, K., & Serriere, S. (2013). Image-based participatory pedagogies: Reimagining social justice. *International Journal of Education & the Arts, 14*(15), 1–21.

Rendón, L. I. (2009). *Sentipensante (sensing/thinking) pedagogy: Educating for wholeness, social justice and liberation.* Sterling, VA: Stylus.

Vinogradova, P., Linville, H. A., & Bickel, B. (2011). "Listen to my story and you will know me": Digital stories as student-centered collaborative projects. *TESOL Journal, 2*(2), 173–202.

Wendell, S. (2013). The social construction of disability. In M. Adams, W. J. Blumenfeld, R. Castañeda, H. W. Hackman, M. L. Peters, & X. Zúñiga (Eds.), *Readings for diversity and social justice* (3rd ed., pp. 481–485). New York, NY: Routledge.

6

PHOTOVOICE AND VISUAL LIFE WRITING

Infusing Participatory Research Into Graduate Pedagogy

Amanda O. Latz and Keri L. Rodgers

M y (Amanda) first foray into the use of visual methods and methodologies was my doctoral dissertation (Latz, 2011). For my dissertation, I employed photovoice (Sutton-Brown, 2014; Wang & Burris, 1997) to inquire about how community college students construct their educational lives (Latz, 2012a, 2012b, 2015). Upon completion of that study, I was convinced of the efficacy of photovoice as a powerful tool in better understanding college students' lives. The research project had a profound impact on me as I engaged in the intellectual work of building local constructivist grounded theories (Charmaz, 2006) from my findings, thereby building a deep and nuanced understanding of my participants' lives. It also gave me the opportunity to sit, listen, engage, and develop a heightened, yet delicate, intimacy with my participants. There is vulnerability in sharing and narrating images, and my participants deftly walked into that vulnerable space, eager to share their educational lives with someone who had been a part of it—me, their former instructor at the local community college.

I was not the only person impacted by my students' stories; the project also affected those who interfaced with the work once the dissertation was complete, and although it is beyond the scope of this chapter, I detail those profound effects elsewhere (Latz, 2017). Individuals who consume photovoice project findings through exhibitions, presentations, journal articles, and/or books are necessarily affected. One of the aims of the methodology is to inspire action, and photographs can be quite visually alluring. In fact, sometimes consumers can be affronted by the images within and narrations of participants' photographs. Again, one of the major purposes of the methodology is to gain the attention of policymakers to influence policy development and change, so this is a desirable outcome. It works, and I saw it happen with my own research.

Becoming a photovoice researcher made me more empathic. It made me decentralize the long-held notion that researchers are to be the sole architects of their studies, the ones unequivocally in charge of logistics, procedures, tone, tenor, purpose(s), and so on. Engagement in photovoice, a form of participatory action research (Whyte, 1991), places the researcher in a role where power is—at least to some degree—dispersed. Further, participatory action research not only produces knowledge but also requires action catalyzed through participant involvement. The photovoice process taught me an enormous amount about the educational lives of community college students. It also taught me a lot about photovoice. When I started teaching graduate-level courses at Ball State University, I was charged with teaching courses about community colleges. How could I carry forward this dissertation experience, build on what I gleaned from it, and ask my students to join me in similar participatory research projects in hopes of fostering for them the atmosphere and circumstances necessary for the type of learning I experienced and mentioned previously?

I have been fortunate enough to be able to address that question for the past four years. Since 2013, I have taught a graduate-level course titled "Community Colleges and Diversity" four times. In what follows, my cocontribtuor (Keri) and I discuss the utilization of participatory research—specifically participant-generated visuals—in pedagogical practice to assist graduate students in not only learning about the lives of community college students but also in meeting the objectives of the aforementioned course. After detailing my (and our) pedagogical experiences with infusing photovoice and visual life writing into my "Community Colleges and Diversity" course, we provide several considerations for others who may take on similar pedagogical pursuits.

Year One: Building a Base

The first time I taught "Community Colleges and Diversity" it did not occur to me to push the pedagogical boundaries of how I would approach the task. Simply surviving as a second-year, tenure-track faculty member with another new course to prepare and building a solid base from which the course could unfold over the semester took center stage. The course was designed similarly to my other courses: readings, discussions, and incremental writing assignments that led to a large final paper. During the course, however, I felt uneasy. It was one thing to read and talk about community colleges and all of the attending diversity (e.g., diversity among the institutions themselves, programs, funding, missions, students, faculty, and staff), but it was quite another to have diversity experiences. We read and talked plenty about diversity, but we were not having diversity *experiences* related to the community college. At the close of the 16-week semester, the course ended. Upon assessing students' writing assignments, noting the progression of our in-class discussions, and reviewing their self-reported learning gains via formal student evaluations, it was clear that the students certainly learned about community colleges and diversity. However, my uneasiness remained. Did my students really understand how diverse community classrooms could be? If they did, was it a nuanced and complex understanding? Where were the potential gaps in my students' knowledge? After settling farther into my position as a faculty member and gaining the confidence to undergo some significant course redesign, I set out to build on the base I created when I first taught the course. It was time to infuse experiences and endeavor toward deepened and empathic understandings.

Year Two: Photovoice Project One

During spring 2014, the students enrolled in the course and I came together as a research team and worked with undergraduates at the local community college on a photovoice project centered on community college students' perceptions of social class, poverty, and financial literacy (Latz, Phelps-Ward, Royer, & Peters, 2016). We partnered with five community college students who volunteered to participate. This project culminated with a photovoice exhibition, which took place at the community college (Figure 6.1).

Although the seven students in my class gained skills and experience related to research, the project also yielded two unanticipated positive outcomes. First, infusing the course with a team-based research project proved to be an effective form of pedagogy at the graduate level. The students in my class experienced authentic learning about community colleges and diversity by being with and talking with community college students, working with community college institutional agents, and spending dedicated time on the community college's campus. This version of experiential and immersive learning was unlike anything my students had previously experienced. Deep understandings were achieved, and student-learning outcomes were met, as was evident through my students' work as well as their reflective essays and course evaluations at the close of the semester.

Second, the experience was important for the community college students involved. They experienced moments of concerted reflection on their own

Figure 6.1. Photovoice exhibition.

lives and, through that process, were able to make new meaning of some of their college experiences moving forward. At the close of the semester, both student groups hosted a public photovoice exhibition within the local community. We worked closely with our community college partner to secure and arrange the exhibition space in a meaningful fashion. In addition, we advertised widely by sending press releases to local news outlets, distributing e-mail invites to individuals through various electronic mailing lists, creating a website and social media accounts, and creating and distributing flyers and posters. Approximately 60 attendees came through our exhibition, which showcased this all-too-uncommon institutional collaboration (Latz et al., 2016). As such, the use of photovoice within this particular course solidified, for me, the utility of photovoice as research, pedagogy, collaboration catalyst, and student development tool. However, there was certainly room for refinement and plenty of other ways to ascertain the *experiences* I so doggedly wanted my students to have. Accordingly, the course changed yet again the third time around.

Year Three: Visual Life Writing

Prior to spring 2015, I became enamored by a book I read over the winter recess called *Syllabus: Notes from an Accidental Professor* (Barry, 2014). Moreover, I had been constantly thinking about visual forms of communication in anticipation of Sousanis's (2015) forthcoming graphic novel, based on his dissertation, *Unflattening*, which arrived in print that spring. Sousanis's work is an ode to visual thinking with clear educational underpinnings and implications. In thinking about how I wanted to design the course for that spring, I knew I wanted my graduate students to work with community college students on a visual life writing/autobiographical life history (Goodson & Sikes, 2001) project. Barry's (2014) work convinced me of that, as she outlined her methods and students' products within the text. My past course experience in addition to my reading at the time pointed me in the direction of using visual life writing.

The goal of the course experience was to create a product that would encapsulate meaningful snippets of community college students' lives, particularly their educational lives. I envisioned the life writing project as being something new students at the community college could use. Who better to narrate and demystify the community college going experience than community college students? So that year, my class partnered with a First-Year Seminar class at the local community college, and this life writing project became a part of that class's curriculum.

I (Keri) was excited to be a partner in this project and served as facilitator of the community college course. Designing an experience to meet both community college students' and graduate students' needs may appear difficult because of the juxtaposition of the two course syllabi, which are intended for different audiences and include seemingly varying course objectives. The first step was to rework the entire course syllabus for the community college course, a syllabus that placed the students in a seemingly subordinate role; the second step was to redesign the course to have the students become colleagues and collaborators in their own learning; and the third step was to consider how, together, we could meet the course objectives while maximizing the opportunity for collaborating with the graduate students presented. With support of community college administrators, we were given the chance to completely rework the course as a part of this unique institutional collaboration.

The community college students recognized the mentoring potential of graduate students learning at their sides. They also desired to share in the totality of the experience as equal partners in their learning. Students' goals for their own learning were discussed alongside the graduate students, who suggested skills and learning outcomes that not only coincided with course objectives but also were based on their own experiences as first-year college students. With these ideas in mind, we developed the curriculum to be responsive to students' needs and objectives simultaneously. Through the use of individual and group visual projects that served as artifacts for discussion, students (community college and graduate) began to open themselves to sharing their stories with each other.

Artifacts were more than class assignments, though, and we never knew what would serve as an artifact. For example, an older student who had been struggling to speak in class one day mentioned 45s and 33s that she played as a kid and saw the blank stares of students half her age, unable to understand vinyl record terminology. The following class she brought examples of each type of record and described how the black discs played music. This formerly silent student had found her voice. It was one of many watershed moments we experienced throughout the duration of the course. Every person in the room became a researcher as well as a participant, examining the visual artifact(s) being discussed, and then probing for a deeper understanding of each other's stories and ultimately their own stories.

My (Amanda) students worked diligently with Keri to make this project come to life. All students were provided a plain composition notebook for their writings, sketches, collages, and diagrams. Across both classes, we all worked together—attending the class sessions and maintaining composition notebooks—for the entire eight-week compressed semester. We provided prompts for the community college students such as the following: (a) Why are you here in college?; (b) Draw your educational journey as a board game; and (c) Create a final reflection on this course and what it has meant to you. In doing so, we mirrored some of the approaches Lynda Barry (2014) has described; composition notebooks are critical in her pedagogical work with college students. In fact, her book *Syllabus: Notes from an Accidental Professor* (Barry, 2014) was created to look and feel like a composition notebook. But as evident from our previous observations, there were many moments of serendipitous visual engagement—with artifacts, photographs, letters, and documents, anything relevant the students wanted to share—throughout the eight weeks.

The resultant project was a *zine* (short for magazine), designed by my graduate students but with content from both student groups and emblematic of many of the handmade, countercultural, underground publications that became widespread in the 1990s (see Friday Night Breakfast (W)rites [2015] to read the zine in its entirety). Figure 6.2, a page from the zine, is a section of a community college student's game board. All involved in this life writing/autobiographical history project experienced similar learning outcomes to those involved with last spring's course. Again, we built empathy across institutions, experiences, and educational journeys. In fact, the zine contains some excerpts from my students and illustrates some of the learning they gleaned from our unique course experience. We encourage readers to engage with the zine; it is available online.

Year Four: Photovoice Project Two

Most recently, when I (Amanda) taught the class for the fourth time, I wanted to blend the best of the previous two course experiences. Therefore,

Figure 6.2. Excerpt from the zine.

Note. Scan QR code to view the full zine (http://fridaynightbreakfastwrites.weebly.com/the-friday-night-writes-zine-2015.html).

I decided we would carry out a photovoice project with community college students enrolled in "Student Success" (a new title for the first-year seminar). This time, after consulting with institutional agents at the community college, we aimed to build an understanding of the diverse needs of incoming students so they could be served optimally—a key to addressing the knotty retention puzzle faced by so many community colleges across the country.

Similar to spring 2014, students across both institutions formed bonds, grew in their understandings of one another, and worked together to showcase the final "product," a photovoice exhibition. In addition to showcasing the community college students' photographs and narrations (Figure 6.3), my students also showcased art installations they made toward the end of the course to illustrate what they learned through the duration of the project (Figure 6.4). This was a particularly thorny aspect of the total experience, as my students wanted more parameters than I was willing to give them. Following is an excerpt from the syllabus:

> One focus of our [end-of-class] exhibition is the photovoice project. A second focus of our exhibition is how each of you experienced the project and the class as a whole. Each of you will create and display an installation that represents what you learned and how you grew as a result of this project and our class overall. I encourage you to use your Course Notebooks as a place to brainstorm and develop your ideas for your installation. **Anything is possible!** During the semester, we will dedicate time to discuss your ideas.

Figure 6.3. Community college students' photographs and narrations.

Figure 6.4. Graduate students' art installations.

Despite not having as many parameters as they thought they needed, my students created thoughtful and meaningful installations that exceeded my expectations. In building this particular installation assignment into my students' course experience, *both* sets of students were able to showcase and talk about tangible items that represented their experiences. This component of the course gave my students another opportunity to showcase how they met the course objectives, and it also provided them with a greater sense of ownership in the overall exhibition experience.

Reflecting on the Use of Photovoice in Pedagogy

In two of the last three examples I (Amanda) provided here, the use of photovoice served a broad range of purposes. First, it was used as a research methodology to advance what is known about the lives of community college students. The journal article that was generated from the project (i.e., Latz et al., 2016) is an example. Because photovoice is a form of participatory action research, it was used to include the community college student participants as both participants and coresearchers, helping to shape and guide the work at various steps in the research process. Moreover, my students had the opportunity to present our findings to the general public as well as institutional agents at the community college with the hopes of affecting positive policy change, which is an aim of the photovoice methodology (Wang & Burris, 1997).

Second, photovoice was used simultaneously as pedagogy. The students in my class were learning by conducting research. Through conducting photovoice research, my students were able to work with our community college student partners in a way that fostered understanding and empathy. Genuine human interactions gave way to relationships, and those relationships—however short and experience-bound—produced authentic experiential learning. Conducting photovoice research meant learning by doing. Third, photovoice was used as a mechanism through which cross-institutional collaboration was ignited and catalyzed. By bringing together students and faculty/staff members from two institutions of higher education—along with members of the broader local area through the exhibitions—community bonds were forged. This was seen, in part, by the myriad positive ways in which the exhibitions were received and experienced by both those involved in the project and exhibition attendees. Fourth and finally, photovoice afforded opportunities to both better understand and advance various forms of student identity development among participants. For example, during the most recent photovoice project, one of our community college student participants noted that the project helped him open up and build confidence; he also referred to his participation in the project as being the greatest experience of his college career. Among college students, participating in a photovoice project can foster a space for identity work.

One of the aims of the photovoice methodology is to make space for individuals to document some aspect(s) of their lives on their own terms; they are the experts. Participation typically entails rumination on a series of photography prompts or questions; photography; and, finally, either writing about, narrating, or discussing the contents of those photographs. For example, during the second photovoice project, community college students had to dedicate energy to considering and acting upon our prompts, which included the following questions: What makes you unique? Why are you in college? What are you inspired by? The time and energy spent on these activities necessarily causes participants to reflect on and make (new) meaning of past and present experiences, realities, and phenomena—actions riddled with potential for identity work. Self-authorship, therefore, is one specific type of student identity development that can be promoted in this kind of work (Latz, 2012a).

Reflecting on the Use of Visual Life Writing in Pedagogy

One of the most salient activities included in the visual life writing project was having the students write about and draw out their educational journeys in the form of a game board (examples are included in the zine illustrated in

Figure 6.2). This was not an in-class activity; it was assigned as homework. But during the class session when the assignment was due, students were given the opportunity to show their boards to the class, narrating them along the way. Through the use of words and images, the students were able to make overt some of the twists, turns, tragedies, and triumphs of their journeys to date. Students were given very little direction for this assignment, which led to a variety of approaches. Some students included a destination, and others did not. Some students included large amounts of texts, and some boards were nearly all images. The community college students told stories about family members being murdered, adjusting to civilian life, and managing drug and alcohol addiction (not an exhaustive list). These stories were often centered on family, personal choices, making comebacks, and having second chances.

As noted previously, the community college course was eight weeks in length, and this assignment was due during the third week. Following the class session when these boards were shared, I wrote the following in my (Amanda's) composition notebook:

> There was truly a beautiful synergy in the room, which is difficult to describe and identify. But I felt like I was in a sacred space—SO HAPPY— to have been there with my [graduate] students so these stories could land HARD on listening ears. A community was born. That session was the epitome of what I thought this experience could be—for EVERYONE there. We made empathy.

This experience—among many others—not only served as a building block to meet the outcomes of both courses but also impacted the ways in which Keri and I now think about, design, and approach pedagogy.

In my work, I (Keri) am more keenly in tune with the importance of visual literacy within my approaches to class sessions, assignments, and assessments. Within my practice, I (Amanda) am much more inclined to encourage multimodal products in student assignments. For example, in one of the graduate courses I teach, students must complete "Reading Notes and Annotations," a product that must showcase students' engagement with the assigned readings. There are very few parameters for this assignment— students have created podcasts, highly visual blogs with embedded relevant photographs, sketches, YouTube videos, memes, and animated gifs. This is most certainly a welcomed path for students to take as their work indicates they are able to bridge our readings, which are textual, with a multidimensional and multisensory visual and/or audio landscape. These approaches to the assignment are emblematic of the broader landscapes within which they live their everyday lives, both personally and professionally.

Considerations for Incorporating Participatory Research

Based on our pedagogical experiences outlined previously, we are strong advocates of infusing participant-generated visual methodologies and methods into the classroom. Although the pedagogical use of such methodologies and methods is the focus of this particular section of the book, we have seen that what begins as a pedagogical application can spill over into work related to both research and student identity development. This kind of pedagogical work is necessarily risky, as it upends many of the hegemonic assumptions that many students, educators, and academic administrators harbor about what education is and how it should happen. Yet, we have found that the risks are worth the reward. If considering this kind of pedagogical approach, which does not necessarily need to take place within the confines of a class-based experience, we offer the following considerations:

- Know your purpose, and articulate the learning outcomes. Here are examples of learning outcomes from the zine project built for graduate students: (a) students will gain an understanding of the complexity, nuances, and diversity of community college students' educational lives; (b) students will deepen their knowledge of community colleges in a general sense; (c) students will become more empathic toward others (i.e., community college students) who *may* be very different from them; and (d) students will be able to articulate all the steps involved in a collaborative project centered on educational multimedia storytelling and life writing.
- Match and map your pedagogical actions to your outcomes and the underlying purpose. Consider the ways in which each task students engage in advances them toward the learning objectives and the project goal(s).
- Make early decisions about who the *participants* are. Will your students be considered the participants, thereby generating the visuals? Will your students be working with others who will be considered the participants? Will all involved be considered participants?
- If collaboration of any kind is a part of the experience, take the time to build relationships and trust among your collaborators. This work never ceases. Keeping everyone updated is an ongoing task, but the payoffs are invaluable.
- Make early decisions about tools needed to generate visuals. In the earlier examples, a variety of supplies were necessary, such as disposable cameras, composition notebooks, markers, colored pencils, and so on.
- Think through approaches, activities, assignments, and products. What steps are necessary along the way? Working backward can be

useful here. In the examples presented in this chapter, the end products were known early, and we knew when the course would end. In two cases, we were working toward public photovoice exhibitions. In one case, we were working toward a zine. What did we have to do, and by when, to make the product(s) before the end of the course? Planning is critical, but there are times when plans must change. It becomes an iterative and ongoing planning process, but having a good map at the start is paramount.

- Know that often your students will show you the way; embrace this. Once the experience is unfolding, encourage students to own the process. Guide them, offer up suggestions, and make decisions when they need you to do so, but ownership yields accountability, which yields results.
- If things feel awkward and discomforting at times, you are doing it right. Dissonance is a sign that you are moving outside of your comfort zone. Trust in the process, your students, and any others with whom you are working.
- Be pragmatic about the time limits of an academic semester or term, especially if the project requires review by a research ethics board. This can be doubly cumbersome if two or more reviews are required. Consider what is reasonable to ask of your students. During the zine project, for example, not all the graduate students came to all sessions of the community college class. In fact, some never attended because of their busy schedules (many of the graduate students have full-time jobs and/or have long commutes to campus). Those who did attend shared their experiences with classmates via discussion, e-mail, and file sharing. We made this possible by dividing roles and tasks based on availability. Regardless, some students will be resistant to this kind of approach, as it is antithetical to traditional pedagogical models of college teaching. Plus, it is a lot of hard work.

Summary

Using participant-generated visuals as part of pedagogical practice has been intensely rewarding in our experience. The use of photovoice and visual life writing as pedagogy reaped significant rewards among the students with whom we worked. The projects in which we engaged meaningfully brought together graduate and community college students in ways that benefitted both student groups. In each case, the graduate students certainly learned a great deal about the prevalence, forms, and nuances of the diversity ever-present within the community college setting. To read about something is very different from experiencing, participating in, and relating to something. Moreover, our experiences illustrated that participant-generated visuals can be a major component of the research, pedagogy, and student identity development that transpires within the realm of higher education—often all at the same time. We are unabashed proponents of this approach. We encourage, you, the reader, to consider the ways in which you might introduce this kind of work into your own practice.

References

Barry, L. (2014). *Syllabus: Notes from an accidental professor.* Montreal, Quebec, Canada: Drawn & Quarterly.

Charmaz, K. (2006). *Constructing grounded theory: A practical guide through qualitative analysis.* Thousand Oaks, CA: Sage.

Friday Night Breakfast (W)rites. (2015). *The Friday night (w)rites zine 2015.* Retrieved from http://fridaynightbreakfastwrites.weebly.com/the-friday-night-writes-zine-2015.html

Goodson, I., & Sikes, P. (2001). *Life history research in education settings: Learning from lives.* Philadelphia, PA: Open University Press.

Latz, A. O. (2011). *Understanding the educational lives of community college students through photovoice* (Unpublished doctoral dissertation). Ball State University, Muncie, IN.

Latz, A. O. (2012a). Toward a new conceptualization of photovoice: Blending the photographic as method and self-reflection. *Journal of Visual Literacy, 31*(2), 49–70.

Latz, A. O. (2012b). Understanding the educational lives of community college students: A photovoice project, a Bourdieusian interpretation, and habitus dissonance spark theory. *Current Issues in Education, 15*(2). Retrieved from http://cie.asu.edu/ojs/index.php/cieatasu/article/view/836/345

Latz, A. O. (2015). Understanding community college student persistence through photovoice: An emergent model. *Journal of College Student Retention: Research, Theory & Practice, 16,* 487–509. doi:10.2190/CS.16.4.b

Latz, A. O. (2017). *Photovoice research in education and beyond: A practical guide from theory to exhibition.* New York, NY: Routledge.

Latz, A. O., Phelps-Ward, R. J., Royer, D. W., & Peters, T. M. (2016). Photovoice as methodology, pedagogy, and community building tool: A graduate and community college student collaboration. *Journal of Public Scholarship in Higher Education, 6,* 124–142. Retrieved from https://jpshe.missouristate.edu/assets/missouricompact/Photovoice.pdf

Sousanis, N. (2015). *Unflattening.* Cambridge, MA: Harvard University Press.

Sutton-Brown, C. A. (2014). Photovoice: A methodological guide. *Photography & Culture, 7,* 169–186. doi:10.2752/175145214X13999922103165

Wang, C. C., & Burris, M. A. (1997). Photovoice: Concept, methodology, and use for participatory needs assessment. *Health Education and Behavior, 24,* 369–387.

Whyte, W. F. (Ed.). (1991). *Participatory action research.* Newbury Park, CA: Sage.

7

PEDAGOGICAL STRATEGIES FOR DEVELOPING VISUAL LITERACY THROUGH SOCIAL JUSTICE

Kathryn S. Jaekel

Despite their overwhelming presence in our world, the examination of visuals in the college classroom continues to be viewed as a "new" activity, by both faculty and students. In discussing the uses of visuals in communication courses, George (2002) wrote that both students and faculty often see the use of visuals "somewhat cynically" and often as a ploy to add "relevance or interest to a required course" (p. 13). What is more, when visuals are utilized in the classroom, students are rarely asked to produce, consume, or even critique the visual. Perhaps most importantly, it is unlikely that students are called on to "acknowledge the visual as much more than attendant to the verbal" (George, 2002, p. 14). Indeed, the verbal, at least in the classroom, garners far more attention than the visual.

Yet, given the digital turn in how we communicate, it is essential that students not only consume information and images but also critically examine them. These literacy practices, such as communications in the digital environment, are becoming necessary skills to have both in educational spaces and in the workplace (Mills, 2010). No longer does literacy center only on the written word; instead, literacy focuses on the multimodal nature of communication, such as visuals and electronic communication and media. This dynamic comes at a time when, like never before, students are inundated with visuals in the media, easily accessed through their computers, tablets, and mobile phones.

Nonetheless, the ideas that visuals are simply add-ons to text-based curriculum in the classroom and that higher education should continue to privilege written discourse over visuals continue to permeate teaching and learning environments. In many ways, both faculty and students in higher education continue to minimize the study and integration of the use of visuals in the classroom. Yet, the use of visuals in college classrooms is indeed powerful and ultimately helps students achieve visual literacy (Metros, 2008), as students are asked to not only interrogate what is represented but also deconstruct the larger implications of what and how something is represented. Critical visual literacy asks viewers to conduct "an analysis seeking to uncover the social and political interests in the images' production and reception in relation to the social effects of power and domination" (Newfield, 2011, p. 92). This type of literacy is more than merely examining what or who is in a visual; it means exploring the social and cultural power that a visual represents. Every image is an argument and has an agenda and larger goals.

Moreover, images have authors who are products of their culture, their time, and their larger political and social beliefs. These ideas are communicated through visuals. Although it may seem that visuals and images merely exist, they are doing far more than existing; they are influencing and mediating experience. Indeed, visuals offer specific arguments, convey points to their viewers, and serve even to convince or sway an audience. They are constructed in a particular time, with a particular purpose, and to achieve a goal (George, 2002).

Engaging in visual literacy, through the examination of the social and political landscapes that aid in both the production and reception of the visual, can be a means of engaging in social justice. Here, *social justice* is defined as a framework that posits the need for equitable and "fair distribution of social, political, and symbolic, as well as economic assets" (Bell, 2016, p. 3). Social justice has a goal of equitable distribution of all resources, but it is also a process, one that requires equitable participation from all social identity groups (Bell, 2016) and incorporates an educational process. This type of education is understood as having the goal and possibility for students to "develop the critical analytical tools necessary to understand the structure features of oppression and their own socialization within oppressive systems" (p. 4). These skills of critical analysis are necessary in order to recognize the institutional and systemic forms of oppression and to cultivate tools to dismantle these oppressive systems. In my experience in the classroom, using visuals can play a crucial role in students' recognition of oppressive systems through the critical analysis of place and examination of the social, political, and cultural elements present in visuals.

In particular, in privileging visuals through the use of a critical place-based pedagogy, students are able to examine the visuals directly around them, including on their campus, in regard to what messages are being sent from an institutional perspective. Although students typically think of their campuses as value free, by examining their surroundings through a critical place-based paradigm, they can begin to evaluate messages of who belongs on campus, who does not, and what messages are sent around the social and political aspects of college and university life.

As a faculty member in an adult and higher education master's program, much of my job revolves around preparing graduate students for a variety of positions at colleges and universities. Some of my students aspire to be student affairs practitioners, whereas others wish to be faculty members at community colleges and universities. Because of their future leadership positions and their engagement with different types of learners, it is essential that my students have solid foundations in teaching, learning, and social justice using multiple modes of content.

Moreover, in my classroom, I seek to integrate a "social justice education [that] encourages students to take an active role in their own education and supports teachers in creating empowering, democratic, and critical educational environments" (Hackman, 2005, p. 103). Students can learn strategies about empowerment, engagement, and educational environments that will help them support their future students. Because these students are future professionals who will engage with their students and inspire learning, development, and participation, it is essential that they demonstrate inclusivity, particularly as it relates to students in higher education. Centering visuals and visual communications in the classroom can help facilitate these goals.

In this chapter, I discuss the use of place-based pedagogy as a way to engage students in examining their campus through a lens of social justice. After providing an overview of place-based pedagogy, I share strategies that I have used to help students begin to conceptualize how visuals can be understood as representing larger systems within a university campus.

Critical Place-Based Pedagogy

Critical place-based pedagogy borrows from critical pedagogy and describes how "intellectuals engage in social change to make the political more pedagogical and the pedagogical more political" (Freire, 1970, p. xii). As such, critical pedagogy engages students in the practice of the social construction of knowledge while simultaneously examining and disrupting systems of power, privilege, and dominance (Sarroub & Quadros, 2015). In examining the social constructions of knowledge and examining how dominance plays a large role in knowledge production, critical place-based pedagogy also pulls from the place-based pedagogy. Within place-based pedagogy, the idea of physical (e.g., the concrete items and messages located in a space) and metaphysical place (e.g., the abstract messages and philosophies) focuses on local and regional politics and systems and connects those to larger global systems and investigates how the local place is impacted (Gruenewald, 2003). That is, place-based pedagogy means investigating the physical landscape, buildings, greenery, and even signage as well as the larger sociopolitical landscape and abstract messages in which a place is housed.

Critical place-based pedagogy takes a critical stance and examines how power and privilege exist and mediate and facilitate knowledge, knowledge production, and participation in an ecological setting. Further, it serves to interrogate assumptions and practices dominant in cultural and educational systems that are too often taken for granted (Gruenewald, 2003). Attention is paid to the "cultural, political, economic and ecological dynamics of places whenever we talk about the purpose and practice of learning" (Gruenewald, 2003, pp. 10–11). In short, critical place-based pedagogy asks students to critically look at visuals and interrogate those representations in how they either uphold or obscure dominant ideals (Jaekel, 2017).

Campuses are not value-free backdrops to learning; their designs, as well as explicit and implicit messages, mediate senses of belonging and serve to either foster or hinder access and persistence. In engaging with my students using this form of critical analysis, we were able to interrogate place through a social justice lens and examine the messages sent to students about whom college campuses serve and how to navigate a campus, as well as larger messages of college attendance. Future leaders in higher education must know how to examine and read their campus environments for these messages and may even find themselves in positions that create campus place-based arguments. These arguments indicate who belongs, who historically has attended campus, and the overarching goals and values a particular campus has.

Cultivating a Critical Visual Literacy

In an effort to begin cultivating students' visual literacy, I engaged in critical place-based pedagogy by beginning my diversity and inclusion in higher education course with the following statement:

> Your campus is a visual argument. Students' campuses, the images they use in signage [and] buildings, [and] even the design of the campus layout is an argument of who belongs, who does not, where people should go, how they should get there, and why they should be in specific spaces.

Students were challenged to think about how they move across campus, the routes they take, and why they take those specific routes. This brief activity served to introduce my use of critical place-based pedagogy.

In order to get students to examine their campus, I assigned a visual diversity audit assignment. The goal of this assignment was to investigate the campus and look for images, visuals, spaces, and places that either cultivate or obscure a sense of belonging for students. A sense of belonging on campus, "perceived social support on campus, a feeling or sensation of connectedness," as well as "mattering or feeling cared about, accepted, respected, valued by, and important to the group (e.g., campus community) or others on campus (e.g., faculty, peers)" (Strayhorn, 2012, p. 3) are critical components to student success. Yet, finding senses of belonging on campus is not always as straightforward as it may seem, often because places can be seemingly nebulous, taken for granted, or an ostensibly neutral backdrop. This assignment gave students a theoretical framework that asked them to critically investigate spaces and visuals on a campus. The assignment allowed them to practice examining their campus for both implicit and explicit messages communicated to students.

Specifically, the assignment asked that students, in groups of three or four, choose a campus (either their own or one to which they have access); physically visit that campus at least three times in the semester; and choose a specific location, visual, or image to analyze. Students could choose buildings, hallways in a building, social spaces where students hang out, routes or pathways students take, or even campus art and artifacts. Each group was asked to document different aspects of those spaces by photographing, drawing, or sketching findings. Depending on what elements the groups selected, it was up to them how they represented their findings.

After documenting their findings, students were then asked to give 20-minute presentations to the rest of the class. They were required to show the visuals they created or captured, give an overview of their analysis, and offer their recommendations and conclusions about what they found. Each group was also asked to create and facilitate some discussion questions to engage the rest of the class about the project. My hope was that groups would share information and insights with the rest of the class and get their classmates thinking about different components of visuals and visual literacy on campus. Because this course centered on diversity in higher education, students were asked to pay close attention to representations (or the lack thereof) of different social identities and systems of power and privilege and make connections to larger institutions and social systems that operate on a national and global level.

Cultivating Critical Literacy

When I started using a critical place-based curriculum with my students and assigned them a visual diversity audit (described previously), I began by having them do a practice exercise. During class, I sent them out to document some aspect of campus. I asked them to use their cell phone cameras to document spaces, places, and items that illustrated senses of belonging and nonbelonging. After half an hour, they were to come back and report to the rest of the class what they found. The purpose of this exercise was to give them some guidance before they set out on their formal assignment.

Interestingly, although most of my students cannot remember a time without access to the Internet, mobile phones with cameras, or a world filled with digital images and visuals, I quickly realized that few of my students had the critical visual literacy that was needed for this assignment. In this exercise, my students overwhelmingly took pictures exclusively of welcome signs and thus stated that campus, overall, was a welcoming atmosphere. Students argued that these signs would create a sense of belonging for students because the word *welcome* was on them. Another student brought in pictures of signage up around campus that indicated there were disability accessible parking spaces and entrances in many of the buildings across campus. Again, students reported that these signs indicated that campus was accessible and thus, welcoming to those who utilized those entrances and parking spaces. The welcome and disability signage was a fine start, but it was not exactly what I was after; I wanted them to critically examine their campus for implicit messages, for representations, and for political and social values.

I realized that my assumption of graduate-level students' visual literacy in documenting the campus did not align with what I initially observed. Critical visual literacy is a skill that must be cultivated and learned over time (Avgerinou & Pettersson, 2011), and I realized that students rarely inherently understand that images, visuals, and their campus are not value neutral or that historical and dominant cultural systems work to design their campuses. I had to first model how critical visual literacy looked, allow my students the time to practice and cultivate these skills, and then have them analyze and document their campus. This practice together proved key as students, from the start of this assignment, seemed to be resistant to both the exercise and the analysis of visuals.

Such resistance took many forms, however; from what students shared with me, exercises that used visuals did not seem to be worthy of their study or time. In short, because they were used to seeing visuals used as a ploy to make things seem "fun," they felt using visuals and images was a waste of time, not graduate student work, and too amateur. Given their experiences and preconceived notions about the seemingly amateur nature and ease of the use of visuals, I knew I needed to craft thoughtful exercises that served to increase interest but that also clearly exemplified course materials. Outlined in the following section are exercises students and I did together in order to begin cultivating their visual literacy skills.

Strategies for Modeling for Critical Literacy

In an effort to help students build their critical visual literacy skills, I projected for them some pictures that I took of the campus. Being relatively new to our campus, I set out to capture more of the spaces and visuals students encounter on a daily basis. One of the first visuals I was struck with was the bust of Martin Luther King Jr. (Figure 7.1). Located in front of our student center and directly across from our library, this piece of campus art is one that students encounter often. What is more, the space where this bust is located is the campus's "free speech zone."

Figure 7.1. Bust of Martin Luther King Jr. on central campus.

After taking the picture of the bust on central campus, I walked around further to explore other buildings, artifacts, and visuals. I was particularly interested in finding our cultural centers and other offices that served students. According to our university website, we had four cultural centers on campus: the Black Cultural Center, the Latino Cultural Center, the Gender and Sexuality Resource Center, and the Asian American Center. After finding the Black Cultural Center (located on the periphery of the south side of campus, next to the Gender and Sexuality Resource Center), I looked around for the other two cultural centers. I had assumed that they would be together, or at the very least, within somewhat close proximity.

After consulting a map, I realized that the other two cultural centers, the Latino Cultural Center and Asian American Center, were located on the periphery of another side of campus, on the extreme north end. Walking across campus, I was struck with how far away from central campus these centers were. After crossing a street and walking into what felt like a residential neighborhood, I finally located the Latino Cultural Center and the Asian American Center. Whereas the other cultural centers "looked" like institutional spaces, the Asian American Center looked much different. In fact, at first, I thought it was one of the homes in the residential neighborhood. I took a picture of the Asian American Center (Figure 7.2) to show my students.

The following week in class, I first showed students the picture of the Martin Luther King Jr. bust and asked if students had seen it on campus

Figure 7.2. Picture of the Asian American Center on the edge of Northern Illinois University campus.

and if they knew its location. Much to my surprise, only about half of the students remembered seeing it or could place its location on campus. We discussed together why some had not noticed it. Some students indicated that they had yet to be in central campus as much of their time was only spent on one extreme end or another. Others discussed how they never really "look around" when they travel on campus.

I asked students about possible larger implications of having a bust of Martin Luther King Jr. be a focal point in a free speech zone. I asked them to think about what message is sent to students, what it might say about the university's stance on the freedom of speech, and how this bust might engage students' sense of belonging and participation. My students discussed that they saw this as a positive piece of art overall. That is, students saw this piece of art as representing freedoms, encouraging active participation on campus, and signifying the importance of critical thought. Given the importance of freedom of speech, as evidenced by Martin Luther King Jr.'s work as well as his gruesome assassination, students talked about how this piece indicates that the university recognized that some have had to pay a large price for engaging in social justice and equity, and working for what you believe in. As we discussed, students began to realize that these visuals serve larger roles of the university's values and concerns, and that visuals could inspire not only belonging but also different types of student participation.

Next, I showed the students the picture I took of the Asian American Center and asked if they had ever seen it before or knew its location. Again, many of the students reported that they had never seen it. Many were surprised that this was a campus building and double-checked the signage to ensure that it was one of our buildings. Students remarked that the center looked like a rental property; asked why it was so far off campus; and inquired about how many students it served, given how small of a building it was. Many showed concern about its size and how it did not "look like a university building" but instead, a "regular house." One student shared that, although she saw the sign and understood it was one of the university's buildings, she would be reluctant to go in because it did not look like a space where she would feel comfortable because it seemed like more of a home than a university space. From there, a discussion ensued about how economic resources are used on campus, who decides where money should go, and where and on whom colleges and universities spend money. Students asked if it seemed like the university cared less about Asian American students than other groups of students given the discrepancy in the characteristics of the buildings. Some students noted that other centers on campus "looked like they belonged to the university," were easier to find, were more centrally located, and were not in houses.

Although some of the students showed concern that the building looked like a "regular house," others shared that they found it refreshing. They said that they had larger concerns about the institutionalization of identity and that in many ways having a "home away from home" may actually serve the students better than having a "university-type" building. From there, students discussed different needs student groups may have, different senses of belonging they may require, and ways in which campus buildings could play a role in meeting those needs. Students discussed that for some of them, having a "regular house" would actually increase their sense of belonging; they shared that they could "relax" and potentially let their guard down while in this space.

Finally, I showed them a map that I sketched of the location of the Black Cultural Center on central campus and the Asian American Center. Roughly half a mile apart, each of the centers was located on the extreme outer fringes of campus. After looking at the map, students talked about how it seemed that the cultural centers were an afterthought on campus and that the initial design of campus simply did not include cultural centers. Although we had read that most U.S. higher education institutions excluded people of color and women until the twentieth century, before this exercise, students had not realized the larger implications of those racist and sexist values on the design of college campuses. They began to realize that campuses were physically designed for specific purposes and for specific people. What is more, although many campuses have attempted to create inclusive centers that serve particular groups of students, when these centers are on the periphery of campus, they continue to reify the notion that these groups of students are afterthoughts. These students are relegated to the fringes of campus; it is on the periphery of campus that they find some support.

In doing this exercise, students began to practice and hone their critical literacy skills. In asking students to examine the pictures as a large group, I was able to mediate the discussion and ask critical questions for them to consider, such as the following: What institutional messages do these visuals send? What do these visuals say about what the university values? And what does this mean for how students participate on campus? Rather than assuming campus visuals and spaces are value free, we were able to coconstruct how these images could be value laden. These discussions helped students conceptualize how spaces, places, and visuals inspired participation and senses of belonging (and lack thereof) by looking at, historically, for whom higher education was designed, who makes decisions about how students can participate and where students can go, and institutional messages of who belongs based on inclusion and exclusion on campus.

Ultimately, student projects were successful. Despite some students' reservations about engaging with visuals, students took the assignment seriously and made connections between visuals and course readings, and the assignment served to help many of the students realize what oppressive systems can look like on a college campus. Some projects focused on a lack of racial representations in campus visuals, such as campus posters and brochures. Other projects looked at a lack of universal design principles in classrooms. Still other projects centered on the fact that there was very little campus public art and how that translated into institutional messages of not supporting creativity or design. These projects helped students see what inequity looks like, how campus designs inhibit participation from different social identities, and how campuses engage in inequitable distribution of resources. Students were able to apply social justice principles to the analysis of the visuals.

Resistance

Although overall the sample exercise was a success, as it prepared the students well for their visual diversity audit assignment, students expressed some resistance to the use of visuals as well as the attention to social justice. Some students continued to privilege the written word over visuals. For example, one student would only engage in "visuals" that were written, such as signs or banners. Although these are important (and certainly written words can create visual messages), the student was unwilling to interrogate more abstract spaces and places. For him, it all seemed "too open to interpretation," and he tried very hard to give other interpretations when students were critical of potential exclusionary practices on the part of the university. For whatever reason, this particular student simply would not accept visuals as having serious or critical implications.

In addition, especially early on, some of the students did not see the connection between campus as a place and how that may affect students' sense of belonging. For them, it was hard to imagine that campuses had particular designs for participation or even traffic flow. This was the case for a few students who held dominant identities, particularly White able-bodied students. They saw campus as a space that was always welcoming and had never had to critically examine spaces for messages about if they belonged or not. Certainly, this type of resistance and the denial of oppression are commonplace when discussing larger social systems of oppression. As Watt (2007) wrote, the "denial defense" is often "identified by a person arguing against an anxiety-provoking stimuli by stating that it does not exist. This defense is usually precipitated by receiving information about an injustice done in American society to a particular group" (p. 120). For some students, the idea that campus was not inclusive of everyone all of the time was difficult for them at times.

Yet, this resistance exhibited by students made the exercise and the class richer, as it opened up discussions about what it means to have a privileged identity on campus. Discussions focused on how students who identified as White, straight, and/or Christian rarely needed to seek out specific spaces that were carved just for them on campus, because, overwhelmingly, campus was designed for them in the first place. These discussions allowed those students to critically reflect on how their experiences were different from students with marginalized identities, such as students of color and students from non-Christian faith backgrounds. It allowed space for students to recognize that their privilege often mediated how they examined, experienced, and engaged in campus as a place and how that affected learning and participation on campus. Although their resistance to this assignment was difficult at times, in the end, it allowed not only for classroom discussion about privileged identity but also space to reflect on what it means to be someone with a privileged identity in student affairs.

Conclusions and Recommendations

Examining visuals on campus can be a powerful exercise for students, particularly future leaders in higher education. It allows them to connect larger social justice ideas to their higher education contexts and provides a tangible space to make sense of students' senses of belonging. Throughout the course, students talked about looking at campus in a different manner and often found themselves investigating different types of visual messages they encountered on campus. The use of visuals offered something unique to students in this diversity course. Many assignments in diversity in higher education courses offer students the opportunity to analyze and reflect on oppression and on institutional missions and values, but using visuals offered students something both concrete and abstract. Students could walk the routes between resource centers, physically see the maps and the art on campus, and have something material to see and feel, as well as experience through visuals how spaces and places felt. They could capture through an image something that words could not; they could feel those spaces in ways that mere words would never allow. They could actually see and feel the campus place. This provided a learning experience that was far richer, far more detailed, and far more intimate than only privileging the written word would have allowed.

Although this chapter discusses the visual diversity audit assignment and a modeling exercise, there are many other ways students can engage in the use and analysis of visuals on campus. Potential project ideas include the following:

- Performing an accessibility audit on their campuses
- Analyzing how campuses engage (or do not engage) in the use of art and the subsequent messages that sends to the campus community
- Designing their own campus using theories of social justice and inclusion
- (Re)purposing existing spaces to create a more inclusive environment

Colleges and universities are rife with visuals and images that illustrate to students what and who are valued as important. Their designs show historical, social, political, and environmental values that serve to mediate how students engage, learn, and feel integrated into the college community. The engagement of students in activities that utilize and analyze visuals can cultivate critical visual literacy as well as inspire these future higher education and student affairs practitioners to influence the formation of spaces in colleges and universities that are welcoming and allow for more equitable participation by all students.

References

Avgerinou, M. D., & Pettersson, R. (2011). Toward a cohesive theory of visual literacy. *Journal of Visual Literacy, 30*(2), 1–19.

Bell, L. A. (2016). Theoretical foundations for social justice education. In M. Adams, L. A. Bell, D. J. Goodman, & K. Y. Joshis (Eds.), *Teaching for diversity and social justice* (3rd ed., pp. 3–26). New York, NY: Routledge.

Freire, P. (1970). *Pedagogy of the oppressed*. New York, NY: Seabury.

George, D. (2002). From analysis to design: Visual communication in the teaching of writing. *College Composition and Communication, 54*(1), 11–39.

Gruenewald, D. A. (2003). The best of both worlds: A critical pedagogy of place. *Educational Researcher, 32*(4), 3–12.

Hackman, H. W. (2005). Five essential components for social justice education. *Equity & Excellence in Education, 38*(2), 103–109.

Jaekel, K. S. (2017). Engaging in inclusion: Cultivating LGBTQ students' sense of belonging through a critical place-based curriculum. *International Journal of Critical Pedagogy, 8*(1), 129–148.

Metros, S. E. (2008). The educator's role in preparing visually literate learners. *Theory to Practice, 47*(2), 102–109.

Mills, K. A. (2010). A review of the digital turn in the new literacy studies. *Review of Educational Research, 80*(2), 246–271.

Newfield, D. (2011). From visual literacy to critical visual literacy: An analysis of 122 educational materials. *English Teaching: Practice and Critique, 10*(1), 81–94.

Sarroub, L., & Quadros, S. (2015). Critical pedagogy in classroom discourse. In M. Bigelow & J. Ennser-Kananen (Eds.), *The Routledge handbook of educational linguistics* (pp. 252–260). New York, NY: Routledge.

Strayhorn, T. L. (2012). *College students' sense of belonging: A key to educational success for all students.* New York, NY: Routledge.

Watt, S. K. (2007). Difficult dialogues, privilege and social justice: Uses of the privileged identity exploration (PIE) model in student affairs practice. *College Student Affairs Journal, 26*(2), 114–126.

8

ENHANCING LEARNING PROCESSES THROUGH TECHNOLOGICALLY MEDIATED DIGITAL VISUALIZATION

Paul Eaton

Online learning offers opportunities for creative educational learning processes not always available in traditional face-to-face course delivery environments. With the proliferation of technologies centered on digital visualization, new opportunities arise for challenging students in online learning environments to present work in formats not traditionally considered "academic," particularly by harnessing digital visualization methods in course assignments.

In this chapter, I utilize my experiences teaching a fully online master's-level seminar, "Leadership in Higher Education," to examine how students' relationships to course content shift through their engagement with digital visualization processes. Based on personal experience, the chapter also offers faculty incorporating digital visualization projects in academic courses critical insights regarding seemingly mundane, yet highly important aspects for successful integration. These include assisting students with unlearning traditional approaches to academic work, rethinking rigor, facilitating the process of providing students with digital visualization tools and technologies, and emphasizing process over product. Such emphasis challenges traditional assumptions regarding aspects of learning centered on grades and achievement, and in this regard, I offer perspectives on viewing the inclusion of digital visualization techniques as more importantly centered on empowering students to challenge themselves with the goal of learning new technologies, fostering creativity, and rethinking the learning process.

Utilizing examples of student work, I highlight how technologically mediated visualization changes students' relationship to learning and processing information from course modules. Further, I discuss strategies for assisting students in overcoming potential anxiety and concern about creating work through technologically mediated visualization.

Teaching Courses Online: Rhizomatic Approaches

Many traditionally trained academics come to online learning with some level of hesitancy, if not outright skepticism, and I was certainly no exception. In accepting a faculty position where I would be teaching primarily online courses I was concerned about many issues labeled as constraints of online learning. These included perceptions of student disengagement due to the often asynchronous nature of online learning, overreliance on video-based lectures, lack of intra-action among students in terms of dialogue and socializing, and time management issues related to balancing grading and individualized insight for students that naturally come as part of the online learning experience.

As I prepared for my first semester of teaching, reading about online teaching pedagogy (Major, 2015), I began formulating possibilities for structuring the learning experiences in online courses differently. Based on my graduate studies, where I took a fair number of courses in curriculum theory and pedagogy, and my reading of Deleuze and Guattari's (1987) *A Thousand Plateaus*, I formulated a pedagogical experiment, creating a rhizomatic learning environment for my online course "Leadership in Higher Education." Rhizomatic pedagogy draws on Deleuze and Guattari's (1987) employment of the rhizome as metaphor, best captured by this quote

> Perhaps one of the most important characteristics of the rhizome is that it always has multiple entryways. . . . Any point of a rhizome can be connected to anything other, and must be. . . . [It] is an acentered, nonhierarchical, nonsignifying system . . . defined solely by a circulation of states. (pp. 12, 7, 21)

Rhizomatic pedagogy creates disruptions in the flow, structure, and experience of traditional approaches to learning through purposeful creation of disequilibrium. It harnesses multiple modes of sensory experience, trusting ambiguity and recognizing the world unfolds through nonlinear relations.

This vision of rhizomatics translated into the pedagogical approach for "Leadership in Higher Education." I decided to harness the structuring proclivities of Blackboard to create a series of modules around broad leadership concepts important for emerging higher education and student affairs professionals. Blackboard allows instructors to create folders, modules, and assignments for students in a variety of ways. Instructors can control when folders and modules are open; track user engagement; and harness tools such as wikis, discussion forums, blogs, videos, and journals to create assignments or share information. Rather than developing a syllabus structured on a linear progression through leadership theory, which would be followed synchronously by all students in a week-by-week format, I created disequilibrium, instructing students they could complete the modules in any order they wished. There was no linear pathway through the course (Love & Estanek, 2004). Thus, each student had a unique experiential engagement with the course.

Within each module I included a selection of readings and multimedia sources immediately pertinent or broadly related to the module topic—including traditional articles, book chapters, podcasts, TED talks, music, and visual images—which harnessed multiple sensory experiences. Rather than forcing students to read and listen to all the same material, students chose one reading and one multimedia source within each module to read/watch/listen to, which created a level of ambiguity; each student engaged different written and multimedia sources. I utilized a wiki—a tool in Blackboard that allows students to add, view, and edit content added by others—within each module and requested that students add an additional resource related to the broad theme of that module. What students added was up to them—it could be an academic or news article, a video, a piece of music, or a selection of poetry—as long as they adequately explained how it related to the overall theme of the module. Students were told they could harness these additional resources if they completed the module after other students; thus, there was a growing number of resources in each module. This created new connections.

For each module students completed one assignment within which they would incorporate, link, and integrate each of the three sources they had engaged in the module (one reading, one multimedia source, and one resource they added). Here is where digital visualization techniques become important. Rather than asking students to simply write a paper or reflection each week, I decided to incorporate a variety of assignment types that would challenge students to utilize digital technologies, thus adding additional ambiguity and disequilibrium into the course. Some of these assignments involved digital visualization of what the student had learned, gleaned, or examined from the module. Examples of these assignment types and the explanation of each offered on the syllabus are as follows:

- PechaKucha Talk: PechaKucha talks are short video talks utilizing 20 slides to examine a topic. For each slide you have only 20 seconds to talk, so this is not like a traditional PowerPoint presentation. Slides rarely contain words, but rather utilize visual images or word images to portray a connection to the topic discussed in the slide.

- Infographic: The digital age has opened opportunities of sharing information in new ways. In this assignment, create an infographic related to one course module.

- Slideshare Presentation: Slideshare, similar to PowerPoint, allows you to create visual presentations to share with a wide audience. You are encouraged to think about the many creative ways you might present information in a Slideshare format.

- Digital Storytelling: Digital storytelling is a way of sharing information using a variety of visual images, music, and other forms of digital technologies. For this assignment create a digital story for one of the modules.

- Quote-a-graphs: Much like infographics, digital tools have allowed us to capture digital text visually, and then share it with the world through our various social and digital networks. In this assignment, create three quote-a-graphs—visual representations of quotes you found memorable from the reading and multimedia sources.

These digital visualization assignment types were options along with more traditional assignments, such as written reflections, video responses, and podcasts. Over the course of the 11 modules students had to complete at least 1 of each type of assignment.

Digital Visualization: Rethinking Learning as Process Creativity

For most students, academic work centers on familiar approaches for articulating and performing learning. Testing, written papers, group work, and formal in-class presentations are common and familiar for students. Digital visualization assignments cause some level of anxiety for many students, who might view the tasks as difficult and challenging due to the necessity of learning new technological tools, or simply because it forces them to think and operate outside their comfort zone regarding academic work. Most students are fairly well trained in preparing for an exam, generally have a solid understanding about what formal academic papers should contain, and have grown comfortable preparing presentations for classmates through now familiar technologies such as PowerPoint. Digital visualization assignments challenge and force students outside of these comfort zones.

Assisting students with understanding the pedagogical rationale behind digital visualization techniques is an important step for faculty seeking to incorporate such approaches into their courses. This involves two important conceptual shifts that should be explained to students: viewing learning as *process* and harnessing *creativity* in the act of learning. Although it should be fairly evident that learning is a process, our educational system has disciplined students into believing that what is important is product and outcome (as measured in grades). This leads students to approach academic work with particular presuppositions in mind, such as the following: What are you looking for? How many references should I have? What will get me an A? Although these are important questions, the focus on product or outcome has taken joy out of how students approach academic work; learning becomes routinized and technocratic.

In explaining my approach to assignments and grading in "Leadership in Higher Education," I emphasize to students that I am less interested in the product they produce through digital visualization and more interested in having them relish the processes of thinking through course material differently; learning to present the material in a manner that appears foreign for many of them; attempting to grapple with skill development through learning a new technology; thinking creatively and imaginatively; and harnessing a different part of their brain than that which they have traditionally used in academic work such as writing, testing, or presenting.

One of the tremendous advantages of digital visualization methods is the ability to foster student creativity and imagination. In her book *Releasing the Imagination: Essays on Education, the Arts, and Social Change*, Maxine Greene (1995) argued that educators should provide opportunities in which students can reflect on larger questions than simply the "right" answer, the rational approach, or technocratic and mundane processing of information. "Teaching and learning," she argued, "are matters of breaking through barriers—of expectation, of boredom, of predefinition" (Greene, 1995, p. 14). She continued:

> When we see more and hear more, it is not only that we lurch, if only for a moment, out of the familiar and the taken-for-granted but that new avenues for choosing and for action may open in our experience; we may gain a sudden sense of new beginnings, that is, we may take an initiative in the light of possibility. (Greene, 1995, p. 123)

One way of increasing student excitement about digital visualization methods in the classroom is by harnessing this language of creativity. Digital visualization allows students to stretch their creativity. Encourage students to view the processes of learning new digital technologies, and their concomitant creative opportunities, as different ways of thinking, processing, and integrating learning.

Part of this creativity involves how students come to match digital visualization assignment types with particular course content. One student reflected on the power of the creative learning process in their course evaluation:

I initially thought that the assignment types were very unusual and I was concerned that they focused more on technology and creativity than on the course content. What I found was I became fascinated by using the assignments to highlight the specific content of each module. When I started the course, being the highly organized, Type-A person that I can be, I made a list of all the assignment types and mapped them to each module. What I discovered along the way was that I made different choices because, for example, the ethics module was a better fit for a quote-a-graph than for an infographic. Those changes forced me to realize that the assignments had to fit the content and compliment [*sic*] each other, which was a real learning moment for me.

In this reflection, the student recognized and demonstrated a few important outcomes that naturally arose from structuring a course rhizomatically utilizing digital visualization methods. The student articulated how they took control of their own learning. Rather than me, the faculty member, telling them which assignment type corresponded to which module (as is traditionally done in much of academia), structuring the course rhizomatically allowed the student to make these choices. Consequently, the student learned that, for them, specific course content more closely aligned with particular assignment types; and often as the student grappled with the content, this forced them to rethink which assignment type they were going to utilize.

Perhaps as important in this student's reflection, and what I have noticed as a faculty member, is that students come to understand learning as a creative process. Students quickly realize they must learn how each particular digital visualization technology and assignment can be used to creatively articulate connections among particular modules' content. For example, when students decide to utilize an infographic, many creative decisions must be made, including the following: Which background, border, or graphic representations best align with the information they are attempting to convey? Which fonts do they use? How do they convey key information without becoming too reliant on the written word? Are there opportunities to incorporate music or voice in addition to visually capturing and presenting information? These are all important aspects of how students utilizing digital visualization think in a creative, process-oriented fashion.

Figure 8.1 is from a student examining the course module Researching Leadership. In this infographic, the student demonstrated a broad depth of understanding regarding the many ways practitioners and scholars measure, assess, and work toward changing people's leadership skills and behaviors. There are visual cues to the multi-institutional study of leadership (MSL), which utilizes the social change model of leadership development and Kouzes and Posner's (2002) leadership challenge. The student utilized a variety of other visual cues—banners, checkmarks, and different shapes—in order to draw the eye toward important content. Further, the student utilized an alternating color palette to organize information. In addition to creatively harnessing different visualization techniques, I chose this particular example because the student also incorporated the academic content with information about the

Figure 8.1. Researching Leadership infographic.

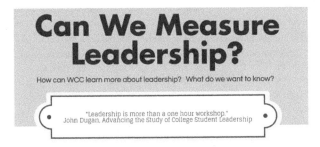

Can We Measure Leadership?

How can WCC learn more about leadership? What do we want to know?

"Leadership is more than a one hour workshop."
John Dugan, Advancing the Study of College Student Leadership

The MSL is an international research program focused on understanding the influences of higher education in shaping socially responsible leadership capacity & other leadership related outcomes (e.g., efficacy, cognitive skills, resiliency).
www.leadershipstudy.net

Multi-Institutional Study of **Leadership**

Measures Outcomes Related To:

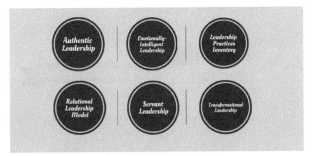

Authentic Leadership · Emotionally-Intelligent Leadership · Leadership Practices Inventory · Relational Leadership Model · Servant Leadership · Transformational Leadership

Link to WCC's Leadership Academy

Waubonsee's Leadership Academy is based on the work of Kouzes and Posner. We have been discussing expanding this Academy and including a student component and it would be key to link the two activities. Kouzes and Posner have also researched leadership development in students using the Student Leadership Practices Inventory (which is measured within the Multi-Institutional Study of Leadership). The Five Practices of Exemplary Leadership are applicable to college employees as well as our students. In a 2012 article, Posner noted that "leadership educators (and student administrators broadly) can take comfort and even pride in knowing that leadership education programs and leadership classes are influencing the actual leadership behaviors that students reports using." (Posner, 2012, p. 232-33).

MODEL THE WAY · INSPIRE A SHARED VISION · CHALLENGE THE PROCESS · ENABLE OTHERS TO ACT · ENCOURAGE THE HEART

(Continues)

Figure 8.1. (*Continued*)

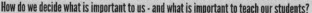

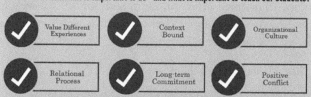

How do we decide what is important to us - and what is important to teach our students?

| ✓ Value Different Experiences | ✓ Context Bound | ✓ Organizational Culture |
| ✓ Relational Process | ✓ Long-term Commitment | ✓ Positive Conflict |

Kezar et. al. highlight a new research agenda for anyone interested in leadership. Those suggestions can provide a strong foundation for any discussion of leadership on a campus and that link clearly to Kouzes and Posner's Five Practices.

1) Conduct explicit examinations of power dynamics embedded in leadership processes (Challenge the Process).

2) Focus on failed examples of leadership (Model the Way).

3) Study the implications of globalization for leadership (Inspire a Shared Vision).

4) Study the relationships between learning and leadership (Enable Others to Act).

5) Focus on cross-cultural leadership (Encourage the Heart).

(Kezar, et al., 2006, p. 175-176)

How Can Waubonsee Integrate this Work?

OUTCOMES

Leadership experiences have a positive impact on the quality of student learning.

ENGAGEMENT

The development of leadership skills among community colleges students is a proactive and strategic investment in retention and completion.

MODELS

Traditional models of hierarchical leadership aren't relevant to college students. We need to find new models that are rooted in values and collaboration.

EMPOWERMENT

"The essential ingredient of effective leadership is helping students develop their talents and attitudes enabling them to become positive social change agents" (Astin and Astin, cited in Jacob, 2006, p. 10).

FINAL THOUGHT

"These approaches suggest that leadership is about developing certain habits of mind, developing emotional intelligence, and connecting to spiritual insights, which takes time. It is a longer-term investment" (Kezar, et al., 2006, p. 158).

powered by

Piktochart
make information beautiful

Note. Reprinted with permission.

unique campus environment. In this visual image, one recognizes that the student processed the information from the course module, understood how it applied to the unique campus environment, and presented the information in a visually appealing manner.

Rethinking Rigor

One of the associated pedagogical challenges for faculty members incorporating digital visualization processes in academic courses involves rethinking rigor. Traditional approaches to measuring learning with which many faculty members are familiar—testing, academic papers, and presentations—are predicated on standardization. Most tests are scored using a normal curve; many papers and presentations are measured against one another through rubrics or other comparative metrics. Incorporating digital visualization processes necessitates slightly different approaches to aspects of grading, evaluating, and providing insight for students.

First, faculty must recognize that students will come to this process with different levels of technological skill. Despite many, even most, students having grown up around digital technologies, familiarity with many of the tools students might utilize will fall along a continuum. From a practical perspective, it is important to recognize and account for the reality that many students are learning these technological tools for the first time. Thus, I account for this learning process as part of the rigor of each assignment. Some tools and digital visualization methods are easier to learn than others, and you can quickly tell by the types of assignments students turn in how much energy and effort has been exerted in completing the assignment.

Second, faculty must recognize that as creative, process-oriented learning, digital visualization affords new opportunities for students to express their own creative capacities. For this reason, I am very careful in constructing instructions for these assignments. If I place too many parameters around *how* particular assignments must be completed, I may unintentionally stifle creativity. Thus, the instructions or guidelines I provide students tend to be purposefully broad, only requiring that students integrate a reading, a multimedia source, and an additional source into the assignment type (while demonstrating rigorous critical thinking and application of creativity).

Students usually exhibit some hesitation, angst, and concern about the issue of grading digital visualization assignments. As a faculty member, you can alleviate these concerns in a few ways. Continuously articulate to students that you are more interested in their application of learning, demonstration of critical thinking, and the process of learning—as opposed to the product. Every student will, at some point, turn in a digital visualization project that is less than appealing to the eye, seems chaotic or messy, or misses the mark. Rather than grading the student on presentation, remember that process is much more important.

Perhaps most critical in rethinking rigor is also committing yourself as a faculty member to the process of providing informative insights for students. In my courses, I call this *feedforward insight*. My language is intentional here. I want students to walk away from this course, and any course in which I integrate digital visualization assignments, with a set of technological tools they can incorporate in future courses and professional or personal environments. Rather than *feedback*, which emphasizes what a student might have done better on an assignment that is already completed, I attempt to provide thorough feedforward insight into my experience with their assignment and perspectives they may think about were they to utilize the digital visualization method again in the future.

An example might be helpful here. One of the visualization methods I incorporate is having students put together a SlideShare presentation—basically a more visually appealing, publicly accessible PowerPoint presentation. For the module Global Perspectives on Leadership, one of my former students designed a visually appealing presentation overall, but some visual images created some difficulties for anyone experiencing the presentation. Specifically, the image incorporated into the slide was blurry, the result of simply downloading an image from the Internet and reshaping the image to fit the SlideShare presentation.

Thus, in providing feedforward insight to this student, I offered a few suggestions for future SlideShare presentations:

> There were a few notes that would improve the overall look and feel of the presentation, which you may incorporate into future presentations. These are: (a) The slide "Clusters of World Cultures" was difficult to read because the image you inserted was a bit too small, and also came out a bit blurry; (b) I would include at least one reference slide so people know where to go to get further information, or how you curated the information in the slideshow.

Here I attempted to provide the student with some key information about how to enhance the experience a user will have with the presentation, while still recognizing that the presentation met the standards of integrating the important information for the module. In other words, I am much less concerned with the overall visual appeal or mistakes students make than I am with integration, demonstration of process-oriented thinking, and inclusion of additional resources. Visual skills can be enhanced over time as students become more comfortable with using a variety of digital visualization tools to create content.

Finally, a word about affirmation. In providing feedforward insight to students, it is also important that faculty incorporate positive messages to students encouraging continued engagement with the new technologies. For example, I have taught "Leadership in Higher Education" utilizing rhizomatic processes and digital visualization assignments multiple times, carefully tracking which assignments students readily embrace and which assignments students avoid until the end of the semester. Each time I have taught this course, a majority of students have completed the digital storytelling assignment last or near the end of the term. Many of these submissions are accompanied by students describing the difficulty of the digital story project, their hiccups with the technology, and their desire to have produced a better project. It is important that faculty affirm students in these cases. While providing feedforward insight to students, I will also provide affirmation. For example, with one student I simply ended my insights with: "Digital storytelling is perhaps the most difficult assignment! Keep playing with it to tell a unique and innovative story." The aim is to ensure students feel empowered to return to the visualization method and try again, rather than walk away from its creative possibilities altogether.

Providing Tools, Insights, and Assistance

A final consideration when designing courses utilizing digital visualization centers on providing the technological tools, insights, and assistance students might require in navigating the projects. Here, a faculty member must once again realize that restrictions placed on the type of tool students might use could unnecessarily limit a student's creative capacities. Digital tools and platforms all come with certain technological affordances. Thus, in some cases you might want to ensure students are using a particular tool or forum for specific purposes, and in other cases you might garner more creative projects as students discover their own tools or ways of creating visual images.

I tend to balance suggestions from my own knowledge and practice with giving students a certain amount of flexibility. For example, in one of the assignments, I have students incorporate what is called a quote-a-graph, where I ask them to select particularly poignant quotes from the readings, multimedia, and additional sources they curate and create a visual image of those quotes. This assignment asks students to think about which content most resonated with them and to reflect on why a particular passage, quote, or moment best captures the message or learning they will carry from a particular module. For this assignment, I have provided students with examples of phone-based applications that easily allow one to design and share such visual imagery. Tweegram and Adobe Spark are two options with which I am familiar, and thus I share these potential tools with students in the course syllabus.

The two quote-a-graph examples (Figure 8.2 and Figure 8.3) demonstrate how one student found an individual way of creating the visual imagery outside of the tools provided in the syllabus.

Both of these examples come from the module Chaos and Complexity Perspectives on Leadership. This particular student did not utilize the tool suggestions provided on the syllabus, but rather found a creative way to develop the quote-a-graph. The use of visual imagery (e.g., the butterfly in Figure 8.2) relates to the module's content (in this case, understanding the butterfly effect). The student is integrating a visual image with textual representation, which enhances the impact of the visual image. As the faculty member, I recognize that the student has integrated the module content while also adhering to the spirit of the assignment—which is to find a memorable quote that speaks to your own resonance(s) with the material. Further, because the student found the means to visually represent this assignment, the student was not reliant on the tools I provided but took initiative to cater the learning to the student's own objectives.

Although some students will take such liberty to discover their own technological tools, others are more reliant on the insights you can provide as

Figure 8.2. Chaos and Complexity Perspectives on Leadership, example one.

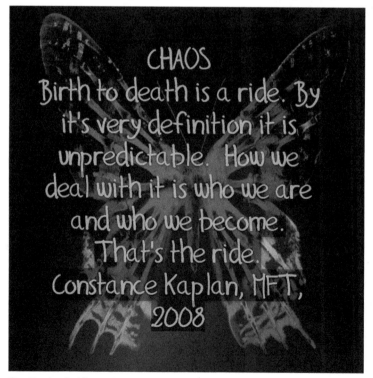

Note. Reprinted with permission.

Figure 8.3. Chaos and Complexity Perspectives on Leadership, example two.

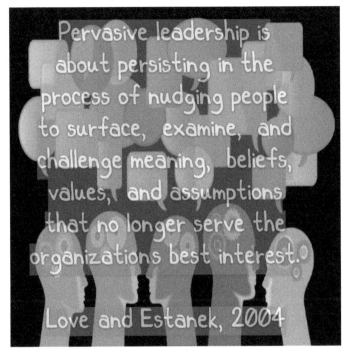

Note. Reprinted with permission.

a faculty member. In my courses, I take this a step further, harnessing the power of our learning community. Because I teach "Leadership in Higher Education" online, I decided to create a discussion forum where students can post tips, insights, and additional tools they are using for each of the assignment types. One benefit to providing students the flexibility of completing assignments in any order is that they can enhance the learning of their peers who may have not completed a particular assignment type by providing tips, insights, and perspectives. Students are quite passionate about doing so, and they often post their tips and insights in the forum for other students. One additional benefit of this approach as a faculty member is that I have been curating additional tools for students. When I teach the course again, I am able to provide future students with a more robust and growing list of potential technological tools they might consider in completing their assignments.

Potential Faculty Concerns

I first incorporated digital visualization methods in my course during my first semester as a tenure track faculty member. Because I was teaching fully online, it was important that I stretch my students to think critically and engage more deeply with material. My reading about online pedagogy (Major, 2015) and subsequent concerns about student disengagement in online learning environments allowed me to experiment with including digital visualization assignments in the "Leadership in Higher Education" course. But just as students express(ed) particular concerns, other faculty may have hesitancies about the process. I want to offer some insights on potential concerns based on personal experience.

First, I was concerned with the amount of additional work the incorporation of digital visualization assignments might entail. Grading and providing quality feedforward insight to students is more time intensive for this course. As noted earlier, grading is also much more ambiguous, particularly if you decide, as I did, to allow for maximum student creativity by avoiding too many restrictions or parameters around assignment submissions. Faculty incorporating digital visualization methods must commit to providing the affirmation and insights students want, need, and deserve. Thus, if you are a faculty member pursuing the integration of digital visualization assignments into courses, think strategically about your time, course load, and other academic obligations. Although I ensconced multiple digital visual assignments in this course, even incorporating one or two assignments will greatly impact the learning, course integration, creativity, and process-oriented learning emblematic of digital visualization.

Second, faculty should become familiar with the ambiguity that may accompany incorporation of digital visualization methods. As noted earlier, most students will turn in at least one visualization assignment that presents poorly. The question you should ask yourself as a faculty member is whether demonstration of process and critical thinking suffices for purposes of grading or whether visual presentation takes precedence. Depending on how one answers that question, faculty should be clear in the syllabus about expectations for visualization projects.

Third and finally, some faculty may have hesitancy about incorporating digital visualization if they lack particular technological skills or familiarity with specific digital tools. Addressing this concern can be accomplished in two ways. First, faculty can think about incorporating digital visualization into their own presentation methods—either in the course where visualization assignments have been incorporated or in semesters and courses preceding the course that will incorporate such assignments. The benefit of this approach is students see that you too have become familiar with the technologies, and you gain experience to provide insights for students on best approaches to grappling with new digital technologies.

Second, I also encourage faculty to trust the process. It is not necessary, in my estimation, that faculty know how every possible digital tool works.

Rather, we must be familiar enough with the process-oriented nature of creating digital visualization projects to encourage students to express themselves creatively. Students can and will learn digital tools if challenged to do so, and in my experience, their ability to harness these tools and their creative capacities produces outstanding work

Embrace Digital Visualization

Although the focus of this chapter is on how I incorporate digital visualization techniques into a fully online course, digital visualization projects can enhance the learning experience of students in traditional face-to-face courses. My experience with incorporating digital visualization techniques into the "Leadership in Higher Education" course has demonstrated that although students are mostly initially hesitant about completing nontraditional assignments or learning new technologies, they come to embrace and value the creative and process-oriented nature of these approaches.

I close with the most important voices—those of students. One student commented that

> the various digital visualization assignments provided opportunities to really think about what your own standpoint is and why. Being able to combine a module you did not feel confident about with an assignment type you did made it fun and easier to work with a difficult module.

Another student stated, "I really did find myself being challenged to think critically on some of the modules and how I would create an assignment to relay my message." Finally, one student closed noting the importance of digital visualization techniques: "I am leaving this course . . . with the ability to use different media techniques to present information." Digital visualization can truly enhance the learning experience—by shifting students away from technocratic and mundane approaches to learning, tapping into creativity, and emphasizing the importance of process over product. Embracing digital visualization as a faculty member will enhance the learning and experience of students in your virtual (or face-to-face) classrooms and challenge you to think differently, teach differently, and be different.

References

Deleuze, G., & Guattari, F. (1987). *A thousand plateaus: Capitalism and schizophrenia.* Minneapolis, MN: University of Minnesota Press.

Greene, M. (1995). *Releasing the imagination: Essays on education, the arts, and social change.* San Francisco, CA: Jossey-Bass.

Kouzes, J. M., & Posner, B. Z. (2002). *The leadership challenge* (3rd ed.). San Francisco, CA: Jossey-Bass.

Love, P. G., & Estanek, S. M. (2004). *Rethinking student affairs practice.* San Francisco, CA: Jossey-Bass.

Major, C. M. (2015). *Teaching online: A guide to theory, research, and practice.* Baltimore, MD: Johns Hopkins University Press.

9

DIGITAL STORIES

A Critical Pedagogical Tool in Leadership Education

Natasha H. Chapman and James McShay

This chapter presents the use of digital stories as visual pedagogical tools to promote critical perspectives in leadership education with undergraduate students. Critical perspectives provide a useful theoretical framework for (re)defining *leadership* because it challenges conventional ideology around leadership and makes experiential knowledge central. Additionally, critical perspectives complement models often used in leadership education that involve epistemological reflection and self-authorship (Astin, 1996; Baxter Magolda, 2014; Higher Education Research Institute, 1996; Komives, Lucas, & McMahon, 2013; Preskill & Brookfield, 2009). Understandings of relational, ethical, and socially responsible leadership have been used to support pedagogies that promote the development of critical perspectives in leadership (Owen, 2015). Such perspectives help learners understand the problematic dynamics that can occur in leadership processes and enable them to challenge their own beliefs and assumptions, as well as consider more inclusive ways of exercising power (Brookfield, 2005; Collinson & Tourish, 2015; Owen, 2015).

Digital stories help to create inclusive learning spaces that allow for honest and authentic dialogue about and across differences, as well as perspective taking (Brookfield, 1993; Pendakur & Furr, 2016). Creating and sharing these stories can lead to sociocultural conversations that help to facilitate students' capacities for socially responsible leadership (Dugan, Kodama,

Correia, & Associates, 2013). The digital story process allows for exploring of individual, group, and societal values while supporting the recognition of peers as knowledge keepers. The process promotes consideration of more complex, non-authority bound approaches to learning and knowledge construction.

This chapter describes the process used to integrate digital storytelling as a pedagogical tool for leadership studies students to explore, examine, and communicate their beliefs and assumptions about leadership. While engaging in the digital story process, students are challenged to use video media to analyze and critique leadership phenomena through critical reflection and by situating their own voice at the center of the meaning-making process. The digital story assignment allows students to articulate a comprehensive leadership philosophy by comparing leadership concepts to their own experiences using an assortment of carefully selected digital and multimedia artifacts. Unlike written assignments, digital stories allow for the use of visuals to help tell stories succinctly with impact and emotion. Powerful visuals can evoke deeper emotions that result in deeper engagement with the content. Unlike oral storytelling, digital storytelling requires the careful selection of narrative and imagery that become fixed once completed. In a way, the final product can stand on its own, apart from the author, and serve as a product for examination and critique. Because of this, students go through an intimate and strategic process of selecting images and audio that best capture their leadership ideas in iconic, symbolic, and deictic ways in a limited visual space, all of which make the digital story assignment unique.

This chapter provides an overview of the benefits of digital storytelling as a visual pedagogical tool, emphasizing its role in enhancing critical reflection capacities in students. We also describe a series of assignments, activities, and guiding questions used throughout a semester to support students in the development of their digital story. We then offer advice and considerations based on our working knowledge of implementing digital stories in the classroom. We close the chapter by discussing the importance of sharing digital stories to promote the exchange of ideas and enhance leadership learning and perspective taking.

What Are Digital Stories?

The educational benefits of digital storytelling as a pedagogical tool used in postsecondary institutions have been well-documented in literature that cuts across fields such as American studies, history, business, education, and leadership (Lambert, 2007; McLellan, 2006; Ohler, 2008; Robin, 2008).

According to McLellan (2006), digital stories' emergence in education can be attributed to the unique way in which visual and textual images enhance students' acquisition of knowledge and facilitate higher levels of critical inquiry and meaning-making. Digital stories tend to consist of relatively inexpensive personal forms of digital technology that use an assortment of media such as video clips, soundtracks, computer-generated graphics, and narration to construct a coherent narrative (McShay, 2010; Ohler, 2008). Some digital stories have incorporated web-based applications such as streaming media, podcasts, and blogs (McLellan, 2006).

All types of media that are employed in digital stories share an essential characteristic: They rely on the use of students' personal voice. Within the context of digital story development, personal voice becomes the central vehicle through which students are given agency to articulate, visually represent, and critique how their lived experiences are shaped by their histories, social beliefs, and institutional systems and practices. Through the use of this tool, students are able to convey both the authenticity and diversity of the human experience, which enables their stories to become powerful learning platforms that support critical inquiry around identity and difference. More specifically, these stories can depict the lived experiences of students in ways that allow for acquisition of academic knowledge and engagement in dialogue about issues of diversity, leadership, and social justice.

Digital stories can take the form of autobiographical narratives, historical documentaries, critical incident analyses, instructional presentations, or other learning modalities. Students' personal voices can be an effective means to evoke dialogue and perspective taking among audience members who view the digital story, and the digital story can also be used as a powerful tool to promote critical reflection for the story developer. Ohler (2008) states that digital stories can facilitate critical reflection by allowing the following:

> Students hear themselves via recorded media for the purpose of listening, self-assessment, and rewriting and/or speaking or recording the narration process. The power of hearing oneself for self-assessment purposes can't be underestimated. It's as though the process of getting words out of one's head and out in the open air exposes them to a quality of critique not available within the confines of one's internal landscape, even if the only people reviewing the narratives are the authors themselves. (p. 58)

This form of critique to which Ohler is referring is deeply embedded in the processes that support critical reflection. Digital stories enable students to use their own words to not only communicate their ideas to others but also self-analyze and make meaning.

Digital stories allow the student to situate his or her experience within the center of the story and use it as a point of critique and analysis. This particular use of digital stories can help develop students' capacities for critical reflection. King and Baxter Magolda (2005) asserted that this type of orientation can best be described as a flexible belief system that increases students' abilities to adapt and make decisions in diverse social and cultural situations. Furthermore, such an orientation would help them resist using an ethnocentric lens to interpret and make meaning of social realities and contexts with which they have limited familiarity. Using digital stories as a learning tool can create opportunities for students to practice essential skills, such as suspending their personal judgment and "trying on" new perspectives in an effort to broaden their own understanding about a particular condition or circumstance.

Educators can pose a number of questions to students that might foster critical reflection both during and after the development of their stories, such as the following:

- What stood out to you the most as you think about the process of developing your digital story?
- In what ways were your perspectives about leadership, identity, and difference informed by this process and how does that make you feel?
- What unanswered questions do you have?
- How do you feel about the themes you explored in the story now and how might that change over time?

As students critically reflect upon the process of developing and listening to their own stories, they are better positioned to identify and critique problems, issues, and themes that explain ways in which they come to understand their own social location and societal participation (McShay, 2010).

Critical Reflection and Digital Stories

The following section outlines the use of digital stories to promote critical reflection in an undergraduate leadership studies course. We share information about the course assignment, the use of critical reflection in pedagogy, and how critical perspectives of leadership were embedded in the course. This section also provides an example of a student's digital story for the course and discusses how that digital story connected to core concepts of the course.

Digital Story Assignment

At the University of Maryland, the leadership studies program offers an advanced leadership course for students who are nearing the completion of their requirements for the leadership studies minor. These students, less than a year away from graduation, spend the semester in a seminar-style course that is formatted heavily around dialogue and critical reflection. The course aims to support students in the examination of their leadership identity development to distinguish benchmarks for continued growth and help them articulate their own personal philosophy of leadership to guide their transition from collegiate leadership environments to new contexts post-graduation.

In this seminar, students complete a final project—a digital story—that reflects their working philosophy of leadership, a synthesis of what they have learned about leadership over time through the leadership studies minor and their lifetime of leadership experiences. The central question of this digital story assignment is as follows: What is your personal philosophy of leadership? Students are prompted to use the digital story to describe their working definition of *leadership* and, more importantly, demonstrate through the use of audio, imagery, and narration, how they have come to this definition. Students are asked to use this medium to document their own socialization of leadership and examine personal assumptions about leadership. They are expected to affirm or critique the leadership concepts, theories, and models they have been taught through the lens of their lived experiences and acquired knowledge, and they are also encouraged to use the assignment to reconstruct normative ideas around leadership by highlighting their unique perspective.

Throughout the semester-long course, students complete a series of assignments and activities that facilitate reflective practice, framed with contemplative prompts and sequenced to developmentally support them in advancing their digital story. Space is created in class for students to respond to digital story prompts in a written narrative. Evolving from the central question previously mentioned, the narrative serves as a working document that develops as students proceed through the semester, completing new assignments, responding to future prompts, and exchanging their ideas with their classmates.

Midway through the course, the narrative is translated into a script and storyboard that serves as a blueprint for the production of the digital story. During a storyboarding session, students share with their peers their narratives and examine each other's themes. This exchange allows students to brainstorm with one another about how to best portray the narrative they've developed through the use of personal photos, symbols, sounds, and video.

Critical Reflection

As an assignment, digital storytelling serves as a beneficial pedagogical tool for a leadership course, because both the process of development and the deliverable itself requires the students to critically investigate their own assumptions about leadership (Brookfield, 1993; Pendakur & Furr, 2016). Preskill and Brookfield (2009) wrote that critical reflection "grounds not only our actions but also our sense of who we are as leaders in an examined reality. We know why we believe what we believe" (p. 45). The digital story assignment allows students to explore their thoughts and emotions and compare subjective experiences to theory or facts through a unique collection of multimedia and digital artifacts (Joint Information Systems Committee [JISC], Leeds Metropolitan University, and the University of Leeds, 2012). Throughout the entire process of making a digital story, the learners are required to make all the creative choices, and they consistently reflect back on why they made those choices. This cycle of reflection—reevaluating why a particular choice was made and why a specific image was chosen—can promote deeper learning and understanding of the self (Sandars, Murray, & Pello, 2008).

According to Sandars and colleagues (2008), "each step of the production of the digital story provides an ideal opportunity to stimulate reflection and this is in addition to reflection on the final overall product" (p. 775). This intentional, persistent reflective process seems especially beneficial in a capstone course for students. Understanding the reflective process will be essential to students as they transition outside of the university setting. This process can inform the future professional practice of students, while simultaneously shaping their growing personal identity. If students can develop into "self-regulated learners," they will be prepared to take on the work of constant self-evaluation and lifelong learning (JISC et al., 2012).

Critical Perspectives

Students are introduced to critical perspectives of leadership early in the semester, starting with an evaluation of a book on leadership. Students select one popular press leadership book to review and write a brief executive summary on the text's central idea(s); the assumptions about leadership that present themselves; and whether, from the student's perspective, the book reflects leadership. This assignment serves as a gateway into a class lesson that highlights the similarities and distinctions among critical thinking, critical reflection, and critical theory. Applying tenets of critical theory allows themes to emerge through the analysis of the popular press books, permitting students to interrogate normative ways of understanding and enacting leadership. Students are encouraged to respond to concerns about ideology, the flow of power, one's value of relationships, and the role of context in the creation of their digital stories.

Throughout the course, students use the same process of critique during class lessons on the historical evolution of leadership studies and on families of leadership theory. They are asked to describe the major components of these theories and their strengths and limitations. They must apply theories to their own life experiences and provide examples of leadership in practice, reflected through an article, video clip, image, or description of a current or historical event. In the process of learning about normative leadership theories, students are challenged to seek evidence in their own lives and in the surrounding world that might support or problematize dominant narratives around leadership.

Inherent in critical pedagogy is the importance of deconstructing dominant discourse around a construct (Leonardo, 2004). Equally important is the practice of reconstructing to develop new, enhanced, and complex ways of understanding and presenting the phenomena. Students are regularly reminded that this practice of critique and collection of digital resources and personal experiences should be applied and utilized in the development of their digital stories. Their digital stories serve as a medium to deconstruct and reconstruct leadership by centering on the student's distinctive voice.

The lessons described previously prepare students to consider the following prompts in the development of the digital stories: What theories and concepts from this course or other courses help to illustrate your understanding of leadership? Which leadership concepts resonate with you and why? How might you incorporate your own language for communicating these concepts? Alternatively, what critique of the literature has informed your understanding of leadership? What leadership experiences have you had that counter the literature or conventional notions of leadership? What is missing from the literature that you would like to communicate in your digital story?

Responses to these critical questions will provide students with some direction in the development of their ideas as they begin with a written narrative, condense the narrative into a script, create a storyboard around the script, and eventually choose visual and audio elements to best showcase their ideas.

Digital Story Example

The following paragraphs highlight aspects of Rui's digital story. As a child, Rui grew up in Brazil and has since lived in different countries. His global perspective is evident in his digital story. Through the use of imagery and movement, he has applied a critical perspective to capture the tension between dominant ideas of leadership and his own experiences (Figure 9.1).

Figure 9.1. Rui's digital story.

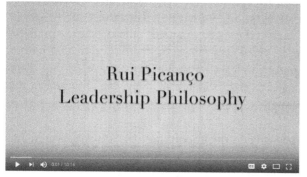

Note. Scan QR code to access Rui's digital story (http://bit.ly/2j9XwBE).

Following is an example of how Rui responded to the critical perspective prompts in his digital story.

> We like to form a narrative, however, we like the idea that Steve Jobs was a wonder kid and a visionary leader. We don't like considering the notion that his leadership was informed by much more than just his character. We don't like to believe that Steve Jobs was a socially awkward kid with wealthy parents, because that doesn't make for a good leadership story. But we need to start challenging these concepts of heroism. Leaders are born out of a context, something bigger than themselves—they are the product of experiences which develop qualities that allow them to succeed. (Chapman, 2017, 5:24)

In the preceding excerpt, Rui used the iconic image of Steve Jobs to represent a cultural archetype of a leader and to reflect a predominant notion of leadership: heroism (Chapman, 2017). This heroic leadership perspective privileges and romanticizes individuals while underestimating the dynamics of power and the influence of context (Collinson & Tourish, 2015). Rui learned about this alternative story about Jobs in Malcolm Gladwell's (2011) book *Outliers* and later contrasted his personal childhood story to support his own conclusion that context plays a significant role in leadership outcomes, efficacy, and identity. He problematized the heroic perspective that focuses on individual traits and minimizes the social construction and interpretation of leadership (Collinson & Tourish, 2015). The image of Brazil followed by carefully chosen clips from his childhood also allowed the viewer to travel across time and space with Rui, creating a sense of authenticity and realism around his conclusions that writing or narrating may not do alone. The following excerpt from Rui's digital story describes the role his childhood played in his leadership development.

> I had a very different childhood growing up in São Paulo, Brazil, than most kids in countries like the [United States]. I bring this up because my parents were in no financial condition to provide me with video games, computers, DVDs, or even LEGOS. I used to get upset because I had friends that had all these new and exciting things that we just couldn't afford. Looking back, I now believe that being deprived of those items gave me an advantage today. Instead of being locked up in my room with computers, I was forced to go outside and engage with other kids at a very early age. I believe accepting my family's financial situation and mustering the courage to go make friends was the beginning of my leadership development. (Chapman, 2017, 6:15)

In his digital story, Rui further emphasized the role context plays in leadership outcomes by contrasting the black-and-white still image of the iconic Jobs to the fast-paced, bright, and dynamic alternating images of people from diverse communities. The center of his digital story reflects the important role of imagery in conveying his conception of leadership in symbolic, literal, and socially relevant ways. His chosen images depict geographic, ethnic, and cultural diversity as colorful, vibrant, and energizing—communicating that context, the human experience, is positive, real, and important. The emotions evoked may have been muted if not for the incorporation of these visual choices to complement his narration.

Leadership Identity

Another lesson introduced students to the leadership identity development (LID) model, a model developed to understand the processes a person experiences in creating a leadership identity (Komives, Owen, Longerbeam, Mainella, & Osteen, 2005). This lesson encouraged students to identify and recognize how significant experiences, relationships, and other developmental factors have contributed to their leadership development and leadership identity. In his digital story Rui highlighted the developmental influences presented in the LID model such as peer and adult influences, meaningful involvement, and reflective learning. In the digital story, through words and images, he was able to provide examples of these development influences in his life. In doing so, Rui demonstrated his ability to apply the leadership model to real life events. He not only demonstrated understanding but simultaneously legitimized this aspect of the literature with evidence from his lived experiences. The visual representation of the model, coupled with Rui's narrated examples, bring the model to life and give the viewer an opportunity to make sense of the model in a relevant way. For instance, in the digital story, Rui voiced the following:

> I developed strong relationships with the kids in my neighborhood. We would play soccer, Simon Says, and compete in foosball tournaments. Even though I didn't recognize it back then, these activities were informing my leadership identity. Most of the kids in my neighborhood had two full-time working parents like me, so it was up to us to organize teams, gather equipment, and communicate with each other. We slowly learned that separate we had very little, but together we could overcome many obstacles. (Chapman, 2017, 7:09)

Social Identity

To supplement the lesson on leadership identity, the class is introduced to identity mapping, adapted from Hannum's (2007) *Social Identity: Knowing Yourself, Leading Others*. Students map the given, chosen, and core attributes of their identity in concentric circles as a way to articulate how they see themselves and as a means to explore how others may perceive them as a leader. Once the map is complete, students respond to questions such as the following: Which items do you believe contribute to your ability to lead effectively? Which items do you believe detract from your ability to lead effectively? This activity gives students an opportunity to consider the intersection of their social and leadership identities and to discuss related implications of how they enact their leadership identities.

The cycle of socialization (Harro, 2000) is also introduced to students to help them understand the ways in which humans are socialized to play certain roles, how we are affected by issues of oppression, and how we help maintain an oppressive system based on power. The application of this concept in the context of leadership development points out to students the ways in which we are socialized into roles of power or powerlessness and can bring to the forefront the explicit and unwritten codes of behavior that reinforce dominant prototypes of leader and leadership. Through these lessons, students had an opportunity to investigate their own socialization of leadership—what they were taught and the messages that they received through social institutions that situated them as powerful or powerless or superior or inferior (Harro, 2000). This reflective process makes visible the ways in which students are socialized into understanding, valuing, and enacting leadership.

Related to these lessons, students are directed to the following prompts for consideration in the development of their digital stories: What is your first recollection of leadership? Who helped to shape your self-concept and your understanding of others? How has your understanding of leadership changed over time? What significant experiences triggered these changes? In what ways do your social identities intersect with your leadership identity? What roles do values, ethics, and social justice play in your philosophy of leadership? How do relationships present themselves in your definition of *leadership* (between and among individuals, groups, organizations, and systems)? Do you believe that leadership is accessible to everyone? Is diversity, inclusivity, or pluralism a priority for you?

Considerations

As indicated previously, much of the class time and deliverables leading up to the digital stories involves the practice of *critical reflection*—the examination of leadership concepts related to one's own leadership learning and practice. Although students are expected to document experiences and respond to the digital story prompts throughout the semester, less class time is devoted to developing competency in the utilization of software and collecting tangible media artifacts, such as clips, photos, and audio, needed to create a digitized product. Students' level of efficacy working in this domain varies, and for some, this variation results in an increase in the amount of time, energy, and stress devoted to learning about software that it could be spent on the clarity of voice and choice of content. This phenomenon is similar to LaFrance and Blizzard's (2013) findings on students' perceptions of digital storytelling as a tool for learning in educational leadership coursework. They shared that due to limited meeting times, their participants also worked independently on their assignment outside of the course, utilizing technologies available to them. Due to these limitations, the authors' findings pointed to the following technology-related recommendation for improving the assignment: Provide a detailed resource sheet, tutorials, specific assignment parameters, and guest speakers to demonstrate resources to help students identify the most effective software for their individual digital storytelling needs (LaFrance & Blizzard, 2013).

Until students are provided with more instructional support on the technological production of their digital stories, in the advanced leadership courses, evaluation of digital stories is based more on the students' clarity of voice, creativity of their construction of meaning, and self-direction (Rossiter & Garcia, 2010) and less on technical acumen. Still, students are expected to utilize their resources to produce a thoughtful, creative, and well-organized deliverable of the highest quality that they are capable of producing. As the advanced leadership course continues to evolve, instructors have identified a few ways to address the current challenges.

Students in the course are also given opportunities to organize their ideas before they produce their digital stories. Developing a script and creating a storyboard allows students to arrange their imagery, audio, and other story elements in chronological order. Storyboarding allows students to physically lay out their entire plan, so that they can conceptualize how the various elements of their story will fit together and address any holes that may exist (University of Houston, 2016). Although a tedious task for some, this allows the students to organize and rearrange the content for maximum effect and can prevent them from feeling overwhelmed if they begin early enough in the semester (University of Houston, 2016). Storyboards can be created manually or digitally. If instructors share storyboarding templates and resources, students can identify a method that they are most comfortable using.

Incorporating class-related activities that allow students to visualize and make meaning of their experiences, ideas, and feelings through the use of images can be helpful. For example, Visual Explorer cards, random postcards, or photographs can be used to provide a visual vocabulary to respond to prompts on leadership topics. Visual Explorer is a tool developed by the Center for Creative Leadership. Based on research and practice that show the power of images and objects, the tool encourages effective dialogue on complex issues about which students can attempt to get at the roots of what they assume and believe (InnovationTools.com, n.d.). To initiate dialogue in the advanced leadership seminar, students are asked to find an image that echoes their definition of *leadership*, a photo that reflects a significant leadership moment in their life, or a card that captures a concern that they have about the world. These images can serve as articles that can be translated into digital form in the development of their digital stories. The Visual Explorer activity allows the two styles of human thought—verbal (analytical) and nonverbal (intuitive)—to work in concert, so that groups and individuals can better draw upon all of their resources to explore complex ideas and issues (Palus & Horth, 2004). In their digital stories, the students' nonverbal thought, which can be neglected in written and spoken assignments, can be reflected through image, pattern, and texture. The imagery allows the students to bring realism to their story and communicate their ideas in a more authentic and emotional way.

Although tutorials on popular and accessible software are also shared with students, it is beneficial to incorporate at least one or two in-class days for students to work on the conceptualization and the production of their digital stories. This not only ensures that students have put in some effort on their assignment but also provides an opportunity for classmates to support one another in the creative process and assist those who are unfamiliar with the video-making software. The popularity of affordable and accessible digital recording technology promotes collaboration and colearning as students create and manage their projects together (Yang & Wu, 2012). Setting aside classroom time to work on the projects offers a convenient space for students to exchange ideas, materials, and resources, which facilitates the coconstruction of knowledge across the learning community (LaFrance & Blizzard, 2013).

Sharing Digital Stories

A necessary and important aspect of the digital story experience in the advanced leadership seminar is sharing and presenting digital stories. Similar to other reflective approaches, the personal learning journey experienced through digital storytelling is greatly enhanced when the process is shared with others (Moon, 2004; Sandars et al., 2008). Digital stories provide not only a means with which students can engage in the practice of self-reflexivity but also a space where student peers can critique, discuss, and explore personal understandings of leadership.

According to JISC and colleagues (2012), the sharing component of digital storytelling spurs discussion and dialogue that not only inspires further reflection for the creator but also stimulates reflection for the audience. Because the sharing contributes so strongly to the reflective cycle, attendance during digital story presentations is emphasized. Unless the class is small, students are divided into smaller groups to allow for deep, meaningful dialogue and greater attention to each digital story. Initially, student peers are most comfortable giving affirmations and identifying commonalities in digital artifacts, so it is often necessary to prepare and challenge students to be curious, seek clarity, and apply a critical lens to fully explore alternative ways of understanding leadership. Additionally, participating in the full digital storytelling experience engages students and their peers in developing competencies helpful in the practice of leadership. The process facilitates social learning, the sharing and receiving of feedback, and emotional intelligence (Robin, 2008). Rossiter and Garcia (2010) suggested that digital stories serve as an exciting option for creating true community within adult learning settings that can bridge differences and foster the capacity for perspective taking among learners. Because this medium of delivery personalizes the learning experience by evoking emotion through images and sound, digital stories may incite curiosities around a particular event, idea, or assumption that was revealed. When intentionally set up, sharing digital stories can foster opportunities for interrogating and affirming leadership perspectives, coconstructing knowledge, and promoting empathy based on the multiple viewpoints offered in the process.

Conclusion

The use of digital stories in leadership education allows for the positioning of one's voice in the examination of constructs such as identity, power, oppression, and privilege as they relate to leadership theory and practice. This makes room for sense-making and perspective-taking that can be displayed through the use of visual and textual images. The reflection that is employed through digital storytelling allows learners to critically examine events and prompts them to analyze their role within those events so that they might learn from the experiences. This leads to the following final reflective prompts for students: How does your philosophy of leadership relate to your hopes for the future? How does your philosophy of leadership empower you?

Ultimately, the process of critical reflection that occurs while developing and sharing digital stories allows students to make meaning of their knowledge and experiences so that they leave the leadership studies minor having committed to and clearly communicating what they believe and value about leadership. As a result, our hope is that students develop a rationale behind their actions; are able to make informed leadership decisions—in which their assumptions have been carefully and critically examined; and, when faced with inevitable challenges, have a sense of confidence that is rooted in their philosophy of leadership (Preskill & Brookfield, 2009).

The digital story as an end-product provides a means for students to share their leadership philosophy in a unique and personal way. However, it is the process of creating and sharing the digital story that is most important to their learning, as they must situate themselves within the complex complex consideration of what leadership is. Students are pushed to engage in higher-order thinking because they are challenged to consider and reconsider each element of the story that they have chosen. At the same time, they must thoughtfully and intentionally consider how they might also help others access their story and make meaning of it. Images have the power to impact how messages are conveyed and received, giving them power to alter understanding. Although digital story telling and sharing can place students in a vulnerable position, it can simultaneously empower and affirm that one can be both learner and teacher in the process.

References

Astin, H. (1996). Leadership for social change. *About Campus, 1*(2), 4–10.
Baxter Magolda, M. B. (2014). Self-authorship. *New Direction for Higher Education, 166*, 25–33.

Brookfield, S. (1993). Self-directed learning, political clarity, and the critical practice of adult education. *Adult Education Quarterly, 43*(4), 227–242.

Brookfield, S. D. (2005). *The power of critical theory*. San Francisco, CA: Jossey-Bass.

Chapman, N. (2017, January 26). *R Picanco digital story* [Video file]. Retrieved from https://www.youtube.com/watch?v=U4Lzp5pKEHc&feature=youtu.be

Collinson, D., & Tourish, D. (2015). Teaching leadership critically: New directions for leadership pedagogy. *Academy of Management Learning & Education, 14*(4), 576–594.

Dugan, J. P., Kodama, C., Correia, B., & Associates. (2013). *Multi-institutional study of leadership insight report: Leadership program delivery*. College Park, MD: National Clearinghouse for Leadership Programs.

Hannum, K. M. (2007). *Social identity: Knowing yourself, leading others*. Greensboro, NC: Center for Creative Leadership.

Harro, B. (2000). The cycle of socialization. In M. Adams, W. J. Blumenfeld, R. Casteneda, H. W. Hackman, M. L. Peters, & X. Zuniga (Eds.), *Readings for diversity and social justice: An anthology on racism, anti-Semitism, sexism, heterosexism, ableism, and classism* (pp. 15–21). New York, NY: Routledge.

Higher Education Research Institute (HERI). (1996). *A social change model of leadership development*. College Park, MD: National Clearinghouse for Leadership Programs.

InnovationTools.com. (n.d.). *Well-designed visual explorer tool enables creative dialogue and collaboration*. Retrieved from http://www.innovationmanagement.se/imtool-articles/well-designed-visual-explorer-tool-enables-creative-dialogue-and-collaboration/

Joint Information Systems Committee, Leeds Metropolitan University, and the University of Leeds. (2012). *Digital approaches to academic reflection*. Retrieved from http://content.yudu.com/Library/A1pi1i/Digitalapproachestoa/resources/1.htm

King, P., & Baxter Magolda, M. B. (2005). A developmental model of intercultural maturity. *Journal of College Student Development, 46*(6), 571–592.

Komives, S. R., Lucas, N., & McMahon, T. R. (2013). *Exploring leadership: For college students who want to make a difference* (3rd ed.). San Francisco, CA: Jossey-Bass.

Komives, S. R., Owen, J. E., Longerbeam, S., Mainella, F. C., & Osteen, L. (2005). Developing a leadership identity: A grounded theory. *Journal of College Student Development, 6*, 593–611.

LaFrance, J., & Blizzard, J. (2013). Student perceptions of digital storytelling as a learning-tool for educational leaders. *International Journal of Educational Leadership Preparation, 8*(2), 25–33.

Lambert, J. (2007). *Digital storytelling: Capturing lives, creating community*. Berkeley, CA: Digital Diner Press.

Leonardo, Z. (2004). Critical social theory and transformative knowledge: The functions of criticism in quality education. *Educational Researcher, 33*, 11–18.

McLellan, H. (2006). Digital storytelling in higher education. *Journal of Computing in Higher Education, 19*(1), 65–79.

McShay, J. (2010). Digital stories for critical multicultural education: A Freireian approach. In S. May & C. Sleeter (Eds.), *Critical multiculturalism: Theory and praxis* (pp. 139–150). New York, NY: Taylor & Francis.

Moon, J. A. (2004). *A handbook of reflective and experiential learning: Theory and practice*. London, England: RoutledgeFalmer.

Ohler, J. (2008). *Digital story telling in the classroom: New media pathways to literacy, learning, and creativity*. Thousand Oaks, CA: Corwin Press.

Owen, J. E. (2015). Transforming leadership development for significant learning. *New Directions for Student Leadership, 145*, 7–17.

Palus, C. J., & Horth, D. M. (2004). *Visual Explorer: Picturing approaches to complex challenges*. Greensboro, NC: Center for Creative Leadership.

Pendakur, V., & Furr, S. C. (2016). Critical leadership pedagogy: Engaging power, identity, and culture in leadership education for college students of color. *New Directions for Higher Education, 174*, 45–55.

Preskill S., & Brookfield, S. D. (2009). *Learning as a way of leading: Lessons from the struggle for social justice*. San Francisco, CA: Jossey-Bass.

Robin, B. (2008). Digital storytelling: A powerful technology tool for the 21st century classroom. *Theory Into Practice, 47*, 220–228.

Rossiter, M., & Garcia, P. A. (2010). Digital storytelling: A new player on the narrative field. *New Directions for Adult and Continuing Education, 126*, 37–48.

Sandars, J., Murray, C., & Pellow, A. (2008). Twelve tips for using digital storytelling to promote reflective learning by medical students. *Medical Teacher, 30*(8), 774–777.

University of Houston. (2016). *Educational uses of digital storytelling*. Retrieved from http://digitalstorytelling.coe.uh.edu/index.cfm

Yang, Y. C., & Wu, W. I. (2012). Digital storytelling for enhancing student academic achievement, critical thinking, and learning motivation: A year-long experimental study. *Computers and Education 59*(2), 339–352.

PART THREE

VISUAL METHODS AND PRACTICE

10

OVERVIEW OF THE USE OF VISUAL METHODS IN PRACTICE

Carrie A. Kortegast

uring my master's program, I held a graduate assistantship in residence life in which I supervised six to eight residence assistants (RAs). One of my roles as their supervisor was to make sure that the bulletin boards on their floors were decorated. These bulletin boards were often used as a form of passive programming where information was communicated through signs, pictures, handouts, and other images. On the whole, my RAs disliked completing bulletin boards. To be fair, we lived in an "active" building in which the materials on their boards would often get ripped down. Aside from that, the RAs did not always see the purpose of passive programming and how the use of visuals could communicate important information about the campus community. Moreover, as a department, we did not do a good job teaching RAs about the importance of visuals in passive programming. The focus was often on completing the task (e.g., hanging a bulletin board) rather than discussing the visual and textual content on the bulletin boards. Conversations about visuals as cultural artifacts that communicated implicit and explicit messages about the community rarely took place. Providing a framework to the RAs during RA training discussing bulletin boards as communicators of community values might have shifted how they saw this task and how their supervisors approached making sure this task was completed. Ultimately, this was a missed opportunity to help students develop visual literacy.

Noted art historian James Elkins (2007) stated that "images are central to our lives. . . . It is time they are central to our universities" (p. 8). Indeed, images are ubiquitous across college campuses. Examples of the use of visuals in learning can be found across different academic disciplines. Although the most recognizable examples might include analysis of art in an art history course or ads in marketing courses, other disciplines use visuals to enhance student learning such as use of pictorial and graphic representation of data in sociology and statistic courses. Moreover, university-sanctioned images can be found on institutional websites, social media accounts, public art, signage, banners, and pamphlets. These images are often used to communicate messages of belonging, diversity, fun, and academic endeavors. Furthermore, students are narrating their lives using images and posting them to social media accounts such as Twitter, Facebook, Snapchat, and Instagram. Although less prominent, participant-generated visual methods such as collages, drawings, photo elicitation, and other arts-based methods are used in various areas of campus life including workshops and trainings as methods to help students reflect and make meaning of their own experience.

The purpose of this chapter is to explore the use of visual methods to enhance college students' out-of-classroom learning, development, and sense of belonging on campus. The chapter describes how visuals can promote college student learning outside the classroom and provides examples of the use of visuals in practice and a framework for understanding campus artifacts.

Promotion of Student Learning

With the new "pictorial turn," Felton (2008) argued that images can "no longer exist primarily to entertain and illustrate;" instead, images are "becoming central to communication and meaning-making" (p. 60). Smartphones, the Internet, social media, and the accessibility of video recording devices and cameras allow college students to narrate their lives in new ways. Moreover, "these everyday tools and artifacts bind adolescents together in a social culture through communication and meaning-making" (Miller, 2007, p. 62). Although students use these methods of communication in their everyday lives, rarely are they asked to reflect on the images and content they produce.

The following discusses three prominent ways the use of visual methods in practice can enhance student learning, development, and experience. These learning outcomes include enhancing visual literacy, engaging in multimodal learning and communication, and facilitating meaning- and sense-making.

Visual Literacy

Visual literacy focuses on "understanding how people perceive objects, interpret what they see, and what they learn from them" (Elkins, 2007, p. 2). Visual literacy can help facilitate learning and meaning-making of particular information and concepts (e.g., diversity, social justice, and inclusion). Moreover, the development of visual literacy is associated with core values—critical thinking, analytical writing, and self-expression—embedded within liberal arts education (Little, Felten, & Berry, 2015). The development of visual literacy requires students to have the "ability to understand, produce, and use culturally significant images, objects, and visual actions" (Felten, 2008, p. 60).

Student affairs practitioners can promote the development of visual literacy in workshops, trainings, awareness campaigns, and individual interactions with students. For instance, advisers working with student organizations can ask critical questions regarding the choices around particular images they are using on T-shirts, posters, logos, and other organizational materials. Conversations regarding what messages and values those images are sending can help students increase their own visual literacy.

Multimodal Learning and Communication

Another learning outcome is multimodal communication. Linguistic modes of communications, such as lectures and written work, often dominate the discourse regarding understandings of promoting and evaluating student learning (Jewitt, Kress, Ogborn, & Tsatsarelis, 2001; King & O'Brien, 2002). However, the focus on linguistic modes of communication fails to take into account other ways students can express ideas, meaning, and information. Multimodal learning and communication combines written, oral, visual, electronic, and kinetic methods of communication. The use of multiple modes of communication provides students with opportunities to represent and integrate knowledge in new and, perhaps, creative ways.

Multimodal learning and communication focuses on the process of constructing meaning and information using a wide range of methods and resources including visuals, audio, numerical, music, and written texts. Multimodal learning and communication engages students in an active process of "remaking" information and messages (Jewitt et al., 2001, p. 6). Students are then tasked with reproducing the information and messages in new, creative formats that draw upon more than one form of communication (e.g., written, oral, visual, electronic). Purposeful multimodal design activities offer a powerful way to engage students in reflection and transformation of their learning environment (Miller, 2007). Examples of the use of multimodal communication in practice include developing videos during service-learning experiences, creating reflective blogs that integrate both text and images for leadership development academies, and requiring students to develop professional ePortfolios.

Meaning- and Sense-Making

The use of visual methods, in particular participant-generated visual methods, can provide students opportunities to reflect, analyze, and share their own experiences and learning through the creation of an image. For instance, Benmayor (2008) stated that through the development of digital stories, students were able to "develop intellectual discourse and critique" (p. 189) as well as engage in critical self-reflection. In a course on Latina life stories, Benmayor used digital stories to connect history and theory with students' own lived experiences. One of her students, Lilly, created a digital story that focused on her struggles inside and outside her ethnic community in understanding and navigating her identity. Lilly ended the digital story discussing how her family and heritage gave her strength. In the written narrative reflection, Lilly connected themes from her digital story and lived experiences to content learned in the course through the use of conceptual frameworks. Specifically, Lilly discussed the process of developing an integrated identity consciousness and recognition of cultural assets she possesses. Benmayor argued that through the process of developing and reflecting, students were able to highlight their own cultural knowledge and experience in order "to transform their thinking and empower themselves" (p. 200). This example is from a classroom assignment, but student affairs practitioners can apply these same steps of reflection, analysis, and sharing experiences through the creation of an image in their work with students outside the classroom.

To summarize, practitioners can incorporate visual methods to foster visual literacy, multimodal communication, and meaning- and sense-making of college experiences. Recall the example at the beginning of the chapter regarding the development of bulletin boards. The creating of the bulletin boards could be reframed from a task that needed to be completed to a possibility for community-building. As a supervisor, I could have encouraged the RAs to engage students on their floor in creating images for the bulletin board. For instance, the RA could poll residents about their favorite study tips by asking residents to take a picture of themselves with a sign with the tip written on it. The residents could then post it to social media using a hashtag with the name of the floor. The RA then could use the images, tips, and other resources to develop a bulletin board for the floor. Through the development of this bulletin board, the RA would have the opportunity to repurpose images, engage the community, utilize multiple modes of communication, and demonstrate the ability to analyze and use visuals. In conclusion, practitioners can utilize visual methods in their work with students. The following section will provide examples of the use of visuals in practice.

Visuals in Practice

There are a variety of ways visual methods can be incorporated into practice to enhance student learning and development. Following are some examples of how visual methods have been used to reflect on out-of-classroom learning for social justice and student activism, professional development workshops, and assessment of campus climate.

Reflection on Experiential Learning

Visual methods can provide an opportunity for students to engage in sense- and meaning-making of their out-of-classroom experiences. For instance, vlogs (video blogs) can serve as a place for students to engage in self-reflection as well as an opportunity for sense-making of their educational experiences. For example, Nadia Honary devloped a series of vlogs about her experiences during a yearlong study abroad experience in Sevilla, Spain. These vlogs can be accessed by scanning the QR code in Figure 10.1. Her vlogs mix self-reflection about her experience, information about Spain, and a chronicle of her travels. In her second vlog, Honary (2011) shared being overwhelmed; confused; and, at the same time, excited about living and studying in a new culture.

Later in the year, Honary (2012) posted a vlog reflecting on why she and other students decided to participate in a yearlong study abroad experience rather than a more common semester-long program. Other vlogs chronicle travels to other cities in Spain and observations about Spanish culture. Overall, her vlogs provided a structured opportunity for reflection and they demonstrate her own growth. Although Honary's vlogs were not required by her study abroad program, study abroad offices often require students to engage in reflection activities about their experiences. Visual methods including vlogs, photo narratives, galleries, and photovoice projects could provide students with structured opportunities to negotiate the meaning of their study abroad experience (Kortegast & Boisfontaine, 2015).

Similarly, PechaKucha presentations provide opportunities for students to discuss experiences, knowledge, and understandings on particular topics through the combination of written text, spoken word, and visual images. PechaKucha, Japanese for "chitchat," is a presentation format in which there are 20 images, each of which stay on the screen for 20 seconds before

Figure 10.1. Seville, Spain vlogs.

Note. Scan QR code to access Honary's vlogs (https://vimeo.com/album/1681575/video/29148883).

advancing automatically (see the PechaKucha website for more information; www.pechakucha.org/faq). In discussing the role of integrity in leadership, Grace Wenzel (2014) developed a PechaKucha presentation about the role of integrity in leadership that was posted to YouTube. In the presentation, she used the images to highlight and enhance her argument about importance of integrity. The quick pace of PechaKucha encourages students to think through what they want to communicate and how to present understandings related to a particular topic. Student affairs practitioners could easily embed the use of PechaKucha in student leader academies; community service reflections; RA trainings; fraternity and sorority conferences; and other workshops, trainings, and programs focused on sharing information, experience, and reflection.

Social Justice and Student Activism

Visual methods can also be used to help students reflect on issues of social justice and diversity as they relate to the campus environment. For instance, Julia Golden-Battle, while serving as the assistant director of residential life at Mount Holyoke, responded to students of color feeling uncomfortable and unseen by creating a documentary highlighting their experiences on campus (J. Golden-Battle, personal communication, February 27, 2017). The documentary followed a few students and asked them about their identities and how they navigated those identities throughout their four years at Mount Holyoke relative to academics, with peers, and as student leaders on campus. She then shared the documentary with other student leaders on campus, which allowed them to learn about their fellow peers, how they identified, and their experiences on campus. After sharing the documentary, the student leaders were asked to discuss what they learned from their peers' experiences. Next, students were asked to create pictures and words to describe themselves and their identities. These images were then posted in the student center to raise awareness regarding how to support one another and ways to create an inclusive community.

The use of visuals in activism and awareness campaigns is a frequently used strategy. For instance, Black students at Harvard started a photo campaign to bring awareness to their experiences (I, Too, Am Harvard, 2014). The photo campaign I, Too, Am Harvard was shared on Tumblr, a microblogging and social network website, and on Twitter using the hashtag #itooamharvard. The photo campaign features students holding a whiteboard with various statements. Most of the statements represent micro- and macro-aggressions of the students' experiences at Harvard (I, Too, Am Harvard, 2014; Figure 10.2).

Similarly, Fordham University student Kiyun Kim (2013) developed a racial microaggression photo series that was published on Tumblr. Again, the focus was to raise awareness about issues facing students and their campus community. Other examples of the use of portraits and text include the

Figure 10.2. "Can you read?" #itooamharvard.

Note. Scan QR code to view #itooamharvard image (http://itooamharvard.tumblr.com/image/78255116303). Figure by Carol Powell. Reprinted with permission.

Dear World (2017) project in which individuals share messages on their skin, the We're a Culture Not a Costume poster campaign, the Ohio University's Students Teaching About Racism in Society (STARS; 2013) student organization, and #MyAllies selfie signs for Gay, Lesbian & Straight Education Network (GLSEN) (2016) Ally Week.

　　Although many of the photo campaigns mentioned here were student-led, student affairs practitioners can support students and student organizations leading these efforts by providing guidance, encouragement, and opportunities to engage. Practitioners could also encourage student groups to partner with other organizations to create more campus-wide social justice and awareness campaigns using visual methods such as murals, videos, and portraits. These opportunities allow students to express their feelings and describe their experience. Finally, student affairs practitioners also need to be prepared to respond to these efforts and address the concerns student activists raise about their experience and the campus environment.

Professional Development Workshops

In addition to enhancing student learning, visual methods can be useful tools to reflect on social identity during professional development workshops for practitioners. For instance, when Jeff Grim was the associate director of academic initiatives and university partnerships in residence life and student housing at Southern Methodist University, he led a professional development workshop for entry-level and midlevel professionals in residence life exploring their personal and professional multiple social identities (J. Grim, personal communication, February 27, 2017). Using the Jones and McEwen (2000) model of multiple dimensions of identity (MMDI), residence life staff were asked to reflect on their own personal and professional identities. The visual representation of the model is shaped like an atom with personal attributes, characteristics, and identity at the core. Surrounding the core are the different social identities that a person holds. Social identities that are more salient to an individual are closer to a person's core than ones that are not. Then, individual understandings of self are embedded within larger sociocultural contexts, family background, and experiences. The model prompts reflection as individuals visually map their own multiple identities.

Although mapping personal and professional identities has the potential of furthering a false dichotomy, these boundaries are often discussed with residential life professionals because of the nature of live-in positions. After participants filled out each of their models, they were asked to reflect on similarities and differences. Grim shared,

> As a manager in the department, I wanted to help entry-level staff reflect on their experience, while providing managers and staff members with more prevalent social identities a glimpse at the type of masking, passing, and code-switching staff members with marginalized identities at work had to do in order to be successful. (personal communication, February 27, 2017)

Moreover, the activity provided a medium for entry-level staff and those with marginalized identities to not only share with others experiences often not discussed but also alert privileged staff to their unique experiences. The process of residence life staff mapping their own multiple identities visually prompted self-reflection on their own identities and how that informs their own praxis. The more practitioners do this self-work, the more they can guide students in reflection and analysis using visual methods.

Assessment of Campus Climate

With increasing pressure for educators to provide evidence related to student learning and outcomes, visual methods might be able to provide new approaches to data-informed decision-making. For instance, in a study about the experiences of lesbian, gay, bisexual, transgender, and queer (LGBTQ) students, I asked students to take photographs that represented the concepts of support/lack of support, inclusion/exclusion, and safe/unsafe. There was some consensus on spaces on campus that were unsafe and exclusive (i.e.,

Greek Life) and supportive and inclusive (i.e., the LGBTQ student center). However, other spaces such as classrooms; interactions with faculty, staff, and administration; and residence life were more complicated and nuanced (Kortegast, 2017). Asking students to represent particular constructs through photographs provided another way to explore student perceptions and experiences regarding the campus environment and sense of belonging.

Similarly, adding a "heat map" to campus climate surveys could provide a visual of places on campus where students feel they belong or do not. For instance, Michigan State University utilized heat mapping as part of a campus climate survey (see Brown, 2016, for full details and example of the heat map). Utilizing the survey software Qualtrics (2017), a campus map was included on the survey instrument (the Qualtrics website has detailed information on how to add heat maps to surveys; www.qualtrics.com). Students were asked to select five buildings where they felt a sense of belonging and five in which they did not feel a sense of belonging. Students were also able to add comments on why they chose the buildings. Using the data from student responses, places on campus where students did not feel they belonged were lit up in red. Places where students found belonging were lit up in green on the campus map. On the Michigan State University heat map, the library was lit up as a place of belonging whereas the administrative building lit up as a place of not belonging. Moreover, there were other spaces that lit up as both places of belonging and not belonging, such as the football stadium.

Whereas the Michigan State University survey used an online survey platform, Kris Renn, professor of higher, adult, and lifelong education, shared that there are other "low-tech ways" to create a heat map (personal communication, February 21, 2017). For instance, place a large map of the campus in the student center with sticky notes for students to identify places on campus they did and did not feel they belonged. Extending on this idea, campuses could then use these maps during focus groups with students to gain more information about the campus climate, but more so, how to make the campus more inclusive and welcoming.

Framework for Assessing Campus Artifacts

The previous sections discussed the use of visuals to enhance student learning and examples of the use of visuals in practice, while this section provides a framework for assessing campus artifacts. Although there are many different approaches to visual analysis, Banning, Middleton, and Deniston's (2008) framework for assessing the equity climate is a useful model for practitioners.

The framework for assessing the equity climate provides a systematic approach to analyzing campus artifacts. The framework identifies four primary types of artifacts (art, signs, graffiti, and architecture) for analysis as they relate to the equity parameters (e.g., gender, race, ethnicity, religion, sexual orientation, ability), the equity approach (negative, null, contribution/additive, transformational/social action), and content of message (e.g., belonging, safety, equality, roles). As Banning and colleagues (2008) stated, "physical artifacts of our educational settings are powerful nonverbal communicators of equity values" (p. 46).

The following is an example of how to use the framework for assessing the equity climate. During fall 2014, across the Northern Illinois University (NIU) campus, large banners were hung on various buildings including the library (Figures 10.3 and 10.4). These banners featured different students

Figure 10.3. Student career success banner featuring a White woman with a violin on the Northern Illinois University campus library.

Figure 10.4. Student career success banner featuring a Black man in a white lab coat conducting an experiment on the Northern Illinois University campus library.

with the tag line "student career success starts here" and the NIU logo. The banners reinforced university-wide initiatives to enhance the university's focus on student career development.

Using the framework, the type of artifact being analyzed is a sign. However, depending on the viewer, these artifacts could also be considered art because they are posters. The images on the posters are of a White woman playing the violin and a Black man wearing a lab coat conducting an experiment. Without knowing for sure how the students identify, presumably, the equity parameters being displayed include gender, race, and ethnicity. The content of the message relates to portraying belonging, equality, and roles. The textual message being communicated is that student career success is a priority of the university. Images of different students engaged in various educational activities (playing the violin, in the lab) reinforce the textual message regarding career development. Given that nearly 40% of students at NIU identify as students of color, visual representation of racial diversity in a wide range of careers (i.e., roles) projects a message of belonging and inclusion. The equity approach for these images is contribution/additive as they are positive and "support equity" (Banning et al., 2008, p. 45). However, they do not necessarily challenge mainstream and/or dominant culture (Banning et al., 2008).

It should be noted that analysis of visual methods and artifacts is often subject to the interpretation of the viewer. Images are not neutral but rather communications of ideas, information, values, and culture. Using the same images in Figures 10.2 and 10.3, a critical interpretation of the visual and textual messages supports concerns regarding the commodification of higher education and neoliberalism. The focus on career success might also raise challenges to the role of higher education as a public good and the value of a liberal arts education. Thus, although these images support a conclusion of being contributive on the equity approach as it relates to race and gender, the overall impression could also be negative as it relates to core values in a liberal arts education. Ultimately, this model can provide a useful framework for higher education practitioners to assess campus artifacts through an equity lens.

Conclusion

This chapter served to introduce how practitioners can use visual methods in workshops, trainings, and assessment practices. Moreover, this chapter discussed how visual methods can provide opportunities for students to make sense and meaning of their out-of-classroom experiences. Finally, this chapter shared different ways visual methods can be used in assessment of the campus environment. The subsequent chapters in part three provide additional information and examples of how practitioners can include visual methods in their work with students.

In closing, I share a story from one of my former master's students, Melanie (pseudonym). At the time, Melanie was interning at a local college in the new student and orientation office. During her internship, she was able to help plan, facilitate, and attend the orientation student leader retreat. In addition to sessions discussing policies, procedures, and other responsibilities of orientation leaders, there were also several activities that focused on getting to know each other and what it means to be an inclusive campus community. One of these activities included students painting self-portraits of themselves. This was an opportunity to discuss topics related to diversity, community, and inclusion. One student, Daryl (pseudonym), was blind. Melanie shared that at first she was nervous about having Daryl participate in the activity. She even second guessed if they should even do the activity fearing that Daryl would not be fully included in it. Daryl painted his own canvas with a peer assisting him with identifying the different paint colors. Daryl wrote his name and the phrase "vision does not equal sight."

I share this story for several reasons. First, the act of creating a visual of self provided a venue for students to be able to share their own stories and to learn from other students' stories. Second, we need to be thoughtful about being inclusive in our practices, but at the same time not put limits on people's potential. Third, it is a reminder that vision and imagery expand beyond what can be seen.

References

Banning, J. H., Middleton, V., & Deniston, T. L. (2008). Using photographs to assess equity climate: A taxonomy. *Multicultural Perspectives, 10*(1), 41–46.

Benmayor, R. (2008). Digital storytelling as a signature pedagogy for the new humanities. *Arts and Humanities in Higher Education, 7*(2), 188–204.

Brown, S. (2016, October 23). "Heat maps" give Michigan State a new view of campus climate. *The Chronicle of Higher Education*. Retrieved from http://www.chronicle.com/article/Heat-Maps-Give-Michigan/238112

Dear World. (2017). *Dear World 2017 college tour*. Retrieved from http://projects.dearworld.me/

Elkins, J. (2007). *Visual literacy*. New York, NY: Routledge.

Felten, P. (2008). Visual literacy. *Change, 40*(6), 60–64. doi:10.3200/CHNG.40.6.60-64

GLSEN. (2016). #MyAllies selfie sign: Full color. Retrieved from https://www.glsen.org/sites/default/files/MyAlliesColor.pdf

Honary, N. (2011, September 16). *My vlog entry2_los primeros 12 días* [Video files]. Retrieved from https://vimeo.com/album/1681575/video/29148883

Honary, N. (2012, February 20). *My vlog entry 7_a preview on the year long perspective* [Video files]. Retrieved from https://www.youtube.com/watch?v=EN2wIMOk-Po&list=PL9F87A7CA6F635749&index=7&t=197s

I, Too, Am Harvard. (2014, March 1). #itooamharvard. "Can you read" [Photograph]. Retrieved from http://itooamharvard.tumblr.com/image/78255116303

Jewitt, C., Kress, G., Ogborn, J., & Tsatsarelis, C. (2001). Exploring learning through visual, actional and linguistic communication: The multimodal environment of a science classroom. *Educational Review, 53*(1), 5–18. doi: 10.1080/00131910123753

Jones, S. R., & McEwen, M. K. (2000). A conceptual model of multiple dimensions of identity. *Journal of College Student Development, 41*(4), 405–414.

Kim, K. (2013, December). Racial microaggressions [Blog site]. Retrieved from http://nortonism.tumblr.com/

King, J. R., & O'Brien, D. G. (2002). Adolescents' multiliteracies and their teachers' needs to know: Toward a digital détente. In D. E. Alverman (Ed.), *Adolescents and literacies in a digital world* (pp. 40–50). New York, NY: Peter Lang.

Kortegast, C. A. (2017). "But it's not the space that I would need": Narrative of LGBTQ students' experiences in campus housing. *Journal of College and University Student Housing, 43*(2), 58–71.

Kortegast, C. A., & Boisfontaine, M. T. (2015). Beyond "It was good": Students' post-study abroad practices in negotiating meaning. *Journal of College Student Development, 56*(8), 812–828.

Little, D., Felten, P., & Berry, C. (2015). Looking and learning: Visual literacy across the disciplines. *New Directions for Teaching and Learning, 2015*(141), 1–6. doi:10.1002/tl.20117

Miller, S. M. (2007). English teacher learning for new times: Digital video composing as multimodal literacy practice. *English Education, 40*(1), 61–83.

Qualtrics. (2017). *Heat map*. Retrieved from https://www.qualtrics.com/support/survey-platform/survey-module/editing-questions/question-types-guide/specialty-questions/heat-map/

Students Teaching About Racism in Society (STARS). (2013). *"We're a culture not a costume" campaign 2013*. Retrieved from https://www.ohio.edu/orgs/stars/Poster_Campaign.html

Wenzel, G. (2014, April 29). *Integrity: A Pecha Kucha presentation* [Video file]. Retrieved from https://www.youtube.com/watch?v=WzNqsGj64Mw

II

IMAGERY IN CIVIC REFLECTION

A Catalyst for Student Development

Elizabeth A.M. McKee

Each year at Northern Illinois University (NIU) we provide opportunities for students to participate in an alternative break trip through which they travel to other communities (both domestically and internationally) to complete service in relation to a current social justice issue. From an educational standpoint, the intended outcome of these trips is to move students along a continuum that progresses them from simply being a member of society toward active citizenship. As a staff, we proactively prepare students for the experience by providing student leaders with "teach the teacher" trainings, because the trips are predominantly student-led, to achieve this outcome. Many higher education administrators would agree that, in general, teaching students about social justice issues can be tough. This is due to students' lack of exposure and understanding of how privilege and oppression impact society, which is why pretrip training for an alternative break is important. We also found that the immersion that occurred in these trips can be especially risky when students experience disorienting dilemmas that result in the inability to competently manage their emotions and/or make mature decisions.

At NIU, our home institution, student leaders returned from trips complaining about one or two "bad apples" who had a negative impact on the trip overall. Typically, this impact occurred when students interrupted the group dynamic by making short-sighted comments about those they were serving both throughout the day and during reflection periods. For instance, students complained about how little time they had to participate in sight-seeing or made disparaging comments about the hygiene of someone they were serving, which not only showed disrespect for the community but also made their peers uncomfortable. As mentioned previously, this was due to the inequities across levels of student development related to managing emotions and cognitive and moral development among trip participants. To mitigate these inequities, we completed a review of the underlying theoretical framework of the alternative break movement (Sumka, Porter, & Piactelli, 2015) and made the decision to implement critical visual literacy and photo elicitation techniques during the pretrip education. This adjustment encouraged students to practice overcoming the disorienting dilemmas they encountered, which led to a transformative learning experience (Mezirow, 1991) that fostered student development in areas where they had room to grow. In turn, this change enabled us to limit the negative impact that students could have not only on the experience but also, more importantly, on the community in which they served.

This chapter provides a brief outline of the format and framework of alternative break programs, as well as an exploration of the theoretical framework that supports the movement. Then, a more in-depth review of the application of critical visual literacy and photo elicitation to the alternative break process is provided, as well as recommendations for educators and administrators looking to implement similar concepts in their classrooms.

Foundation of Alternative Break Programs

Alternative break opportunities at colleges and universities have grown in popularity across the United States since the turn of the century as a way for students to make a positive impact on a community they visit while on university break (Sumka, Porter, & Piactelli, 2015). This movement was started to counter the damage done to communities when the typical "spring breaker" visited to party and let loose while on vacation. To support alternative break trips, most universities work with a parent organization, which provides an outline of the appropriate structure that should be used for pre-, on-, and post-trip service experiences.

NIU collaborates with Break Away, one of these parent organizations whose goal is to move students along the active citizen continuum throughout their alternative break experience (Sumka et al., 2015). This continuum focuses on various developmental stages students experience as they engage in service and allows programs and individuals to set goals in regard to progress

Figure 11.1. The active citizen continuum.

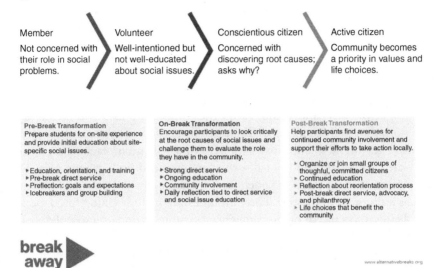

Note. The active citizen continuum is utilized to help educators plan educational experiences geared toward creating active citizens through alternative break programs.

along the continuum. According to Break Away (2017), students move along the continuum as depicted in Figure 11.1.

As outlined earlier, the goal of an alternative break is to teach students to be community-centered leaders, or active citizens. To do this, Break Away requires programs to train student leaders on how to provide the triangle of quality community service, which is a theoretically based model that utilizes education, service, and reflection to encourage student development (Sumka et al., 2015).

The triangle of quality community service model is derived from Kolb's experiential learning cycle (Sumka et al., 2015). This is important to note because this model is utilized to ensure that students create meaning of their experiences through a balance of challenge and support (Sanford, 1966). This results in a transformative learning experience, rather than simply "helping" a community and leaving. That is, this is Break Away's method of ensuring that students are provided with ample opportunity to move along the continuum as well as have a positive impact in the community.

As students cycle through this model, they experience a variety of student development growth opportunities, ranging from managing emotions to cognitive and moral development, due to the varying challenges presented to them throughout the trip. These challenges run the gamut but could include students' completing eight or more hours of hard labor, pushing themselves outside of their comfort zones, and speaking with their peers about differing perspectives. The support provided to students often occurs prior to the trip through training in regard to the triangle for quality community service.

Generally, through this pretrip training (e.g., support building) students are taught the facts and figures about the community they will be serving, the work they will complete, and some skills needed to be successful in that work. They are also informed that reflection will occur each night while they are on the trip. Additionally, they are provided with ground rules for processing through their experiences, which they practice throughout the weeks leading up to the trip. These ground rules include taking turns speaking, being respectful of others' thoughts, listening to understand rather than respond, and putting phones away.

Yet, as many student affairs professionals have experienced, when students face concepts that stretch them developmentally, they may act in a manner or use language that is insensitive to the issues of the community they are serving (Jacoby & Mutascio, 2010; Sumka et al., 2015). For example, a student might post a picture on social media of him or herself holding an orphan and caption it with verbiage that explains how his or her work is elevating an underprivileged community, which only succeeds in further stereotyping the issues the community faces and portrays them as being helpless. Others might find themselves making negative comments about community members, without understanding the members' full life experiences, which further alienates them from those they are serving. Thus, even though most students experienced some form of development throughout the trips as a result of training, we noted that the complaints we received from student leaders indicated the need for a change in the way students were prepared for the trip. Some students were getting stuck in the volunteer stage whereas others more closely aligned with the conscientious or active citizen viewpoints, and we needed to work to bridge that gap. In the end, we turned to Kolb's (1984) experiential learning cycle, the base of the program experience, to identify ways to better support and prepare students to overcome the challenges they experienced on their trips.

In previous sections, the foundation and components of an alternative break were reviewed. In the next sections, to better understand where critical literacy and photo elicitation fit into enhancing the students' experience, the components of an alternative break will be broken down to show how they relate to Kolb's cycle and identify where and how visual methods were incorporated into the program.

Theoretical Overview and Visual Method Application

There are four major components of Kolb's (1984) experiential learning cycle. The first is the concrete experience, which is simply the experience a person goes through and eventually utilizes for meaning-making. The second and third are reflective observation and abstract conceptualization, which encompass the internal and external processing that occurs as the result of an experience. The fourth is active experimentation, which happens when the person moves through the previous phases and uses the knowledge gained as a result to participate in the next concrete experience (Kolb, 1984).

This model, applied to the alternative break experience, manifests as follows: Participants engage in a service experience (concrete experience) relevant to a particular social justice issue, then reflect on their personal experiences and challenges at the end of the day (reflective observation). They then engage in abstract conceptualization as they think about their experience throughout the day, listen to others and process information during reflection periods, then make plans for how they would use that information for the next service day. Through the next day of service, they engage in active experimentation as they implement the plans they formed from the night before, and then begin the cycle again with a concrete experience, each time with more understanding and experience than the day before. Using this model, students often walk away from the overall experience with a wider worldview; however, the community may have suffered from students' original lack of understanding or engagement at the beginning of the experience, as they fought through the unexpected challenges they encountered while on the trip.

After brainstorming with colleagues about the best way to mimic this type of experience for students before they left on their trips, we were introduced to the methods behind photo elicitation and the concepts of critical visual literacy. These methods were appealing to us because images, as with any type of art form, leave room for multiple interpretations of what is presented. Additionally, with careful image selection, the prompts would provide the perfect avenue for students to encounter the "this is not what I thought it was" concept that occurs so often during an alternative break experience. The following section outlines the methods we used and includes specific examples of how we used images to reach our goals.

Outline of Photo Elicitation Approach

Photo elicitation is a visual method that leverages photographs in the interview process to gain information about participants' experiences and perspectives. This method often provides information about individual experiences that might not have been gained from prepared questions alone (Harper, 2002). We took this visual method approach and applied it to the alternative break experience to create a simulated concrete experience akin to that in Kolb's (1984) cycle. To ensure the creation of a disorienting dilemma during this experience, we provided students with a picture that initially appeared to be connected to a specific social justice issue or societal stereotype (e.g., homelessness) but could actually challenge the conventional stereotype through information provided to the students after their first reaction was given.

In the exercise, we guided students through an initial reflection that focused on what the students saw in the picture and what they thought their interpretation represented. Then, we provided students with more information or asked guided questions about the picture with the intention of challenging the students' preconceived notions. This exercise mimicked the on-trip experience of finding that reality did not meet expectations and served as the disorienting dilemma that would lead to transformative learning (Mezirow, 1991). It also allowed us to understand where students were developmentally, as they analyzed the picture.

Next, we helped students recognize the negative feelings they were experiencing, where they came from, and the outward impact of the manifestation of those feelings, as well as how to recognize those feelings while they were on the trip. To do this, we were intentional with the questions we asked and created questions and discussion points that highlighted the fact that these experiences would likely occur on the trip and that students' reactions could have a big impact on the trip's success overall.

Additionally, rather than form questions that would encourage students to argue their perspectives, we asked students about why they thought they had formed their opinions. At that point, students would begin to understand that their previous experiences were affecting their viewpoints. We then moved on to how it felt when they realized that what they learned as true or others' viewpoints conflicted with their original thought, how they might avoid making those assumptions in the future, and how they could work through their emotions while they were on the trip. This framework, put into practice, is further detailed in the following section.

Practical Application of Photo Elicitation Approach

To begin the simulated concrete experience, students were presented with a photo of a person who was homeless sleeping on a bench. There were no words or specific landmarks in the photo. To begin Kolb's (1984) reflective observation stage, students were provided with the following questions to spur the initial reflection: What do you see in this photograph? How do you think that person got to be there?

After reflecting on these two questions, students were asked to share what they wrote down. Some students expressed that they saw a person who was homeless; others thought that the person might simply be sleeping there for the night. When they began to speak about how the person got there, the conversation shifted to students' assumptions about the person's predicament. Some stated that the person likely had dropped out of school, did not have a job, and could not afford a place to stay. Others remained silent at this point due to their familiarity with homelessness (whether personally or through a close friend or family member), which sometimes came out and helped to disorient other students.

After they were given time to share their assumptions about the photograph, the students were informed that the photograph was of a current student on their campus who worked 20 hours each week but could not afford a place to stay because most of the student's money was sent to the student's family. This information challenged some students' assumptions about why people were homeless (e.g., the person was lazy, uneducated, did not have a job).

Students were then asked to reflect on the following four questions:

1. Why do you think we waited to share this information with you?
   1a. What made you assume this person was uneducated?
2. Please write down the emotions/feelings you felt when you found out the additional information provided by staff.
3. Please share one of those emotions and why you think you felt that way.
4. How did those feelings impact the way you spoke or wanted to speak about the subject?

After the first question some students expressed that they were unsure why we did not share context information with them about the subject of the photograph. Other students figured it was because we were trying to get students to identify their assumptions about homelessness. When the students were unable to answer the question, we would follow up with the subquestion (1a), and students typically began to understand the intent behind the question. In question 2, students were prompted to identify all of the emotions they felt. We would ask them to choose one to share with the group. In sharing how they felt, we tried to provide a forum for students to reflect on their feelings and their perceptions about homelessness. Most participants felt safe saying that they were surprised by the additional information due to the negative perception of homelessness that has been depicted in the media. Students were also asked to write down their answer to the last question in this set, which forced them to recognize the other feelings they listed, whether or not they chose to share those feeling within the group.

The following final set of questions was designed to begin preparing students for the active experimentation phase of Kolb's (1984) cycle:

1. What impact could these assumptions and feelings have on your experience when participating in an alternative break?
2. How can you avoid making assumptions like this in the future?
3. What are three takeaways that you have from this conversation?

Using the "surprised" emotion as their reference point for answering the questions immediately preceding, students would express that they might enter into an interaction with someone assuming that they knew how that person got to where he or she was. Through this reflection, students started to realize that they should avoid making assumptions and ask questions of the person directly. This discussion also allowed us to affirm that it was okay for students to talk to people about their lives, but it needed to be done with sensitivity and thoughtfulness. Students also discussed trying to recognize assumptions they might have about a community before they entered into an interaction, as well as the feelings that might warn them of the fact that they had encountered a situation that was challenging them.

With the last question (3), students were asked to write down their answers and were encouraged to share one takeaway with the group. After students shared their takeaways, we summarized the intention of the exercise by reminding students that everyone comes to an experience with preconceived notions that help them to process and make judgments about that experience. We also noted that it is important, especially when working with social justice issues, to evaluate those assumptions and their impact on either perpetuating or stopping stereotypes pertaining to that issue. Additionally, we reminded students that although it can be painful to realize that our assumptions are wrong, it is important to process those feelings in a mature manner in order to ensure that the experience is positive for both the participants and the community in which they are immersed.

At the end of the exercise, and upon reviewing the students' written reflection answers, we worked to facilitate discussions with students so they could begin to recognize their preconceived notions. Moreover, we discussed the importance of suspending judgment and interrogating bias. As expected and evidenced through the final reflections, this photo elicitation activity was the beginning of a process; thus, we facilitated the activity multiple times to provide several opportunities for students to reflect on their own assumptions and beliefs. We found that over time, students began to recognize their own assumptions and biases regarding topics related to the service they would be participating in during an alternative break.

Outline of Critical Visual Literacy Approach

In order to avoid too much repetition, we practiced overcoming disorienting dilemmas through the enhancement of students' critical visual literacy skills as well. Within the critical visual literacy technique, participants are asked to analyze an image and critique the implications of the choices the artist made in regard to what they chose to depict from a sociological viewpoint (Newfield, 2011). In our application of this approach, similar to that used in photo elicitation, we provided students with a photo and asked questions to encourage reflection regarding what they thought was being portrayed by the photographer. The students were then introduced to a new concept pertaining to the photograph, which induced the disorienting dilemma necessary to spark a perspective shift. After being introduced to this new information, students were asked why they thought the photographer made the choices he or she did, how people on other trips might make the same decisions, and what the impact of those decisions could be for the community. They would then discuss how learning about the new ideas made them feel, because the ideas challenged the students' original notions of what was portrayed. Finally, students were asked to explore their feelings, the impact they might have on the community they were serving, and how to navigate those feelings while on the trip. This concept, put into practice, is outlined in the next section.

Practical Application of Critical Visual Literacy Approach

For this exercise, a picture was chosen from a satirical social media account called Barbie Savior, which depicted farcical images of volunteers "doing good" in the community they were serving. These images also included satirical commentary that alluded to the issues we wanted to address regarding the intent of the image and its contents. The idea behind the account and the pictures posted was to point out that, often, the photographs people choose to take, what people say about those photographs, and the kinds of work they do can be harmful to the community they wish to serve.

In this example, students were first told that the social media account belonged to a Barbie who was documenting her service trip in Africa. Then, the students were provided with a picture from the website (Figure 11.2)

Figure 11.2. "Orphans take the best pictures. So. Cute."

Note. This photograph is an example of an image used to frame guided questions in critical visual literacy skill development exercises. Reprinted with permission.

which showed a White Barbie holding an orphaned African infant from the community in which she had been working. The students were asked the following questions about the picture (Figure 11.2) to engage in content reflection.

1. What do you see here?
2. What do you think the photographer was trying to depict?

Students identified that the volunteer and the infant looked happy to take the picture together. They also shared that photographs were a good way for them to document the trip and remember the feelings that they had serving others. After this initial discussion occurred, we introduced the idea that some communities were not as willing to accept outside volunteers due to the fact that the volunteers saw themselves as saviors and were looking more for personal gain and affirmation than to help the community (Sumka et al., 2015).

Next, we shared the following satirical commentary that accompanied the picture:

Orphans take the BEST pictures! So. Cute. #whatsyournameagain #orphans #wheredemorphansat #kingdomcome #blackbabiesarethecutest #strangers2secondsago #attachmentproblemsarentcute #notazoo. (Barbie Savior, 2016)

This is the point at which most students became disoriented because they had been under the impression that their service would be greatly appreciated by the community that they served. Through the commentary, students also picked up on the idea that the pictures further perpetuated the stereotypes associated with the social justice issue they were serving, rather than bringing awareness to or fighting against it. After the introduction of this new information, the following questions were asked:

1. How did you feel when you realized that the community might be skeptical about your arrival and view you as attempting to be a savior?
2. How might these feelings impact your experience?
3. How can you navigate these strong feelings if you experience them on your trip?

Students were asked to write down their reaction to the first question, and then were asked to share as they felt comfortable. Students, as they often did throughout these exercises, expressed surprise, but other emotions similar to resentment were also reported by students who were able to admit that they might not feel as committed to their work if they did not feel appreciated. This conversation allowed the group to discuss the core purpose of the work of alternative breaks, which is to serve a community, rather than to receive gratification from the work completed as a result of the trip. This discussion also led to the development of strategies through which trip members could graciously point out if another participant was approaching a task from a self-gratification standpoint or a community-centered service standpoint.

Two other questions were asked to help students better understand that photos could be taken, but that they should carefully consider the implications of their photos in order to ensure that they did more good than harm in the community.

1. What would the impact of pictures like this be on your trip?
2. How can you avoid doing this within the community you work?

Through the conversation sparked by these questions, students identified that they would need to work to tell the full story of the community through photographs rather than simply taking pictures of "cute" kids or anything they found particularly intriguing. This helped them to make deeper meaning of the experience as they found viable solutions to the disorienting dilemma they had encountered. As with the previous exercise, we reviewed the written reflections to gain a sense of where students fell on the active citizen continuum, which allowed us to identify opportunities and exercises for further development or reflection.

Recommendations

Visual methods, as demonstrated previously, have the potential to enhance student learning. However, when making the decision to implement visual methods, educators must be diligent in the measures they take before doing so. From the amount of time allotted or the rules set for discussion, to the groundwork laid from both a theoretical and social justice standpoint, one must not simply *decide* to integrate visual methods without first understanding how the methods will achieve one's programmatic or educational goals.

When making these considerations, educators must study the educational theory and practical approaches that undergird their chosen visual method(s). This will prepare them to identify the most appropriate method through which they will be able give new life to old exercises. This includes, but is not limited to, introducing students to the concepts of privilege and oppression in conjunction with and/or prior to implementing a visual method so that students have access to the tools needed to engage in conversations sparked by the images. To this end, visual methods should be incorporated with the learning outcome in mind, rather than with the thought of simply making a class more relevant in terms of pop culture. Educators can fall into the trap of trying to freshen up their classroom or exercises by including online videos and images that are popular but may not be successful in achieving the learning outcome. There is merit to using visuals to make a class more interesting, but these visuals should be utilized primarily to achieve program goals.

Educators must also thoroughly examine the visuals chosen for each exercise to ensure, to the best of their ability, that the visual will have the impact intended. They must also be prepared to facilitate the conversation that ensues as a result of exposure to the visuals. This was especially apropos for us because we were working with populations that struggled to manage emotions or had little exposure to disorienting dilemmas. For example, images that depict extreme situations may lead students to focus on the emotions invoked by their initial response, rather than dive deeply into the impact of the photographer's decision to depict such a graphic image. At the same time, educators must be trained in how to properly facilitate discussion in which students' emotions have the potential to spiral out of control due to those strong emotional reactions. For instance, it was always important for us to build group trust by starting with an exercise in which students identified a common set of ground rules related to respect and sharing within the group. In the exercises mentioned in this chapter, we were successful only because students felt safe expressing opposing worldviews. Thus, it is recommended that educators study group facilitation techniques in order to be prepared to mitigate any concerns students might have about sharing within a group.

Conclusion

Student concerns prompted us to review our program structure and enabled us to determine that although we were seeing student growth, our program had potential to be more successful in promoting active citizenship. To do this, we identified that students needed more practice with the skills necessary to overcome the challenges they faced. Thus, we delved into the theoretical foundation of our program and identified that we could strengthen the entire experience through visual methods. In this endeavor, we incorporated photo elicitation and critical visual literacy approaches to foster the development of skills that would enable students to better manage their emotions and make more mature decisions while on site. In terms of active citizenship, we have truly seen our program grow as students who started our program as participants evolved into advocates for social justice on our campus and in the community. Furthermore, those participants became the well-educated site leaders of the next generation of alternative breakers at NIU. Our current student leaders are much more prepared for challenge and have set the tone by letting other students know that alternative breaks are not about having an excuse to *see* more of the world. Rather, they are meant to provide students with an avenue through which they can *change* the world.

References

Barbie Savior. (2016). Orphans take the best pictures! So. Cute. [Photograph]. Retrieved from https://www.instagram.com/p/BDivxtLsfX8/?taken-by=barbiesavior

Break Away. (2017). Active citizen continuum. Retrieved from www.alternativebreaks .org/about

Harper, D. (2002). Talking about pictures: A case for photo elicitation. *Visual Studies, 17*(1), 13–26.

Jacoby, B., & Mutascio, P. (2010). *Looking in: Reaching out.* Boston, MA: Campus Compact.

Kolb, D. A. (1984). *Experiential learning: Experience as the source of learning and development.* Englewood Cliffs, NJ: Prentice Hall.

Mezirow, J. (1991). *Transformative dimensions of adult learning.* San Francisco, CA: Jossey-Bass.

Newfield, D. (2011). From visual literacy to critical visual literacy: An analysis of educational materials. *English Teaching: Practice and Critique, 10*(1), 81–94.

Sanford, N. (1966). *Self and society: Social change and individual development.* New York, NY: Atherton.

Sumka, S., Porter, M. C., & Piactelli, J. (2015). *Working side by side: Creating alternative breaks as catalysts for global learning, student leadership, and social change.* Sterling, VA: Stylus.

12

USING VISUAL METHODS TO EXPLORE STUDENT AFFAIRS PRACTITIONERS' EXPERIENCES

Jillian A. Martin

During the second year of my student affairs masters' program, I met with a professor to discuss a class project on career development. The project required developing a metaphor for my career development and creatively presenting this metaphor to the class using visual aids. While in graduate school, many of my professors designed similar assignments to encourage novel approaches to academic material. I often felt incompetent when asked to think abstractly and then creatively express my thoughts in some tangible form. I shared these concerns with the faculty member during our conversation, and she offered some suggestions for the project. She shared how she created the project to elicit a holistic understanding of career development for student affairs. Instead of just focusing on student affairs, for example, she encouraged me to reflect on how I first started thinking about "what I wanted to be when I grew up," how it got me to my current work as a graduate student, and where I saw myself in the future of the profession. When I shared my story, she asked me to think about some of the high points of each of those positions and how they connected with my vision for my work in student affairs. Through that conversation, we brainstormed a few concepts that captured those concepts.

Centering on the idea of love, I decided to use the human heart as the representation for my career development. I saw the heart as the place from which all of my passions and interests flow, so I decided that a visual of the human heart and its functions served as the perfect metaphor for the class project. I represented blood flow as my experiences, the ventricles as the mechanism through which those experiences flowed, and the aorta as the strong connection to my undergraduate experiences. By using visual methods for this class project, I embraced my career development philosophy centered on passion, love, culture, and stories. In addition, I discovered a new passion to inform my reflexive student affairs practice: visual methods.

One of the intermediate outcomes for student affairs practitioners' personal and ethical foundations competency is the ability to "analyze personal experiences for potential deeper learning and growth, and engage with others in reflective discussions" (American College Personnel Association & National Association of Student Personnel Administrators [ACPA & NASPA], 2015, p. 17). For continued professional growth, student affairs practitioners should engage in opportunities that allow them to analyze, reflect, and discuss their perspectives and experiences. As discussed throughout this book, visual methods provide many benefits for student development, engagement, and learning in higher education. These methods are also useful in exploring how student affairs practitioners reflect on their experiences as practitioners. In this chapter, I explore the use of visuals in two qualitative research projects titled "Scholarship in Student Affairs Practice" (SIP) and "Exploring Student Affairs Socialization" (ES). Each of these studies incorporated visuals as elicitation tools for individual and group interviews about student affairs practice (Pauwels, 2011). In this chapter, I provide an overview of the visual research methods used for both studies, examples of the visuals submitted by the participants, and an explanation of how these visuals guided discussions about student affairs practice. I conclude with a discussion of the implications of visual methods as a useful tool for promoting reflective student affairs practice.

Overview of Scholarship in Student Affairs Practice and Exploring Student Affairs Socialization Studies

The SIP study was a qualitative research team project conducted at the University of Georgia. We used photo elicitation and narrative interviews to explore how new student affairs practitioners engaged scholarship in their practice. *Scholarship in practice* was defined in this study as how practitioners engaged scholarship (research studies, theories, evidence-based practices) within their respective on-campus roles (Jones, Martin, & Linder, 2016). In conjunction with a narrative qualitative methodology, we used photo elicitation interviews as a method to more actively engage the participants "to enhance their active role in the research project" (Meo, 2010, p. 152). The inclusion of visual methods with qualitative narrative interviews enhanced our understanding of the multiplicity and complexity of how student affairs practitioners engaged with scholarship in practice.

We recruited 13 participants for this study who identified as new student affairs practitioners (within 5 years of their master's graduation). We conducted individual and group interviews with the participants. Prior to their participation in the study, participants shared demographic information, their definition of *theory to practice*, and supplied photos that represented their use of scholarship in practice. We instructed the study participants as follows:

> Take pictures of events, activities, or things that represent theory to practice to you. You may use your own camera phone, digital camera, or check out a digital camera on the campus on which you work to participate in this study. This may take up to an hour of time over the course of a month. Submit these pictures electronically to the research team to consolidate for a focus group with other participants in this study.

In addition to the photo, participants also submitted a photo description and how the photo represented scholarship in practice (Figure 12.1). We compiled the photos submitted by the participants and, during the interviews, each participant discussed his or her photo and its relevance to the study. We used those photos as the foundation of additional questions about how participants conceptualized and incorporated scholarship in practice.

The ES study was a publishable paper I designed and implemented during my first two years as a doctoral student. In this study, I explored how six new student affairs practitioners conceptualized their professional socialization experience (Martin, 2015). Originally, I designed the study to be a phenomenological exploration of practitioner socialization using interviews as the primary data collection method. However, after working with the SIP study and engaging with the richness of the conversations as a result of using a visual method, I wanted to incorporate a similar method to engage participants. Instead of using photo elicitation, however, I wanted to include—similar to the creative career development project I did in graduate school—aspects of participants' creative individuality in the study. In discussion with my doctoral adviser, we decided to have the participants develop a creative conceptualization of their socialization experience. A *creative conceptualization* was defined as an original, tangible object created by participants that represented how the participants interpreted their socialization experiences.

Figure 12.1. SIP study example photo.

Note. This SIP photo was submitted by Avery (a participant) with the following description: "My use of theory to practice is just like the river. . . . It naturally flows most of the time, [but] there are seasons where it is slower or stops altogether while there are other moments where I can flood a program with theory and drown out learning for the sake of a theory."

Similar to the SIP study, the ES study included 6 new student affairs practitioners with 1 to 5 years of full-time experience in student affairs. The participants engaged in two 60- to 90-minute interviews for this project, and either selected or were assigned a pseudonym. During the first interview, I asked participants about their entry into the field of student affairs, their graduate school experiences, their transition into their new role, and their definition of *socialization*. At the end of the interview, I asked the participants to prepare a representation of their socialization experiences in student affairs or a creative conceptualization using the following prompt:

> For our follow-up interview, I would like you to use the definition of *socialization* you provided to creatively represent your socialization experience in student affairs. Include any aspects—people, places, symbols, and experiences—that highlight your socialization into the field and into your institutional role(s). (Martin, 2015, p. 19)

During the second interview, I explored the creative conceptualization of each participant. The participants responded in a variety of different ways, creatively conceptualizing their socialization experiences between the two interviews. Both of these studies highlight the utility of visual method as a tool for reflective student affairs practice and professional learning.

Visual Methods for Reflective Student Affairs Practice

The use of visual methods in this study helped us understand several aspects of the participant experience. First, visual methods are a valuable tool for facilitating reflexivity. *Reflexivity* "is a reciprocal process that asks practitioners to consider the relationship between their beliefs, experiences, the environment, and others" (Ryder & Kimball, 2015, p. 34). Second, as a continuous feedback loop, practitioners' reflections on these interrelated elements should then inform an adaptation of practice (Reason & Kimball, 2012; Ryder & Kimball, 2015). Third and finally, for this study, we used a photo elicitation prompt as the impetus for participants to engage in reflexivity in relation to their use of scholarship in practice. For example, having to think about scholarship in practice and how to capture it with photos prompted Victoria, one of our participants, to reflect on this process. During her interview, she stated:

> When I had initially signed up for this [research study], I was wondering what photos [I would take]. I don't sit down every day and think, "Okay, I'm going to make sure that I'm using this theory for that." So for me, personally, I don't do that and I know some people do but then to go back through and have a moment of reflection and see that we actually do engage with it on a daily basis, just maybe not as intentionally as I always hope or plan to.

The need to translate the phenomenon of scholarship in practice to a visual medium precipitated the reflection process for Victoria. Similarly, Hannah, another participant, discussed the process of reflection on scholarship in practice precipitated by having to capture the phenomenon with photos. She decided, like many of the participants, to capture scholarship in practice in books (Figure 12.2). She outlined her thought process during her interview as follows:

> When I first heard the prompt I was like, "Well, I got to take some pictures of some books, because that is where the theory lives." That was my first, and I challenged myself to reflect upon that and I eventually took—well I actually took two—book pictures, but when I decided I was going to take book pictures I couldn't just take pictures of my text books. Because, it's not just about the textbooks for me. That is why there is a little bit of diversity in the book type there. What struck me, is that most of my pictures are not about the books. It is about the actual practice of what we are doing.

Hannah intentionally chose books that directly represented her practice in student affairs. The reflection and use of the visual method helped Hannah to modify her thoughts about the source of scholarship and its use in practice.

Figure 12.2. SIP study collage of participant's creations.

Note. This collage depicts participants' photos of books and their planning processes as visual representations of their conceptualizations and incorporations of scholarship in practice.

In the ES study, participants conceptualized and reflected on their definitions of *socialization* into the student affairs profession. Another participant, Philip, conceptualized his socialization in the field as having to "learn on the fly," a concept that was present in his undergraduate, college, and work experiences. He drew "a train speeding down the tracks" as a representation of his socialization experiences (Figure 12.3). Each of the elements of the train had a particular meaning. Philip saw himself as the conductor of the New Professional Express that proudly flew the university's flag, which represented his institution's past, present, and future. Philip described the second car behind the locomotive as "a freight car" that encompassed all of his life experiences. Philip saw his experiences in student affairs as cargo that he carried on his journey through student affairs that helped inform and guide his student affairs practice. He further described being the conductor but not being sure

Figure 12.3. Philip's socialization train.

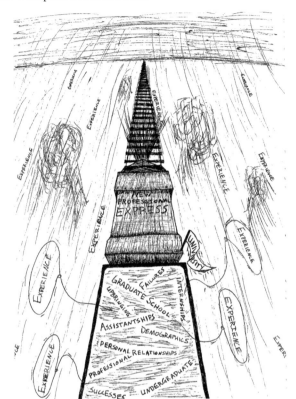

Note. This is an original drawing done by study participant Philip that describes his socialization experience in student affairs. He depicted his socialization as the "Professional Express" with his experiences, relationships, demographics, success, and failures as part of the cabooses on the train.

where he was going in student affairs. This was further illustrated by Philip's following description of the train tracks, which was what he called "the most important thing" for him.

> If there is a horizon and the train tracks show that it's going to the horizon, but . . . at this point in my new professional career [and] at this point in my position, I'm not exactly sure where those tracks are going to lead. I don't know if there's going to be a left turn up ahead. I don't know if there's going to be a right turn or if I'm just going to kind of stay this course. But you know, I think the overall message that I've tried to get across: I'm the one that's conducting this train. I'm moving forward. And . . . I'm going to work, I'm going to give everything my all in this current position so that I can do the best that I can and sort of work like there's no tomorrow.

Although unsure about his destination, Philip's sense of agency of his experience was clear. As his career continued, Philip discussed the importance of slowing down and taking perspective to be more mindful of his career direction. At the end of the second interview, Philip remarked how he appreciated the time to reflect on his student affairs career and trajectory provided by the research project:

> Our first conversation was great, and then the talk between that, then and now . . . I've thought . . . and reflected . . . and I guess I've reflected more in this last month between the interviews than I probably would have. So thank you for helping me do that.

By using this visual method, Philip reflected on his experiences and thought about his trajectory in the field of student affairs. This reflective practice is critical for how student affairs practitioners are mindful of how their own experiences influence their work within the university community.

This awareness was also key for how Nefertiti discussed her socialization experience. Nefertiti represented her socialization as a shield, depicted in Figure 12.4 as a photograph:

> The whole thing is holistically a shield because I do a lot of work with students' [values], so we create a coat of armor. A lot of times a coat of armor is seen as a shield, so I think a large part of what I've been doing culturally and as a new professional is shielding myself from things that I would be asked to do that accounted to my value while I continue to build on my

Figure 12.4. The shield of Nefertiti.

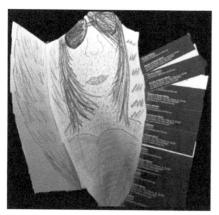

Note. This is a photographic rendering of a decoupage shield or coat of arms, front (left image) and back (right image). Each element of the shield represents some aspect of Nefertiti's personal values (left image) and her professional values (right image).

value. So when things come up that I haven't dealt with before my coat of armor becomes more of a shield until I'm able to kind of figure out what my values are and [effectuate] to that issue or ideology and then once I know that, I add it to my coat of armor and I'm able to make decisions based on my value structure.

Similar to Philip, Nefertiti depicted additional metaphors on the shield. The person depicted on the shield is Nefertiti and represented who she shows to the world as a person who is "hip and cool," as well as professional. The tiny dots on her skin represented the following:

All of those people along the way or all of those lessons along the way that have really kind of helped to compose the kind of person I am. So you can't really see it on me, on the inside. . . . So I made that a physical representation of my students, the professionals above me and the professionals representing levels, my grad school cohorts and all those little dots kind of represent those lessons on the skin. Those are things that have constantly been with me. Whether I like it or not they will affect me personally later on.

She also discussed her experiences as having made impressions on and sticking with her, even though they are not always visible. Her affinity for service and leadership was represented on the left as a wing "to swoop in and help whenever [people] need it."

On the other side of the shield, which Nefertiti described as "more of the professional," she depicted a tree with a flourishing side and a barren side. The flourishing side represented times when she is empowering herself, whereas the barren times represented the times when she did not feel empowered and needed to recharge. The outline of the shield was of her business cards that are visible on both sides of the shield because she viewed her student affairs role as dually representing her personally and professionally. The lines between the business cards and the inside of the shield represented "energy" for Nefertiti:

Those . . . kind of electric things are like these shaky lines that go back and forth to my business cards because sometimes I feel like I seem the same, and sometimes I'm not being the same professionally as I am personally. But that's how people are going to identify me so that's why those lines are a little bit rocky because I'm still trying to figure out where I am in that.

Nefertiti's depiction of her socialization experience in this way symbolized the tenuous nature of navigating personal, professional, and institutional values. Further, she had not reached full resolution on her socialization but saw it rather as a dynamic process that she would continue going through when faced with value-based decisions at work. In addition to participating in the study, Nefertiti was also part of the national student affairs conference presentation of this research, where she discussed how the opportunity to reflect and clarify her values using visual methods helped to jump-start the next phase of her career journey.

Visual Methods as Symbolic of Lived Experience

In addition to reflexivity, participants also used visual media as symbols of their lived experience as student affairs practitioners. In the SIP study, participants took photos of their writings, drawings, and visualizations that depicted their processes of incorporating scholarship into practice (Figure 12.2). These photos represented participants planning and developing programs, services, and initiatives. The interview site became another site of reflection for the participants as they viewed, described, and discussed each other's photos. Cody remarked on a photo from another participant that resonated with him as it relates to engaging others in scholarship:

> I think that that photo—it's the picture of the notebook paper that Avery talked about and I think that you mentioned that making theory accessible to people . . . and people that maybe are using it more tacitly, I think that that really resonated with me because it is kind of that constant battle . . . . It's still guiding your work but I think that there are some people that are immediately kind of turned off and switch off if you hear, "Well, he's just talking about theory, there he goes." So I think it really is—when you said that, that really resonated with me like, okay, that makes a lot of sense.

Here, Cody was referring to Avery's photo of a brainstorming session with colleagues on how to use critical pedagogy for practitioners engaging in identity-based work. The visual representation and Avery's discussion of the photo resonated with Cody and his own experiences with how others may perceive scholarship as part of student affairs practice. The visual method underscored the communal experience of sharing and learning inherent in the foundation of the student affairs professions in the first gatherings of deans of men and women, the professional associations of the present, and graduate preparation programs that use the cohort educational model (Gerda, 2006; Kuk & Cuyjet, 2009).

Nefertiti's shield from the ES study represented not only her socialization into student affairs but also her lived experience of being "the only Black person" in her department:

> Being the only Black person in my department. . . . That is something I deal with every day. But is it on my professional role? No. So I don't know

if . . . I haven't challenged anybody but I don't know if people understand what that means for someone in that position and having students come up to you and say why aren't you doing the BSU [Black student union] presentation? Well, I'm not everything Black, I can deal with that. You just deal with it too.

Nefertiti's shield also represented her socialization as a Black woman in student affairs and having to accomplish her job duties in addition to being expected to support Black students on the campus even though that is not directly related to her job role. For her, socialization into student affairs was about the assertion and negotiation of values between the personal and the professional. This negotiation is represented by a shield that dually reflects the integration of her personal and professional values.

Participant Affinity for Visual Methods

Finally, the use of visual methods highlighted participants' affinity for using visual mediums in their own professional learning process. For example, Philip's decision to draw his conceptualization was due to him being "very right brained" and being a visual thinker (he earned an art minor as an undergraduate student). Accordingly, Philip knew immediately that he would depict his socialization experiences in the form of a drawing. In contrast, Nefertiti initially struggled with her creative conceptualization, but the project prompted her to reflect and consider what elements of her socialization were salient for her as a new student affairs practitioner. The reflexivity by both participants demonstrates how critical visual methods can be in helping student affairs practitioners to clarify their values and experiences. Similarly, participants in the SIP study used visual mediums to devise their conceptualizations of scholarship. Figure 12.2 depicts whiteboards, drawings, jottings, and other visual means in students' reflexive process that were captured in their study-related photos. The participants' affinity for visual mediums of reflection and organization emphasizes visual methods as a helpful tool for reflexive practice and professional learning for student affairs practitioners. Avery's epiphany when reflecting on the commonalities in the photos of all the participants highlights this aspect:

We took pictures of visuals ourselves and what that means in practice, because I think so often, at least in my program, . . . the models that stick with me are those that had visual representations or things that I picture very easily, and so I think about—I think the reason I remember Kohlberg and Gilligan so well is because I was walked through examples of them and talked about the same—and so that—so that's a very visual metaphor for me, or something like Bronfenbrenner sticks with me because it's very visual and I can latch on to that in a really powerful way.

Avery discussed how visual representation of theories "stick" more than theories without a visual representation. This stickiness created a "powerful" connection between the learner and scholarship. This is an important implication for using visual methods as part of professional learning for student affairs practitioners.

Philip's drawing, Nefertiti's shield, and the SIP study photos represent the integration of the personal, professional, and contextual elements in the socialization and professional learning experiences of new student affairs practitioners. All media used in both studies reflect the participants' analysis and reflection "for deeper learning and growth" (ACPA & NASPA, 2015, p. 17) that is necessary for demonstrating proficiency in the personal and ethical foundations competency. Similarly, the participants in the SIP study demonstrated proficiency in this competency by analyzing and capturing their conceptualizations and incorporations of scholarship in practice as well as "engag[ing] with others in reflective dialogue" (p. 17). Central to both of these studies was the use of visual methods to engage participants in reflexive practice and create moments of critical reflection where individuals could begin to formulate a feedback loop that informs their practice (Merriam & Bierema, 2014; Reason & Kimball, 2012). Visual methods, then, were essential to this process and helped to elicit depth in the participants' perspectives on student affairs socialization and use of scholarship in practice. Visual methods provided a holistic and comprehensive view of the participants' socialization experience that would have been absent if relying solely on numerical or written data. Using visual methods to help student affairs practitioners engage in reflexive practice is an important implication from both of these studies.

Implications for Practice

As stated previously, student affairs practitioners benefitted greatly from the opportunity to reflect on their practice. In addition, both studies illustrate how the practitioners clarified and articulated their personal and professional values using visual methods. Reflection is key to both socialization and use of theory in practice, as it creates a feedback loop for the practitioner's professional identity, which begins in graduate school and continues throughout the practitioner's career (Hirschy, Wilson, Liddell, Boyle, & Pasquesi, 2015; Liddell, Wilson, Pasquesi, Hirschy, & Boyle, 2014; Reason & Kimball, 2012; Wilson, Liddell, Hirschy, & Pasquesi, 2016). These feedback loops also help practitioners develop in terms of student affairs competencies by building their ability to evaluate and improve their skills (ACPA & NASPA, 2015; Reason & Kimball, 2012). To aid in this reflexivity, I offer three perspectives on how visual methods can be incorporated into student affairs practice.

Visual Methods for Student Engagement and Graduate Preparation

As stated at the beginning of this chapter, my interest in visual methods began with a faculty member's incorporation of a creative project that required a visual medium in her class curriculum. That project not only helped me reflect on my experiences but also provided me with the opportunity to engage a different learning system. As a result, I was able to think more critically and deeply about being a scholar-practitioner. So, for trainings, workshops, and classes, I include an activity or assignment that, at the very least, allows the use of a visual medium like drawing, photography, or a creative conceptualization. I design the activity or assignment for participants to reflect upon their experiences and create a tangible representation of that reflective process. For example, for a class I taught on socialization into student affairs, students submitted reflexive journal entries as part of their assignments. Although written journal entries were accepted, I also permitted students to explore other mediums of reflection conducive to their style of expression.

Onboarding, Supervision, and Professional Learning of Student Affairs Practitioners

Supervision and mentorship is critical to professional identity development (Pittman & Foubert, 2016), and supervisors can use these visual methods to engage practitioners in discussing their experiences in their new roles. This technique can be used when onboarding new employees, to help staff grasp new division and office-wide initiatives that require their buy-in, and to provide opportunities for practitioners to reflect during the annual reporting process. If the practitioners conceptualize their experiences visually, they have another medium through which to engage and articulate their professional identity, which can complement supervisor meetings and job performance evaluations. The practice of using visuals can also help the practitioner articulate his or her values and effectively build the relationship between the supervisor and practitioner.

Another implication for student affairs practitioners can be using the visual methods as part of a larger framework to create professional learning communities in student affairs. These learning communities can help facilitate camaraderie among practitioners around a central topic that uses visual methods to explore and engage student affairs practitioners within that topic. These learning communities could be held in conjunction with or modeled after faculty learning communities that are part of faculty development programs (e.g. Adams & Mix, 2014; Gordon & Foutz, 2015; Jackson, Stebleton, & Laanan, 2013; Michel, 2014; Sheehy, Bohler, Richardson, & Gallo, 2015).

Visual Methods for Individual Reflective Practice

In the two studies highlighted in this chapter, visual methods provided practitioners the opportunities to reflect on their practice for their individual professional learning. Although they were part of a study, participants discussed how the active experience of reflection created a feedback loop to help them better understand themselves as practitioners. I have included both prompts in this chapter as tools for faculty, supervisors, and student affairs practitioners to use when incorporating visual methods. Student affairs practitioners, especially, can use these prompts to demonstrate agency in their own learning and development in the field of student affairs. Although the studies in this volume focused on the experiences of new student affairs practitioners, visual methods can also be helpful for mid-level and senior-level practitioners seeking ways to engage in reflective practice.

Conclusion

One of the primary strengths of using visual methods is in eliciting a more in-depth understanding of student affairs practice through the participants' experiences. Without these visuals, participants could definitely provide responses to interview questions, but the visual methods helped practitioners to more intentionally reflect on their experiences. Further, as in the case of the SIP study, participants in the group interviews were able to view and reflect on others' photos. This element contributed to rich discussions about the limitations of scholarship and the ways in which practitioners critique and reimagine scholarship for their practice. In addition, using visual methods adds to the multiplicity of perspectives in the field of student affairs, where we have relied primarily on responses to questionnaires and interview transcriptions to guide research on student affairs practice. Finally, the use of visual methods helped participants to further clarify their perspectives and experiences as student affairs practitioners. Visual methods not only helped participants to communicate their perspectives on aspects of their socialization and professional learning processes but also provided examples of their lived experiences as student affairs practitioners.

Although there are many strengths in using visual methods, researchers may encounter some challenges as well. Primarily, participants may hesitate to engage in visual methods as part of their reflective practice, as I did as a graduate student. Participants in both studies discussed the challenge of visually developing a conceptual piece on their socialization and with taking photos that accurately depicted their use of scholarship in practice. Along with the creative conceptualizations in the ES study, participants also discussed the effort and time that went into reflection and creating the piece and/or taking photos. As a researcher, it was challenging to find an analytical method that could fully encapsulate the different conceptual pieces and photos as well as the overall themes in the study. In the analysis and final reports for both studies, I focused on general themes from the written transcripts rather than incorporating the visual mediums as part of the analysis. By analyzing each visual medium and participant description of that medium, I could have a more robust understanding of the participants' lived experiences.

Even with these challenges, student affairs leaders can become more competent in using visual methods to engage students by engaging student affairs practitioners using visual methods. Throughout this volume, there are many examples that highlight the outcomes of student engagement using visual methods. This success can extend to student affairs practitioners and can empower them to reflect on their practice, improve their practice, and impact the student experience. Further, visual methods provide a valuable tool to understand the student affairs practitioner experience and aid in retention in the field.

References

Adams, S. R., & Mix, E. K. (2014). Taking the lead in faculty development: Teacher educators changing the culture of university faculty development through collaboration. *AILACTE Journal, 11*(1), 37–56.

American College Personnel Association & National Association of Student Personnel Administrators (ACPA & NASPA). (2015). *ACPA/ NASPA professional competency areas for student affairs practitioners.* Washington, DC: Authors.

Gerda, J. J. (2006). Gathering together: A view of the earliest student affairs professional organizations. *Journal of Student Affairs Research and Practice, 43*(4), 1343–1359.

Gordon, L., & Foutz, T. (2015). Navigating the first-year program: Exploring new waters in a faculty learning community. *International Journal of Teaching & Learning in Higher Education, 27*(1), 81–93.

Hirschy, A. S., Wilson, M. E., Liddell, D. L., Boyle, K. M., & Pasquesi, K. (2015). Socialization to student affairs: Early career experiences associated with professional identity development. *Journal of College Student Development, 56*(8), 777–793.

Jackson, D. L., Stebleton, M. J., & Laanan, F. S. (2013). The experience of community college faculty involved in a learning community program. *Community College Review, 41*(1), 3–19. doi:10.1177/0091552112473145

Jones, G., Martin, J. A., & Linder, C. (2016). *Troubling theory: Examining new student affairs professionals' perspectives on using student development theory for social justice.* Manuscript submitted for publication.

Kuk, L., & Cuyjet, M. J. (2009). Graduate preparation programs: The first step in socialization. In A. Tull, J. B. Hirt, & S. A. Saunders (Eds.), *Becoming socialized in student affairs administration: A guide for new professionals and their supervisors* (pp. 89–109). Sterling, VA: Stylus.

Liddell, D. L., Wilson, M. E., Pasquesi, K., Hirschy, A. S., & Boyle, K. M. (2014). Development of professional identity through socialization in graduate school. *Journal of Student Affairs Research and Practice, 51*(1), 69–84. doi:10.1515/ jsarp-2014-0006

Martin, J. A. (2015). *Exploring socialization: Perspectives on student affairs professionals.* Unpublished manuscript, Department of Counseling and Human Development Services, University of Georgia, Athens, GA.

Meo, A. I. (2010). Picturing students' habitus: The advantages and limitations of photo-elicitation interviewing in a qualitative study in the city of Buenos Aires. *International Journal of Qualitative Methods, 9*(2), 149–171.

Merriam, S. B., & Bierema, L. L. (2014). *Adult learning: Linking theory and practice.* San Francisco, CA: Jossey-Bass.

Michel, R. M. (2014, Spring). Finding the SurPriSe: A case study of a faculty learning community. *Academic Leadership Journal in Student Research, 2.* (EJ1055329). Retrieved from http://files.eric.ed.gov/fulltext/EJ1055329.pdf

Pauwels, L. (2011). An integrated conceptual framework for visual social research. In E. Margolis & L. Pauwels (Eds.), *The Sage handbook of visual research methods* (pp. 3– 23). Los Angeles, CA: Sage.

Pittman, E. C., & Foubert, J. D. (2016). Predictors of professional identity development for student affairs professionals. *Journal of Student Affairs Research & Practice, 53*(1), 13–25. doi:10.1080/19496591.2016.1087857

Reason, R. D., & Kimball, E. W. (2012). A new theory-to-practice model for student affairs: Integrating scholarship, context, and reflection. *Journal of Student Affairs Research & Practice, 49*(4), 359–376.

Ryder, A. J., & Kimball, E. W. (2015). Assessment as reflexive practice: A grounded model for making evidence-based decisions in student affairs. *Journal of Research & Practice in Assessment, 10*(2), 30–44.

Sheehy, D. A., Bohler, H. R., Richardson, K., & Gallo, A. M. (2015). Professional learning community: Thriving while facing the challenges of faculty life together. *Transformative Dialogues: Teaching & Learning Journal, 8*(1), 1–13.

Wilson, M. E., Liddell, D. L., Hirschy, A. S., & Pasquesi, K. (2016). Professional identity, career commitment, and career entrenchment of midlevel student affairs professionals. *Journal of College Student Development, 57*(5), 557–572.

13

ART RESISTS. ART HEALS. ART IS RESILIENCE

Utilizing Creativity in Postsecondary Education

Heather C. Lou

Resisting and navigating microaggressions, bias incidents, hate crimes, and politically charged demonstrations is exhausting labor for students with multiple marginalized social identities. Moreover, they heighten chilly physical and psychological learning and living climates for students. In a U.S. context in which President Trump has attempted to "Make America Great Again" by appointing White nationalists to his cabinet and officials in the House and Senate proposed to eliminate ethnic studies, accessible health care, and protections for people who are transgender, students, faculty, and practitioners with marginalized identities have felt a heightened threat to their livelihoods due to the legislature and rhetoric that impacts their civil rights. Whether students are in the classroom, actively engaging in activism, or processing current events in practitioners' offices, they are activated by different crises, or what Bettez (2011) called "sitting in the fire" (p. 7). These interactions are challenging and require practitioners to understand their own identities as they interact with students, bipartisan political landscapes at public institutions, positionality, and boundaries around physical and emotional labor in order to sustain productive learning environments. Beyond active listening and traditional crisis response, what nontraditional tactics can student affairs practitioners utilize when these events negatively impact postsecondary education campuses? How might practitioners help cocreate identity-based counterspaces that allow students to express vulnerable emotions, ask for support, navigate our complex institutional structures, or simply process or heal from cycles of oppression?

There is not a single solution to these questions—students, faculty, and practitioners live complex and multifaceted lives navigating power, privilege, and oppression. Postsecondary education in the United States has a colonial legacy of White supremacy, which privileges White, cisgender, straight, able-bodied and able-minded men in physical and psychological environments of the academy. Practitioners at both minority-serving institutions (MSIs) and predominantly White institutions (PWIs) must acknowledge this reality within current hxstorical[1] and political contexts and find ways to utilize more inclusive critical pedagogy that allows for the increasingly diverse student populations to build, share, express, and center their narratives in educational contexts that were not made for their academic and personal success.

Visual arts methods such as poetry, performance, sculpture, painting, coloring, and drawing can allow for critical community (Bettez, 2011) development and a deeper understanding of campus climate issues that traditional dialogues or focus groups cannot provide. If students are able to own and share their narratives in ways that are authentic to their leadership and cultural communication style, they can develop critical communities and a deepened understanding of their experiences on campus. Practitioners can utilize a borderlands lens (Anzaldúa, 1987) and a critical mixed race studies (CMRS) lens (Jolivétte, 2014) to center narratives of students with subordinated, fluid, and intersecting identities. These perspectives can help practitioners and students unveil the complicated meanings of the learning environments around them in order to heal, resist, and practice resilience against White supremacist, neocolonial, and neoliberal power structures of postsecondary education.

From conceptual theory to practice, critical visual arts practice has the potential to support student identity development and facilitate difficult dialogues that ultimately enhances student belonging and mattering (Schlossberg, 1989). This chapter explores theoretical considerations and opportunities for practitioners to adapt in political and professional contexts with the following grounding assumptions: (a) everyone can be an artist and create, (b) art heals, (c) art resists, and (d) art is resilience.

Developing a Borderlands and Critical Mixed Race Perspective

As a queer, multiracial, Asian, cisgender womxn of color artist working in postsecondary education, art has become a critical practice that has helped me make meaning of my fluid social identities. I attended San José State

University for my undergraduate education and worked in the cross-cultural center at the height of California state budget cuts in the late 2000s. I recognized in my art hxstory and humanities courses that a majority of the artists and authors we studied were White men or monoracial artists of color. I noticed that administrators and legislators making decisions about my education were also people with dominant identities. Why were people who looked and identified like me absent from my educational courses and learning environments? How was I supposed to navigate education when I clearly didn't belong? How was I supposed to be a student, an employee, and a member of a community and somehow succeed when I felt like the people making decisions didn't care about my experiences or identities? Did other students with marginalized identities experience this questioning, too?

I learned quickly that writing research papers and developing petitions and campaigns only conveyed some of the issues of racism, sexism, classism, and genderism in my collegiate experiences. With the support of my supervisors at the cross-cultural center (who were the first people to challenge me to think about my own nuanced understandings of my own White privilege and minoritized multiracial experiences), I developed a community-centered visual arts campaign based on Kip Fulbeck's Hapa Project. This project empowered me and other students with fluid racial identities to take photos and share narratives via prose or other visuals about navigating monoracism and developing counternarratives and to find affinity in shared experiences. This experience has been foundational to my praxis as a current student affairs practitioner, as it allowed me to share my own narratives with peers and scholar-practitioners, challenge my internalized White supremacy, find belonging, and engage in self-care and healing during a politicized period in my collegiate experience. Since this intentional programmatic experience, I have aspired to utilize nontraditional teaching and learning methods, particularly visual arts and creativity, as a tool for identity development, community-building, and healing for marginalized and minoritized student populations in postsecondary education.

Before engaging in self-care, healing, or transformative social justice work within communities, student affairs practitioners must have grounding in theoretical frameworks that guide praxis. *Community* can have multiple definitions, and for the purpose of utilizing visual arts in student affairs and postsecondary education in practice, *critical community* (Bettez, 2011) is defined as

> interconnected, porously bordered, shifting webs of people who through dialogue, active listening, and critical question posing, assist each other in critically thinking through issues of power, oppression, and privilege.

Critical communities are not necessarily fixed in location or even in present time; they are dynamic, fluid, and shifting. (p. 10)

Within this understanding of critical community, participants must be actively learning and exploring their social identities and narratives, interrogating power and privilege, and actively listening and exchanging with members of the group(s). The concept of critical community, when coupled with a borderlands lens (Anzaldúa, 1987), recognizes that these physical and psychological counterspaces can "represent intensely painful yet also potentially transformational spaces where opposites converse, conflict, and transform" (p. 319). *Counterspaces* can be understood as intentional, subversive critical communities where people with similar minoritized identities and experiences come together to develop tools and tactics to navigate White supremacy, as well as find support and validation in navigating the detrimental effects of racism, sexism, homophobia, and other forms of oppression.

Practitioners must recognize that multiple truths are valid, and that in such critical communities and counterspaces, it is possible that students might navigate multiple truths within themselves (e.g., a student who identifies as multiracial, Asian, and White; a student who identifies as queer and cisgender). Critical community viewed through a borderlands lens allows for intentionally interrogating and questioning the meaning of such narratives. Living within a borderlands lens recognizes that multiple truths might require and/both approaches (e.g., multiple, fluid, subjective identities, among others) to understand our shared learning environments, versus an either/or binary approach (e.g., Black or White, queer or straight, transgender or cisgender, among others). This perspective also challenges the ways that students, faculty, and practitioners have internalized and perpetuated White supremacist ways of knowing (e.g., bureaucracy/hierarchy, funding, reason versus emotion) in their everyday lives. A borderlands lens allows for students, faculty, and practitioners to recognize White supremacy and combat it directly to honor ambiguity, multiple truths, and alternative ways of expressing its impact through poetry, art, performance, or challenging dialogue in critical communities.

In recent years, students with multiple marginalized identities vocalized social justice inequities correlated with White supremacist ways of knowing on their home campuses through activism. Examples include the San Diego State University Shit-In (2014), Mizzou Concerned Student 1950 (2015), University of Minnesota Twin Cities Whose Diversity? (2015), and University of California Davis Fire Katehi campaign and sit-in (2015–2016). Practitioners were challenged to consider not only students with marginalized identities in their responses but also students with dominant identities. For example, in advocating for queer students, sometimes practitioners have to respond to student questions such as, "But what about White/cisgender/straight students?" Attitudes and questions like these often continue to perpetuate a postracial, postgender, and neoliberal lens beyond the tension of multiple truths on campuses.

With this in mind, Jolivétte's (2014) CMRS framework, in addition to a critical community and borderlands lens, enhances practitioners' ability to support students' identity development within postsecondary education. CMRS stems from the concept of multiracial consciousness (Osei-Kofi, 2012) and centers people with the most marginalized identities and experiences. The goal is to transform social systems to the "highest common denominators" for a socially just community (Jolivétte, 2014, p. 151). Focusing on the highest common denominators means that if practitioners develop spaces and practices that support students who do not equitably access the resources needed to graduate (e.g., housing, tutoring, healthcare), students with dominant identities will also benefit. This can also be understood as trickle-up social justice (Spade, 2015).

This reframing of centering in critical community through dual borderlands and CMRS lenses provides the necessary framework for practitioners to utilize creativity for healing, resistance, and resilience in postsecondary education. The following case study discusses an event that triggered multiple forms of art and creativity and ultimately provides examples of healing, resistance, and resilience. The case study demonstrates that everyone can be an artist and create, regardless of skill level.

Everyone Can Be an Artist and Create: A Case Study

At the beginning of the fall semester student organizations and departments at the University of Minnesota, Twin Cities (UMN) gather for a campus-wide event to paint publicity on panels bordering a high-traffic pedestrian pathway. This event has been regarded as a vital community-building and resource-sharing event that helps first-year and transfer students better understand ways to get involved, develop as leaders, and enhance their academic experience. As a large, public, predominantly White, research university, free speech and expression is paramount, including bipartisan political perspectives. In 2016, members from the College Republicans (a student organization), decided to paint the phrase "Build the Wall" on their panel (Figure 13.1). This is a popular phrase coined by the 2016 Republican presidential candidate. The politically charged phrase referred to building a wall between

Figure 13.1. UMN College Republicans' "Build the Wall" panel painting (Hirsi, 2016).

Mexico and the United States to ensure that all immigrants would cross the border legally or not at all.

This immediately evoked a range of responses from students who identified as undocumented, first-generation citizens, people of color, religious and spiritual minorities, refugees, native and indigenous populations, and aspiring allies. Students and community organizations quickly vocalized feeling unsafe when passing the racist and xenophobic panel painting and engaged in protest within 48 hours of the event.

Immediately, faculty and practitioners focused on policies and First Amendment rights on a public postsecondary education campus via e-mail, phone calls, or in-person bias response team meetings. Should practitioners address the College Republicans' "Build the Wall" panel painting? Were institutional policies violated? Would this be demonstrating a partisan bias during an election year? What about providing space for civil discourse about politics and impact of phrasing? How might college practitioners address students feeling unsafe passing the panel? Should there be a dialogue around intention versus impact? Could this expression of political perspective insinuate a chilly climate, especially when using a borderlands/mixed race theory approach to developing critical community? These were all questions administrators and faculty were grappling with in discussing how to respond to this incident.

There are many potential responses universities could take to address this case study. One thing was for certain: The College Republicans engaged in an artistic and creative expression of their political beliefs. The following responses to the initial "Build the Wall" panel provide concrete examples of a wide range of ways to address the case study and accompanying questions. In each example, applicable recommendations are provided for practitioners to utilize creativity as an education methodology for students, practitioners, faculty, and other members of critical community, in order to expand dialogue during politically tense and chilly environments.

Art Resists

Sigma Lambda Beta ($\Sigma\Lambda B$) is a hxstorically Latinx organization, and the student leaders recognized the negative impact of the College Republicans' panel. $\Sigma\Lambda B$ immediately responded by painting "Build Bridges, Not Walls" on a neighboring panel. Other student organizations participating in the panel painting event also began painting this phrase on their panels. Additionally, the College Republicans' panel was painted over with the phrase "Stop White Supremacy" in gold paint within 48 hours (Figure 13.2). Over the next few months, other forms of resistance art began appearing across campus in the form of stencil art that said "Stand Up, Fight Back" and "Resist."

These examples of visual arts are examples of ways art serves as a form of resistance on college campuses. For the purpose of this chapter, *resistance* is defined as actions that address and oppose behaviors and actions that reinforce systems of oppression. The immediate challenges to racist and xenophobic artwork empowered students of color to express the negative impacts

Figure 13.2. "Stop White Supremacy" painted in gold paint over the UMN College Republicans' panel painting (Hirsi, 2016).

of the phrase "Build the Wall" and explore tactics to support each other as incidents of bias and hate increased on campus and nationally. Reports of students of color being told to "Go back home," or being physically assaulted after the College Republicans painted their panel, was a curious correlation, but perhaps not causation. The Muslim Student Association's panel was also spray painted with the word "Terrorists," which only heightened students' fears of being targeted by bias and hate crimes. Students gathered at these physical sites of resistance to protest and rally against the Trump and Pence campaign. They stated that "Build the Wall" was one of many examples of incidents that were not congruent in values with their educational environments and principles.

Practitioners responded to artistic acts of resistance differently, according to their positionality, understanding of policy, and activism. Members of ΣΛΒ were publicly praised for their quick response, as well as for following university policy in doing so. They created a response on their own panel painting and helped organize students that followed the sanctioned time, place, and manner policy. Time, place, and manner policy notes that any activities that take place during hours of instruction must not impede or inhibit students' ability to learn and faculty/practitioners' ability to teach or provide services. Practitioners partnered with students to make and hand out pins that said "Build Bridges, Not Walls" and "No Hate" across social justice and inclusion events across campus. However, the "Stop White Supremacy" spray painting sparked a different conversation. It was immediately painted over with white paint and labeled as vandalism. The university president sent an e-mail condemning all forms of vandalism and stating that incidents of free speech should be addressed only with more free speech, negating any issues of campus climate that resulted from the original "Build the Wall" painting.

Although there are practical implications to ensure that all community members understand expectations about policy and free speech to preserve physical and psychological learning environments, resistance art can be pieces of critical community development for students, practitioners, and faculty. Resistance can be understood as a form of cultural capital that encompasses "those knowledge and skills fostered through oppositional behavior that challenges inequality" (Yosso, 2005, p. 80). This kind of education engagement can be challenging during election years; there can be general points of dialogue that embrace the nuances of the borderlands and centers marginalized voices in reactions to events on campus.

As demonstrated, resistance art can be organized formally through administrative policy or occur organically overnight. How might practitioners navigate art that resists on their college campuses? The university president engaged in due diligence to address the spray paint incident but missed a vital conversation defining expectations of inclusion and the meaning of White supremacy. If practitioners are able to address the impact of political rhetoric, without necessarily endorsing a particular political party, they can successfully support students in their identity development. It should be noted that the university administration initially addressed only the intent of the College Republicans, not the impact of their artistic interpretation of "Build the Wall," which incited fear, intimidation, and hurt for many on campus. When experiencing this kind of art, whether policy abiding or not, the ability to hold space and facilitate dialogue can help critical community members reach a common-ground understanding of intent versus impact of messaging or behavior. Critical community members should also reflect and better understand issues of power and privilege, as well as create actionable items to prevent harmful incidents moving forward. Dialogues can occur individually, in small groups, and among people with different roles and statuses at a university. Ask questions such as the following:

- What does it actually mean to build bridges and not walls?
- What is White supremacy? Do you think that it occurs here on campus?
- What is free speech? How might we create a common understanding, while using policy or community expectations?
- Why do you think the panel was painted over?
- Who was impacted by the original panel? Who might have been impacted by it being painted over?
- Do you think identity impacts the way each of us understands the impact? Why?
- What other methods or tactics can different community members use to share their political ideologies, while also recognizing the (un)intended impact on other people?
- What do you think can happen next so that we can better understand or heal as a community?

In this specific incident, practitioners serve a key role in empowering critical community members to utilize tangible tools and tactics to clearly communicate expectations and understandings of identity politics, power, and privilege in their educational contexts. Remembering that identity and resistance are intricately intertwined, administrators also must understand that resistance is a brave and daring act for students with marginalized identities.

By continuing the varied and difficult conversations and processing the impact of resistance art, practitioners can implement resistance capital building with a culturally conscious lens.

Art Heals

Healing can take many forms through the vehicle of art. The mechanisms can be planned, spontaneous, or a mixture of both. When supporting critical communities navigating incidents, it can be astonishing for practitioners to experience the tactics that organically develop in response. Once the "Stop White Supremacy" painting was painted over, students began having dialogues, protests, and community speak-outs about feeling unsafe or unwelcome on the pedestrian pathway. Increased reports of students of color being physically or verbally assaulted started flooding the bias response team inbox. One morning, colorful chalk drawings appeared on campus. The drawings had phrases such as "You are loved," "You are welcome here," "You matter," or "You belong here" (Figure 13.3). The pedestrian pathway was covered with pieces of paper and sticky notes with affirmations, quotes, encouragement, and ways the campus could continue to be more inclusive. Soon enough, students began gathering on the pedestrian pathway and adding their own notes. The community had navigated trauma, hurt, and pain over the past few weeks and wanted to start finding ways to make meaning.

Figure 13.3. "You belong here" chalk art on a UMN campus walkway.

The chalk art and sticky notes were community-organized efforts to help the people most impacted (e.g., undergraduate students, immigrants, Chicanxs, Muslims, among others) find healing and a sense of belonging. Practitioners can support these efforts by helping students navigate policy, accessing resources needed, and simply showing up to support. This might include creating similar messages in offices and communal spaces (e.g., lounges, study rooms, conference rooms) or helping develop continued programming that allows creative expressions for healing.

Other structured forms of art-as-healing might include holding processing or debriefing spaces for critical community members to dialogue. These spaces are not "safe spaces" but sites for dissonance, question posing, expressing emotions, or just physical or psychological counterspaces to reflect silently. At academically rigorous institutions, these kinds of spaces are often treated as nonacademic (and therefore undervalued), but they can serve to support or enhance students' ability to engage in persistence. Instead of having structured dialogue, practitioners can recognize the impact of resistance capital, borderlands, and CMRS so that students can express their sentiments in order to advocate for a more inclusive environment.

Practitioners can provide prompts and invite students to answer in a media of their choice. Students might paint on canvases provided, draw a diagram with paper and colored pencil, use markers to scribble out emotions, make a zine or comic book, author a short story or poem, or write a direct response. Providing coloring pages with self-care techniques might also help students process their own desires for healing or resolution. As students explore their answers, practitioners can check in with them and ask about their process, the feelings coming up, and/or how answering in this way makes them feel. Example questions and prompts include the following:

- How are you doing . . .
  - Emotionally?
  - Physically?
  - Psychologically?
  - Spiritually?
- Which identities or narratives inform your response to this event?
- What does a more inclusive space feel/smell/look/taste/sound like?
- What colors or shapes do self-care or healing take on?
- Create a map/action plan of how you will take care of yourself.

Art can be a helpful tool for processing and healing. There are not specific recipes for practitioners to utilize this method. However, if practitioners engage with faculty, peers, and students to inform the needs and structures of these kinds of visual arts-centered spaces, they can be effective in promoting continued self-care, healing, and tactics for students to form their resistance capital understanding and implementation.

Art Is Resilience

A key component to student affairs practice is helping students build resiliency skills to better navigate complex systems. Art can be a mechanism for students to not only process events but also move forward and create tangible action items to enhance their ability to graduate. Many students with marginalized identities, particularly ones navigating the borderlands, understand ways to recuperate from challenging events. These particular students may have high resistance and resilience capital due to their narratives and life experiences, and art can only enhance their ability to develop as scholars and leaders on postsecondary education campuses.

Upon experiencing the various forms of creativity and art resistance and healing that addressed the "Build the Wall" panel, faculty and practitioners cocreated a teach-in about immigration and student activism to continue to foster healing and action on campus. It was clear to the faculty and practitioners that students had already explored resistance and methods of healing, and faculty and practitioners wanted to provide additional information and community accountability space for students to enhance their resilience. The teach-in included setting the context, providing immigration and migration facts, offering resources on- and off-campus, and creating critical community-identified projects to help foster a more inclusive environment on campus. A majority of the teach-in utilized lecture and dialogue formats. Recognizing different learning styles and identity dynamics, the facilitators decided to end with an artistic brainstorm for participants to imagine ways to stay involved moving forward (Figure 13.4). Participants were asked to reflect individually, write their answers on the communal artistic brainstorm, and then share with the group as they were able. Students decided to engage in multiple ways, including repainting panels, creating an art gallery with immigration facts, and exploring ways to make the campus physically more welcome through walking each other to classes.

Practitioners can utilize art as a resilience tool in other forms. Whether taking notes by creating images; allowing students to engage through photo essays or videography; or simply brainstorming schedules, timelines, or

Figure 13.4. Photo of action plan artistic brainstorm.

narratives through drawings, visual arts can prove to be an inclusive and radical way for students to notice patterns, trends, and relationships relative to navigating postsecondary institutions. Students can also apply art and creativity for resilience in visioning goals, developing professional skills, or making simple affirmations as tools for self-care (e.g., coloring, mood tracking, making destress items such as glitter jars) during stressful events as scholars.

Educators facilitating each of these activities or programs should identify learning outcomes to help effectively communicate the knowledge, skills, and awareness to constituents and participants. Better understanding the purpose of creativity, critical community, and identity development in relationship to current events allows for the ability to assess if the outcomes are met, as well as if students have developed skills that they will continue to utilize for resilience. These creative skills can become practices that students, faculty, and practitioners adopt for a lifetime. Quite simply, practitioners can ask questions such as the following:

- What does it mean to be resilient?
- What are triggers or topics that make it hard to be a student? How will you notice when those start impacting you?
- How you will take care of yourself moving forward? Tell me two or three tactics you will utilize.
- What do you need to be a thriving member of our community? How will you get those needs met?
- What are resources you can access to find support?
  o Emotionally?
  o Physically?
  o Psychologically?
  o Spiritually?
- What is one affirmation you have for yourself?
- What color makes you feel empowered? How will you incorporate it into your everyday?

Conclusion

When provided with options to be creative, students, faculty, and practitioners often wince and say "I'm not an artist." Faculty and practitioners also often default to methods that are academically respectable (e.g., writing papers, dialogues, common readings), which can be valid methods of navigating challenging incidents but might not be inclusive for students with different learning styles, social identities, or cultural practices. These traditional learning methods can feel safer or more comfortable for some, but an educational shift is needed to serve students in regard to the highest common denominators (Jolivétte, 2014). As students experience microaggressions, bias, and hate incidents, as well as chilly climates due to political landscapes, faculty and practitioners need to find other practical tactics to develop and sustain critical community and to enhance outreach and retention efforts.

Administrators need to find new and innovative methods for making meaning of hurt, confusion, or even despair to address events that impact critical communities on college campuses. By encouraging critical dialogues and "sitting in the fire," there is an inevitable free and democratic exchange of diverse ideas that holds people accountable for the impact of hate or bias speech or behavior (Bettez, 2011, p. 7). However, when candidates and elected officials share rhetoric and promote legislation that targets or harms people with marginalized identities, it is student affairs practitioners' ethical duty to address the harm and help provide educational environments that encourage culturally competent dialogue. If practitioners can utilize critical theory such as the borderlands lens and CMRS, it is certain that students with dominant identities will be supported as well. Now is the time to move from safer methodology to taking a creative risk in order to better support a wide range of students. Creating inclusive critical community and environments that recognize the ways that art is a radical teaching methodology can allow student affairs practitioners to expand their helping skills. There are a variety of methods that can center students with marginalized identities and expand understandings of perspective and reality, including collaborative brainstorms, coloring sheets, community art galleries, self-care spaces, and many more.

Art resists. Art heals. Art is resilience. Everybody can be an artist and create, especially in heightened divisive, political, and social environments. Utilizing creativity can help students, faculty, and practitioners develop more socially just and inclusive environments to transform the self, critical community, and landscape of institutions.

Note

1. The term *hxstorical* recognizes the patriarchal roots and male privilege in narrative story telling. By removing "his," the phrase honors and recenters the narratives of people with marginalized and minoritized identities. This also can be applied to the terms *womxn* and *Latinx* throughout the text.

References

Anzaldúa, G. (1987). *Borderlands: La frontera*. San Francisco, CA: Aunt Lute Books.
Bettez, S. C. (2011). Critical community building: Beyond belonging. *Educational Foundations*, 25(3–4), 3–19.
Hirsi, I. (2016). "Build the Wall" mural at University of Minnesota sparks protest. *MinnPost*. Retrieved from https://www.minnpost.com/new-americans/2016/10/build-wall-mural-university-minnesota-sparks-protest
Jolivétte, A. J. (2014). Critical mixed race studies: New directions in the politics of race and representation. *Journal of Critical Mixed Race Studies*, 1(1), 149–161.
Osei-Kofi, N. (2012). Identity, fluidity, and groupism: The construction of multiraciality in education discourse. *Review of Education, Pedagogy, and Cultural Studies*, 34(5), 245–257.

Schlossberg, N. K. (1989). Marginality and mattering: Key issues in building community. *New Directions for Student Services, 48,* 5–15.

Spade, D. (2015). *Normal life: Administrative violence, critical trans politics, and the limits of law.* Durham, NC: Duke University Press.

Yosso, T. J. (2005). Whose culture has capital? A critical race theory discussion of community cultural wealth. *Race Ethnicity and Education, 8*(1), 69–91.

14

IMPLICATIONS AND FUTURE DIRECTIONS FOR VISUAL METHODS IN RESEARCH, PEDAGOGY, AND PRACTICE

Bridget Turner Kelly and Carrie A. Kortegast

Individually and collectively, humans are storytellers and "lead storied lives" (Connelly & Clandinin, 1990, p. 2). Visuals often help tell these stories. Increasingly, college students are recording and narrating their lives in new ways through the use of visuals. We believe student learning and development is conveyed in part through the use of visuals. Astin's (1999) theory of student involvement strove to understand the "mediating mechanism that would explain how these educational programs and policies are translated into student achievement and development" (p. 520). Visual methods provide a new approach to understanding student learning and development.

Visuals help "broker" experiences. *Brokering,* in this sense, is the act of "transferring some element of one practice into another" (Wenger, 1998, p. 109). For instance, several students in Kortegast's (2015) study on short-term study abroad discussed hosting viewing parties for their friends and families. During these parties, the students narrated their study abroad experience via the use of photographs. The visuals helped students explain, demonstrate, and translate their experience for their friends and family. Ultimately, "through the medium of photography, students engaged the listener while providing the opportunity to highlight the most significant pieces of their [study abroad] experiences" (Kortegast & Boisfontaine, 2015, p. 826). Throughout this book, our goal was to help broker the transfer of understanding the potential and use of visual methods for research, pedagogy, and practice.

The power of the visual to evoke affect (feeling) and cognition (thinking) from students involved in research, pedagogy, and practice is evident in the examples described by authors in this book. Student learning and development often require getting in touch with the heart and the head, particularly when it comes to areas of inclusion and social justice. Although we never asked authors to provide examples rooted in any specific topic, each chapter showed how visual methods assisted students' growth and development, particularly in areas of inclusion and social justice. In this chapter, we overview the insights from research, pedagogy, and practice sections of the book, and discuss future directions in visual methods.

Visuals in Research

In part one on research, both in the structure (how) and in the content (what) of the research, issues of power, oppression, and social justice surface in Branch and Latz's chapter on photo elicitation. The decision to use participant-generated photos as data in their studies relinquished some control Branch and Latz, two White women professors, had in the study. Branch's topic of African American students' belonging at predominantly White institutions addresses oppression and inclusion through students' taking their own photos of spaces on campus and talking with each other and the researcher about their racial identity work in relation to those spaces. Student development was fostered through the increased time on task and engagement of student participants in both Branch and Latz's research.

Similarly, Nguyen's chapter describes how the National Study of Lesbian, Gay, Bisexual, Transgender, and Queer-Identified (LGBTQ+) College Student Success used participant-generated photos, campus map drawings, identity illustrations, and other visual methods to understand LGBTQ+ students' college success. Centering student voice and visual representation allowed students to define *success* for themselves and offer counternarratives to dominant policy and research on the topic. Nguyen's research showcases student learning and development by focusing on a traditionally marginalized student population, seeking out their experiences through nondominant visual methods, and validating their understandings in research.

Rounding out part one on research, Linder describes how visual methods in research helped her understand issues of sexual violence activists, gender, race, and socioeconomic class on college campuses. Examining posts on social media uncovered the ways college students learn and develop as activists and as participants in campus cultural traditions. Linder helps us understand student development through firsthand, unfiltered, visual images that students generate and disseminate. The visual method in research fosters student voice, engagement, learning, and development, particularly as scholars examine issues of inclusion and social justice.

Visuals in Pedagogy

All college students take classes and a majority are consuming and creating visual images in social media and mainstream media. Pairing the ways students engage with each other and society outside of the classroom with their experiences inside the classroom models student development practice of meeting students where they are. Authors in part two on pedagogy demonstrate how using a variety of visual methods in curriculum and teaching promotes student development and learning. Latz and Rodgers show how photovoice and visual life writing prompted students to engage in identity development work, and engage in experiential learning. The content of the courses, community college and diversity, also centered on inclusion and social justice. For example, by focusing on community colleges that are open-access and diverse in socioeconomic class, race, ethnicity, language, and nationality, among other social identities, the visual pedagogy enabled students to explore the richness of the institutional type through the considerable time they took to take and reflect on photos and visually chronicle their own life stories.

Jaekel's chapter also centers issues of inclusion by focusing on how using a critical, place-based visual pedagogy assists students' learning and development in social justice. The visual diversity audit assignment, for example, gave students concrete and abstract ways to feel, see, and experience places on campus that impacted marginalized students' sense of belonging on a predominantly White campus. These two chapters from Latz and Rodgers and Jaekel highlight how identity development could be fostered through the visual in graduate preparation courses, and the next two chapters in the pedagogy section focused on leadership courses infused with visual methods.

Eaton's chapter describes an online leadership course that used digital visualization. His focus on empowering students and fostering creativity and imagination is aligned with social justice practice and student development. Giving students the freedom to express themselves visually runs counter to dominant forms of expression that are rooted in patriarchy, competition, and Western standards of academic rigor (Kelly, McCann, & Porter, in press). Chapman and McShay's chapter also discusses how the use of visual digital stories in their leadership course disrupts notions of dominant approaches to learning and how knowledge is constructed. For example, the identity mapping assignment invites students to visually depict how their social and leadership identities intersect, thereby promoting reflection on students' leadership development. The critical pedagogical approach they champione through the visual digital stories and identity mapping helps students develop inclusive ways of enacting leadership.

Visuals in Practice

If students realize the power of visual research and pedagogical methods and do not have an opportunity to utilize these tools in their practice, development can stop. Chapters in part three on practice highlight how visual methods can not only spur student development outside of the classroom but also development of practitioners who work with college students. Again, this development centered largely on areas of inclusion and social justice. McKee's chapter evidences how infusing critical visual literacy and photo elicitation techniques during pre-alternative break trip training promoted student development in managing emotional, cognitive, and moral development. The alternative breaks related to particular social justice issues and the photo elicitation visual methods provide students with a concrete experience to disrupt stereotypical notions of communities they held prior to engaging in service. The critical visual literacy exercises students participate in prior to the trip also encouraged their development in being inclusive and socially just when they took pictures of their alternative break experience. Practitioners who guided students through being both consumers and creators of visual images in alternative break service is one application of visual literacy used in McKee's chapter.

Martin's chapter shows how applying learning from visual literacy and visual methods should be a continuous process for practitioners that allows them to reflect on their own development, even as they are responsible for students' development. Martin found that if practitioners create their own visual depiction of their identity journey in student affairs, it results in reflection on racial identity development within the professional role of practitioner.

Lou's chapter picks up this theme and notes how critical visual arts assisted practitioners in creating counterspaces for students to express vulnerable emotions and navigate oppressive structures. Lou found students developed in areas of belonging and mattering through creating art (e.g., poems, drawings, sticky notes, and paintings, among other forms) and having practitioners guide them through critical reflection and dialogue about their feelings, beliefs, and actions.

It is clear that inviting chapter authors to share examples of how visual research, pedagogy, and practice promoted student development and learning elicited examples of social justice, inclusion, and critical visual literacy. There is power in utilizing a nondominant, left-brain-oriented modality to help students and practitioners unearth and reflect on their own learning and identity development. The chapter authors showed how taking a critical theoretical lens to their work promoted critical visual literacy whereby students, researchers, and practitioners gained tools in understanding how to be socially just and inclusive when creating and consuming visual images.

Future Directions for Visual Methods

Although this book showcases current uses of visual methods, technology will continue to evolve and change how individuals interact and engage in the social world. As new technology emerges, we as educators need to learn to use it to enhance students' visual literacy, both inside and outside the classroom. The ability to narrate and interact with our world visually through social media, for example, requires increased critical literacy. Focusing on visual literacy gives researchers, teachers, and practitioners new ways to gain insights into the lives of students.

Confidentiality and Consent

New methods also bring challenges to overcome. Visual methods pose new ethical and practical questions that researchers need to negotiate. Issues of confidentiality, ownership of images, and editing of images can feel like shifting questions. Understandings of privacy and what individuals are willing to share publicly might be changing in a digital world where students, in particular, are narrating their lives via social network. For instance, most of the photographs Kortegast's participants shared of their study abroad experience were also posted to Facebook. Thus, the images that were collected as part of a research project were also publicly available on students' Facebook accounts, making confidentiality in the study difficult to maintain. Anticipating this problem, informed consent documents and the institutional review board (IRB) application included language that discussed confidentiality not being guaranteed (Figure 14.1).

Ultimately, the goodness of the research study is not completely about the ability to maintain confidentiality or not. Rather, it is about participants

Figure 14.1. Consent document sample language.

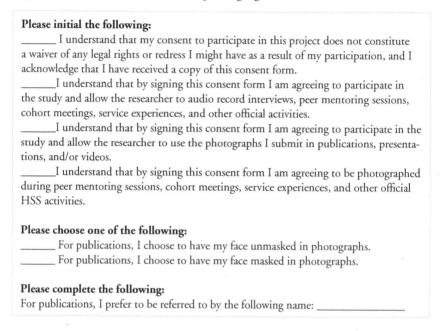

Please initial the following:

_____ I understand that my consent to participate in this project does not constitute a waiver of any legal rights or redress I might have as a result of my participation, and I acknowledge that I have received a copy of this consent form.

_____I understand that by signing this consent form I am agreeing to participate in the study and allow the researcher to audio record interviews, peer mentoring sessions, cohort meetings, service experiences, and other official activities.

_____I understand that by signing this consent form I am agreeing to participate in the study and allow the researcher to use the photographs I submit in publications, presentations, and/or videos.

_____I understand that by signing this consent form I am agreeing to be photographed during peer mentoring sessions, cohort meetings, service experiences, and other official HSS activities.

Please choose one of the following:

_____ For publications, I choose to have my face unmasked in photographs.

_____ For publications, I choose to have my face masked in photographs.

Please complete the following:

For publications, I prefer to be referred to by the following name: _____

being fully informed regarding the risks before participating. One way to utilize consent documents is to highlight the risks involved and provide options regarding participation. Figure 14.1 is an example of language on an informed consent document from a current visual ethnographic study Kortegast is undertaking.

The document allows students to choose to have their photographs used in publication. The document also allows participants to choose if they want their faces masked or unmasked. The goal is to encourage participation while providing participants some control over the use of their image.

It is not just at the initial conception of research that confidentiality need be considered. For researchers who want to publish their work in scholarly journals in higher education, the "blind" review process journal reviewers engage in also has to be thought about in new ways. I (Kelly) consulted with Kortegast and other contributors to this book when, as associate journal editor for media and book reviews, I was tasked with developing guidelines for reviewers assessing studies that involved visual, video, or audio data. Items that I addressed were whether the video was publicly available; tied to an author's name; or had identifiable images of campuses, for example, if the institution in the study was anonymous. Providing guidelines on visual data served to level the playing field with reviewers who were already well-versed in assessing quality, fit, and rigor of studies with word or numerical data.

Although navigating issues of confidentiality and usage of images in studies that utilize participant-generated methods can be mediated via informed consent documents and guidelines for reviewers, research utilizing publicly available images on social media, such as Instagram and Twitter, pose different ethical questions. Linder, in chapter 4, addressed some of these ethical and practical questions. But new questions might be raised regarding consent, usage, and (re)presentation of information and images with the increasing sophistication of facial recognition software. Again, as researchers, we need to not shy away from data and information that can provide new insights into students' learning, development, and experience in college. We need to ask good questions about purpose, risk, and (re)presentation of information.

Connections and Connectivity

Advancements in video technology have allowed everyday people to record and produce videos. Facebook Live, YouTube, and other streaming options provide new opportunities for data collection, course assignments, and connecting with individuals via video conferencing services. For instance, we (Kelly and Kortegast) participated in a recorded session about innovative methods in qualitative research with Amanda O. Latz and Jessica Harris, organized and hosted by Chris Linder for her qualitative research course (Linder, 2017). Through the use of Google Hangout, we were able to interact and connect in real time, virtually face-to-face; record the session; and post it on YouTube. Linder's students, as well as others, were able to access and view the video online. Although it is a fairly simplistic form of video recording and watching, technology has allowed others to connect and share information in new ways. Additionally, technology has also opened up how interviews can be conducted and visual information shared.

Moreover, digital natives, raised in an era of the Internet and smartphones, communicate with each other often through the use of visuals. This includes sending picture messages through Snapchat, using GIFs to highlight points, or narrating their days through images on Instagram. Images are centered that sometimes include text for context. Although images can serve as entertainment, we can also harness these forms of communication in research, pedagogy, and practice. Searching the Instagram feed of Northern Illinois University and Loyola students brings up images of students engaging in various student organization and attending major campus events, as well as pictures of food, working out, and friends. These platforms are used to enhance connection and connectivity with each other. Thus, practitioners, educations, researchers, and faculty may tap into these platforms to promote student learning, belonging, and community.

Stable, Authentic Self or Situated Self

The use of visual methods in research, practice, and pedagogy can also challenge the notion of a stable, authentic self. Instead, visual methods can highlight the complexity of identity and multiple ways students engage in the university. How a student shows up online might be different than how he or she shows up in the classroom or during a research study. This opens the door to think about how individuals navigate and negotiate a situated identity.

Paul Eaton's (2016) article "Tag-Untag: Two Critical Readings of Race, Ethnicity, and Class in Digital Social Media" provides some insight into how students manage, negotiate, and construct their identities on social networking platforms. Centered on a participant named Miranda, Eaton provides two interpretations of Miranda's active process of untagging herself from pictures that "mark her body within a specific racial, ethnic, or socioeconomic strati" (p. 74). The article pushes the reader to consider the construction of a situated identity and a "non-unitary subject" (Braidotti, 2013, p. 100). Eaton concludes that "her identity [was] not as static, essential, or predictable but as an emergent phenomenal unfolding through intra-active relationships with human and non-human actors across physical environments and distributed social medial ecologies" (p. 74). With that, the use of visual methods, including multimodal forms of communication and interactive digital platforms, are going to challenge how researchers, practitioners, and educators come to understand student engagement, learning, and development. At the same time, visuals can help understand how individuals develop, create, and express a situated, polyvocal identity.

Low Tech, High Tech

Although it is easy to think about the future and the use of technology regarding visual methods, we must not lose sight of the power of lower tech construction and production of visual methods. The physical act of creating a drawing, collage, or painting provides opportunity for reflection, remembering, and (re)producing experiences. For instance, cutting up fashion magazines and (re)imagining the images into new shapes, structures, and designs could be a powerful way to discuss gender, sexism, and body images. Through this process, students have opportunities to (re)create new and different potentials regarding bodies and inclusion. Again, it is not about how high-tech the materials or the medium are; it is about the opportunity to engage in tactical learning.

Additionally, arts-based activities can provide opportunities for students to connect highly theoretical work to their own lives. Figure 14.2 is a collage Maryann Rainey, a former master's student of Kortegast's, made as part of

Figure 14.2. Collage for self-authorship assignment, by Maryann Rainey.

an assignment exploring the use of self-authorship (Baxter-Magolda, 2001, 2008). The assignment asked students to develop a collage to reflect on their own learning and development as it relates to the following questions: Who am I? How do I know? How do I want to construct relationships with others? Salient identities such as sister, wife, bicultural, and Christian are evidenced by her collage. Other values and aspirations are also present such as the light bulb for knowledge, and creativity, optimism, learning, and being happy. The physical act of having to create a collage rather than just writing a paper to discuss the application of theory to self and others allowed students to slow down and take time for reflection and consideration of the theory. In this case, the low-tech nature of cutting and pasting, painting, and drawing actually enhances the opportunity for reflective learning. Sometimes what is old (students may have made collages in K–12) becomes new when done as an adult for a graduate-level course.

Final Reflections

We return to the statement James Elkins (2007) made, "images are central to our lives . . . it is time they are central to our universities" (p. 8). For us, this book has taken seriously the call to center images and visuals as frameworks to understand and promote student learning and development. Throughout the book, we have explored the production of images by students such as digital storytelling, collage making, and photo elicitation to enhance student learning as well as to understand student development. Additionally, we have discussed the importance of developing critical visual literacy as an analytical framework to explore the campus environment and student engagement through visual artifacts. Ultimately, our goal was to highlight possibilities regarding how visuals can enhance student learning and development through the showcasing of various examples across research, pedagogy, and practice.

We opened the book by sharing how each of us began our journey using visual methods in our research and pedagogy to enhance student learning. We close with two final reflections that highlight developing the next generation of scholars, educators, and practitioners utilizing visual methods in their praxis.

Bridget Turner Kelly's Reflection

As Carrie A. Kortegast and I embarked on editing and writing chapters for this book, I was inspired by reading Eaton's chapter to shift the way I taught an online version of "Multiculturalism for Social Justice." I taught the face-to-face version for over 15 years, and dialogue facilitated by the students was a central component. When I first began teaching the course online a few years ago in an asynchronous format with students based all over the world, it worked okay for students to facilitate dialogues that spanned over several days and included text/writing back and forth to student-generated questions about the readings. However, reading Eaton's chapter helped me rethink how I could capitalize on the online format and utilize the power of visuals to deepen students' learning and engagement. I utilized VoiceThread, which is a completely web-based application that enabled students to use images, video, and voice in their asynchronous online presentations. Through VoiceThread, a new assignment invited students to upload recorded 15-minute visual presentations accompanied by video narration of personal and professional stories that affirmed or refuted ideas in that week's reading. Students then had the option of responding back to the presenter on VoiceThread through audio, text, or video.

As I Skyped with a student in my class to assist her in preparing the VoiceThread presentation, she noted that the presentations that had already occurred were much more intimate and engaging than she realized they would be. In a paper for this class, another student wrote how she was excited to share her critique and insights on the readings with the class in the VoiceThread presentation responses. From the perspective of the presenters and the students responding to the presentations, the power of the visuals and videos captured students' attention and energized them. As all of our topics are dealing with systems of privilege, oppression, power, and social justice, the opportunity to hear and/or see classmates as well as infuse meaningful visuals in the presentation made the class personal and vulnerable in ways that were harder to discern when students only had the option to use written rather than spoken words.

This example highlights for me how communication is enhanced when we can use more of our senses, head, and heart; when we are not afraid of new technology; and when we rely on support mechanisms when utilizing visual methods. The act of visually depicting stories, connecting to ideas in the readings and then responding to each other in video (I encourage them to use video and audio as much as possible so we can capture the 70% or so of communication that is nonverbal), cuts down on students' apprehension to only have one method of communication, the written word, to convey biases, prejudices, hurt, anger, affirmation, and joy. The technology of VoiceThread allowed facial expressions, tone of voice, pictures, drawings, and models, among other visual and audio to be communicated. VoiceThread is new to me and my students, but it is supported by my university so we can contact the Help Desk as needed. As an educator, I did not wait until I was an expert/authority to try something new with my students. Leaning into my discomfort with new technologies is rewarding when it inspires students to share and connect in courageous ways. My hope is that finding ways to incorporate visuals in research, pedagogy, and practice gives your work new vitality.

Carrie A. Kortegast's Reflection

In March 2017, I was having lunch with a former master's student named James. We were catching up and discussing recent projects we were working on. I mentioned to James that I was coediting this book. He indicated that he was not surprised that I was involved in a book project about the use of visual methods as he had taken several courses with me that used visuals. One of the assignments in particular for a diversity in higher education course required students to conduct a campus art audit. In the campus art audit, students were asked to analyze public art on campus with the following questions in mind: What are the messages being espoused? What is the curriculum or hidden curriculum being communicated? What messages of belonging (or not belonging) are being projected? James confirmed to me that at the time he and his group members were a bit suspicious of the project.

Now as a practitioner, James shared that he has adapted the campus art audit assignment and incorporated it into the training for new student government association (SGA) officers. He has the officers analyze the pictures and images in the student union. In one section of the student union are portraits of all of the former SGA presidents and a timeline of students through the years. The images of students, in particular SGA presidents, provided

striking visuals of who has been elected to represent the student population. Of the more than 100 photographs of former SGA presidents, only 12
were not of White men. The collection of portraits allowed for conversations
about race, representation, inclusion, and their roles as student leaders.

For me, this story represented two things: First, it represented the flexibility of visual methods to be used and transferred from one place and practice to another. The activity started as a classroom assignment to explore
belonging and inclusion but was repurposed by a practitioner as part of a
development program for student leaders. The activity could also have been
transformed into a research project. Second, it represented the power of visuals to prompt awareness regarding inclusion and social justice. The visual of
seeing the race and gender of previous SGA presidents forced the students to
grapple with tough questions regarding White, male privilege. The images,
in many ways, circumvented discussions of plausible deniability or excuse
making regarding representation. For me, the power to evoke, question, challenge, and (re)imagine the social world is one way visuals can enhance student learning and development.

References

Astin, A. W. (1999). Student involvement: A developmental theory for higher education. *Journal of College Student Personnel, 40*(5), 518–529.

Baxter Magolda, M. B. (2001). *Making their own way: Narratives for transforming
higher education to promote self-development.* Sterling, VA: Stylus.

Baxter Magolda, M. B. (2008). Three elements of self-authorship. *Journal of College
Student Development, 49*(4), 269–284.

Braidotti, R. (2013). *The posthuman.* Malden, MA: Polity Press.

Connelly, F. M., & Clandinin, D. J. (1990). Stories of experience and narrative
inquiry. *Educational Researcher, 19*(5), 2–14.

Eaton, P. (2016). Tag-Untag: Two critical readings of race, ethnicity, and class in
digital social media. *Journal of Critical Scholarship on Higher Education and Student Affairs, 3*(1), 61–78.

Elkins, J. (2007). *Visual literacy.* New York, NY: Routledge.

Kelly, B. T., McCann, K., & Porter, K. (in press). Women faculty's socialization:
Persisting within and against a gendered tenure system. *The Review of Higher
Education.*

Kortegast, C. A., & Boisfontaine, M. T. (2015). Beyond "it was good": Students'
post-study abroad practices for negotiating meaning. *Journal of College Student
Development, 58*(8), 812–828.

Linder, C. (2017, February 14). *Innovative methods in qualitative research* [Video
files]. Retrieved from https://www.youtube.com/watch?v=j-WkGXEThxY

Wenger, E. (1998). *Communities of practice: Learning, meaning, and identity.* New
York, NY: Cambridge University Press.

ABOUT THE EDITORS AND CONTRIBUTORS

Editors

Bridget Turner Kelly, PhD, is associate professor of higher education at Loyola University Chicago. Her scholarship focuses on marginalized populations in higher education, such as women faculty on the research tenure-track, in which she used the visual method of participant drawing in a longitudinal study. She has authored over 20 publications, including 2 articles that have received over 100 citations each and 2 that have been cited in amicus briefs for U.S. Supreme Court cases. For over 15 years, she has taught in graduate preparation programs using visual methods in pedagogy and made national presentations about visual research and pedagogy at the Association for the Study of Higher Education and the American College Educators International annual conferences. Kelly served on the editorial review board of the *Journal of College Student Development* for 10 years and is the executive editor for the *Journal of Student Affairs Research and Practice*.

Carrie A. Kortegast, PhD, is an assistant professor at Northern Illinois University. Kortegast's scholarship focuses on topics related to identity, diversity, and social justice as it relates to how educational environments mediate student learning and development. She has written about out-of-classroom learning during short-term study abroad and post-study abroad negotiating of learning; the experiences of lesbian, gay, bisexual, transgender, and queer (LGBTQ) students and student affairs professionals; and the use of visual methods in research and pedagogy. In research, she has integrated photovoice methodology to explore how the campus environment mediates the experiences of LGBTQ students and understand out-of-classroom student engagement during a short-term study abroad experience. In her teaching, she has utilized a wide variety of visual methods including reflective collages, digital storytelling, campus art audits, and drawings. Kortegast is the associate editor of media features and reviews for the *Journal of Student Affairs Research and Practice*.

Contributors

Katherine Branch, PhD, is an associate professor at the University of Rhode Island. Branch's teaching and research interests center on adult development and learning in relationship to diverse students in collegiate settings, environmental theory and assessment in higher education, and college student persistence and educational attainment. She has expertise in qualitative inquiry, including using photography as a visual research method.

Natasha H. Chapman, PhD, serves as the coordinator for the leadership studies program at the University of Maryland, College Park, where she has oversight of curriculum design, instructional delivery, and evaluation of undergraduate leadership courses. Her scholarly interests include pedagogy in leadership education, critical perspectives in leadership studies, the experiences of multiracial college students, and college student development.

J. Michael Denton, PhD, is the program coordinator and an instructor for the college student affairs degree program at the University of South Florida. Denton has used arts-based methods as a form of ethical, queer, and participatory research with gay college men living with HIV. His research interests include LGBTQ college student populations, college student sexuality, students living with chronic illness, the social construction of HIV/AIDS and illness, and poststructural perspectives on higher education research and practice.

Paul Eaton, PhD, is an assistant professor of educational leadership at Sam Houston State University. Eaton's research interests include inquiries into digital technologies in education and human identity-subjectification-becoming, complexity theory's application to educational research, postqualitative and posthumanist inquiry, and curriculum theorizing-philosophy in the realms of postsecondary education and student affairs.

Kathryn S. Jaekel, PhD, is an assistant professor at Northern Illinois University in adult and higher education. Her background includes preparing novice educators and teaching assistants at the graduate level to teach writing, communication, and visual literacies. Her research interests include critical discourse analysis, queer theory, and teaching critical pedagogy.

Amanda O. Latz, EdD, is associate professor of adult, higher, and community education at Ball State University. Some of Latz's research interests include the lived experiences of individuals within the community college setting, particularly students and faculty, and qualitative research methodologies, especially visual methods such as photovoice. She is the author of *Photovoice Research in Education and Beyond: A Practical Guide from Theory to Exhibition* (Routledge, 2017), a book dedicated to the photovoice methodology.

Chris Linder, PhD, is an assistant professor in college student affairs administration at the University of Georgia. Linder's research interests include building and maintaining inclusive campus environments, specifically in regard to race and gender. Additionally, she has explored the identity development of student activists and the role of social media in campus sexual violence activism. She has used a variety of visual methods in her work, including photo elicitation, participant-generated visual representations, and online visual ethnography.

Heather C. Lou is an angry Gemini earth dragon, multiracial, Asian, queer, cisgender womxn of color multimedia artist and postsecondary education administrator based in Minneapolis, Minnesota. Her art and writing is a form of healing, transformation, and liberation, rooted in womxnism and gender equity through a racialized borderlands lens. Lou works at the Metropolitan State University as the director of student life and leadership development, where she focuses on campus climate, inclusion, and intersectionality in her daily practice.

Peter Magolda is a professor emeritus in Miami University's student affairs in higher education program. He received a BA from LaSalle College, an MA from The Ohio State University, and a PhD from Indiana University. His scholarship centers on ethnographic studies of college subcultures and critical issues in qualitative research. In 2016, he wrote *The Lives of Campus Custodians: Insights Into Corporatization and Civic Disengagement in the Academy* (Stylus Publishing). He currently resides in Elliston, Virginia.

Jillian A. Martin is a doctoral student in the college student affairs administration program at the University of Georgia. Her research interests include the socialization and preparation of new student affairs professionals, student athlete transition, and African student affairs and higher education. She serves on a research team exploring scholarship in student affairs practice and is currently conducting her own case study about new student affairs professionals' experiences with socialization.

Elizabeth A.M. McKee is assistant director for community service in student involvement and leadership development at Northern Illinois University (NIU) in DeKalb, Illinois. Her research interests are grounded in determining the best way to meet the unique needs of students at NIU, which has manifested through critical analysis of the theoretical components of the Huskie Alternative Break program as well as research about the experience of the population of students who experience food insecurity at NIU.

James McShay, PhD, is an associate director for the Adele H. Stamp student union at the University of Maryland, College Park. His areas of supervision include multicultural involvement and community advocacy; leadership and community service-learning; and Stamp human resources, training, and development. He has taught undergraduate and graduate courses in multicultural education, ethnicity and learning, antiracist education, and multicultural practice in student affairs. Some of his research interests include uses of critical pedagogy in K–16 education, multicultural curriculum development and assessment, and digital learning technologies and critical multicultural education.

Carrie Miller is a doctoral candidate at the University of California, Los Angeles, in the Graduate School of Education and Information Studies. Her research focuses on causes and consequences of educational inequality related to college access and completion.

David J. Nguyen, PhD, is an assistant professor of higher education and student affairs at Ohio University. His research agenda leverages theoretical insights from behavioral economics, organizational theory, and sociology to examine issues of access and equity in postsecondary education. Two interrelated strands of inquiry anchor his research agenda: examining how individual and organizational factors promote success for underserved and underrepresented students; and exploring how financial aid policies and circumstances shape student decision-making toward academic and social outcomes, such as high-impact practice participation, campus employment, and postgraduate career choices.

Keri L. Rodgers is a doctoral student in educational studies at Ball State University. Her major is curriculum with cognates in cultural, educational policy studies, and educational technology. She has taught in secondary and postsecondary educational institutions.

Ester U. Sihite is a PhD candidate in higher education at Loyola University Chicago's School of Education. Her research interests include the cultivation and use of multicultural and antideficit frameworks by faculty and staff at community colleges; racial stratification, educational access, and equity in higher education; and the collegiate experiences of low-income Asian Americans and immigrant populations.

academic success. *See also* student
success
from external support, 53–54
funding incentives for, 45
graduation and credentialing as,
43–44
of LGBTQ+ students, 43–45
student success, 45–46, 51–53
as success and belonging, 51–53
activism, 170–74, 178. *See also* political
acts
alternative break programs for, 169,
216
anti-racism, 158–59, 161–64, 203–6
anti-sexism, 43, 45, 59–64, 159,
161–64
anti-sexual violence activism, 59–64
creativity in education as, 197–201,
202–3, 206, 208–9
critical pedagogy disrupting privilege
as, 107–8
as formal or organic, 204–5
images in, 17–18, 60
Latinx, womxn, hxstory terms
countering privilege as, 211n1
LGBTQ+ students selfies in, 159
photovoice interviews in, 93–94
from professional development, 160
on satirical website, 175–77
as savior, 175–77
as social justice, 85–86, 105–17, 167
social media for, 59–60, 62, 64, 214
by student affairs within institutions,
204, 208
as trickle up in social justice, 201
visual literacy with critical pedagogy
for, 105–17, 179

visual methods for, 5, 214, 224
visuals used by, 158–59
administrators, 24, 92, 167, 201–3
African American students, 18, 190–91
anti-racism images by, 60–61, 159,
199
campus culture for, 19, 32–37,
111–15
racial stereotyping and, 18–19, 174,
216
alternative break programs
racial stereotyping identified in, 216
spring break spent on, 168–71
visual methods assisting, 171–78
anti-racism activism, 60–61, 199. *See
also* racial stereotyping
visual audit for, 158–59, 161–64
against White supremacy, 203–6
anti-sexism activism, 199. *See also*
privilege
inequality in, 43, 45, 59–64, 159
visual audit for, 161–64
White male photos in, 223–24
womxn and hxstory as terms for,
211n1
anti-sexual violence activism, 59–60,
62, 64, 214
anxiety
by educators on digital tools, 133
over digital tools, 120
visual methods provoking, 115–16
arts-based elicitation interviews
in classrooms, 3–4
empathy increased by, 21–22
paintings, drawings, self-portraits
and poetry in, 23
arts-based pedagogy

skills developed in, 114–15
for social justice, 105–17
strategies for, 111–15
student affairs practitioners
promoting, 156
websites utilized by, 175–77
visual methods
for activism, 214, 224
alternative break programs assisted
by, 171–78
anxiety provoked by, 115–16
challenges in, 194–95
drawings and photos as, 186–88,
191
in experiential learning, 190–91
for inclusion and identity
development, 214
lasting impressions from, 186–89,
191–92
leadership developed with, 215
learning objectives achieved by, 178
participants affinity for, 191–92
personal voice supported by, 215
photo elicitation in, 182–84
photos in, 188–90
power promoted by, 217
privacy concerns in, 217–19
privilege acknowledged with, 178
professional development shown by,
188–91
in research, 3–7, 13–25, 16, 31,
37–39
resistance on, 25, 110, 115–16
as retention tool, 194–95
student affairs and reflection in, 182,
185–90, 192
student affairs experiences in, 24,
159, 181–95
for student development, 5, 7–8, 31,
37–39
visual pedagogy, 6–7
anti-racism activism assisted by,
158–59

digital stories as, 80–82
empathy from, 116
in experiential learning, 157–58
with graphs, symbols and spatial
arrangements, 78, 122, 124–27
higher education methods in, 80–89
image theater in, 83–84
for learning, 77
learning styles assisted by, 78–80
photo elicitation in, 84–89
in practice, 153–65
as relevance ploy, 105
resistance to, 25, 110, 115–16
steps in, 85–88
as underutilized, 9
visual research methods
for activism, 5
administrators benefitted by, 24
contemporary life shown in, 31–32
digital tools as messy in, 68
discussion forum of, 186, 190
future of, 213–24
hashtags in, 68
higher education research use of,
8–9, 18–24
institutional use of, 5
for interpreting meanings, 5
learning objectives from, 5
on LGBTQ+ college environments,
48–49
LGBTQ+ students success
understood by, 47–48
NSLGBTQSS use of, 44–48
participants represented in, 5,
191–92
photos in, 16–17, 33
privacy concerns in, 5
for recognizing meanings, 8
in research on students, 3–7, 13–25,
31, 37–39
for scholarship in practice, 193
student affairs benefitted by, 24, 159,
181–95